Angela Liddon, author of the *New York Times* bestselling *Oh She Glows* cookbooks, shares a vibrant collection of protein-packed, plant-based salads designed to nourish, satisfy, and make you glow from the inside out.

Designed to keep you glowing through every season, *Oh She Glows Salads* is brimming with fresh, flavor-forward recipes, from refreshing spring and summer bowls to cozy, hearty salads for autumn and winter. Inside, you'll find soon-to-be favorites like the Glow Up Pesto Dream Bowl; Roasted Chickpea and Parm Romaine Crunch Salad; The Ultimate Ranch Barbecue Tofu Cobb Salad; Warm and Cozy Roasted Mediterranean Lentil Salad; and Fall Crunch Farro Kale Salad—each crafted to power you through busy days.

You'll also discover an abundance of satisfying plant-based protein toppers, creamy dressings, vibrant vinaigrettes, savory cheeses, and crunchy nut clusters—everything you need to create satisfying, restaurant-worthy salads at home. To strike the perfect balance, Angela has included an indulgent-yet-wholesome dessert chapter, because sometimes the best way to finish a veggie-packed meal is with a little treat!

With her signature creativity and warmth, Angela makes eating well joyful and inspiring. Whether you're a longtime *Oh She Glows* fan or new to plant-based living, *Oh She Glows Salads* will ignite your love for the power of plants—one flavor-packed bite at a time.

oh she glows salads

oh she glows salads

Get Glowing: Protein-Packed,
Plant-Based Salads for Every Season

Angela Liddon

PENGUIN
an imprint of Penguin Canada, a division of Penguin Random House Canada Limited

Canada • USA • UK • Ireland • Australia • New Zealand • India • South Africa • China

Penguin, an imprint of Penguin Canada
A division of Penguin Random House Canada
320 Front Street West, Suite 1400
Toronto, Ontario, M5V 3B6, Canada
penguinrandomhouse.ca

The authorized representative in the EU for product safety and compliance is Penguin Random House Ireland, Morrison Chambers, 32 Nassau Street, Dublin D02 YH68, Ireland, https://eu-contact.penguin.ie

LIBRARY AND ARCHIVES CANADA CATALOGUING IN PUBLICATION

Title: Oh she glows salads : get glowing: protein-packed, plant-based salads for every season / Angela Liddon.
Names: Liddon, Angela, author
Description: Includes index.
Identifiers: Canadiana (print) 2025017605X | Canadiana (ebook) 20250176068 | ISBN 9780735250215 (hardcover) | ISBN 9780735250222 (EPUB)
Subjects: LCSH: Salads. | LCSH: Cooking (Natural foods) | LCSH: Vegan cooking. | LCGFT: Cookbooks.
Classification: LCC TX740 .L53 2026 | DDC 641.83—dc23

Cover and interior design by Terri Nimmo
Typeset by Daniella Zanchetta
Front cover photo and interior photos by Angela Liddon
Back cover photo and interior photos on pages ii, xi, xiii, 4, 7–10, 20, 31, 68, 322, 340, 356 by Eric Liddon
Prop and food styling by Angela Liddon

Printed in China

10 9 8 7 6 5 4 3 2 1

To my favorite dreamers, explorers, and free spirits:

Chase your passions with wild abandon,
and do it with a big heart.
I'll never stop cheering for you—
this, by far, is my favorite part.

Love, Mom/Ange

contents

about this book

There was once a time in my life when a salad felt like a punishment. A wilted bag of lettuce and dried-out shredded carrots on their last legs, topped with a few mushy tomato slices and some fat-free dressing made of who knows what. Thankfully, over the years, the fat-free and low-calorie chokehold that had its grip on me for far too long started to release as I decided that restricting myself in such a way was no way to live. There was a whole other world of food out there that I wanted to explore. Healthy fats became my BFF, and variety became the spice of life!

Some days, it's still hard for me to believe that a bowl so energizing and nutritious can also be so indulgent and mind-blowingly delicious. In fact, that became my goal as I delved into the world of creating plant-based recipes. When I'm not in mom-on-the-go mode—protein bar in hand, kids in tow—you'll usually find me in the kitchen, recipe testing my latest obsession: hearty, feel-good plant-based salads. I could live off these fresh and vibrant salads for the rest of my life (well, along with green smoothies and chocolate desserts!).

Since embarking on my journey to health in my twenties, I've always been the one among my family and friends to bring salads and desserts to social gatherings. I love big salads because they bring people together and they are the perfect take-along dish for any gathering. Not to mention, they help your skin glow from the inside out and can be endlessly customized to suit your preferences, the season, or even your mood. I may be a recipe nerd (okay, that's probably a fact), but I find them so fun to dream up and create! And let's be real, when done right, they feel like a multivitamin in a bowl.

Salads can get a bad rap, as they're often imagined to be these boring, sad little bowls of wilted greens and tired veggies. If you've ever asked for a vegan salad in a not-so-vegan-friendly restaurant, you've probably been served this a million times. I know I have. Maybe, like me, you've grown tired of plain-Jane salads and you're ready to reignite your passion for these healthy plant-based bowls of joy. To me, "salad" encompasses a huge array of different recipes that are bursting with creativity, varied ingredients, warm and hot components, raw and roasted, or steamed or pickled—really, there are too many variations of salads to count, and I prefer a broad definition to include them all. That said, I'm also a firm believer that salads should be accessible, with easy-to-source ingredients.

I truly hope *Oh She Glows Salads* inspires you to reimagine what salads can be—and shows just how satisfying it is to create restaurant-quality bowls right in your own kitchen. This cookbook has been such a joy to create because, while health is important, food is so much more than nourishment—it's about connection, and salads and desserts are my favorite meals to share with the people I love. These salads are created, prepared, and shared from the heart. My wish is that you'll return to these recipes again and again, in a dog-eared cookbook weathered by years of use and love—the kinds of recipes your family and friends ask for so often that you eventually just hand over your cookbook, and never get it back. (Raise your hand if that's happened to you, too!)

To make this cookbook easy to revisit throughout the year, I've organized my salads by seasonal groupings of "Spring and Summer" and "Fall and Winter." In the warmer months, I love to use crisp, hydrating, and in-season vegetables, with fresh herbs and fruits, served raw or grilled. I find them satisfying yet refreshing and perfect for welcoming spring and for taking along to summer gatherings. Colder months find me craving hearty, warming bowls brimming with caramelized roasted root veggies (hubba, hubba), warm legumes, robust greens, and smoky spices. I love bringing them to holiday get-togethers or simply for cozy nights indoors. Even though I distinguish the recipes by seasons, you'll find that many of them can be made any time of the year, so I encourage you to flip through all the seasons when choosing your next perfect meal.

Once you've crunched your way through the wide array of salads, if you find yourself craving a little something sweet after a meal (you're not alone), that's when it's time to turn to the Desserts chapter and indulge in one of my decadent but healthified plant-based sweets. You know that I just had to create a dessert chapter to balance out the healthy goodness of the salads. Whether it's a birthday, a holiday, or simply a Friday night sweet tooth, you'll find something here to bake and love. From my Autumn Spiced Carr-oat Cake with Vegan Cream Cheese Frosting (page 289) to my Triple-Layer Mocha Fudge Torte (page 297) and Chocolate-Coconut Zucchini Bundt Cake (page 293), there is truly something for everyone and for every occasion throughout the year!

my journey continued

It feels like my entire life has changed wildly and flipped upside down and right-side-up a couple times since my last cookbook, *Oh She Glows for Dinner*, came out in 2020. In 2021, our family embarked on a big move from Ontario to Alberta, where we are now only a hop, skip, and a jump from the gorgeous Rocky Mountains, a dream of ours for a long time. Having lived in Ontario for almost half my life (and for my husband, Eric, since he was a baby), it was the change we were looking for in our lives. Our children, Adriana and Arlo, were still quite young at the time, and luckily they were on board with this new adventure, too.

During that life-changing year, I was also pregnant with our third baby (what made me think it was a good idea to move across Canada while pregnant . . . we shall never know!), so it was a bit of an emotional roller coaster (mainly for me). Luckily, we were moved and somewhat unpacked before our sweet son Levi made his grand arrival in late October, just as fall was settling in, the evenings were getting darker, and Halloween was a few days away. It was also during that busy year that I stepped back from my career and decided to focus all my energy on motherhood and our family of five (it was survival mode most days . . . gulp!), not to mention discovering our friendly new community and nature-loving province in our downtime. Stepping back was the best thing I could've done, as I went through some months when I just felt plain ol' burned out (and suffered from some health issues, too) and I knew that I couldn't keep going full speed in every part of my life. Motherhood has changed me in so many ways, and one of those has been learning when to put my foot on the gas pedal and when to brake.

Kananaskis Village, Alberta

Kisses for little brother Levi

During my time away from recipe creation and photography, something totally unexpected happened to me. I was hit with this immense passion for art. One day, after talking to my mom about one of her new paintings, it struck me that I desperately wanted to paint. I had this urge to paint that couldn't be ignored! It was so strange; never in a million years would I have guessed that I'd develop an interest in painting. My mom is a talented artist, and there are many more in our family, so maybe I was destined to pick up a brush, too. I took a months-long art course, followed by the next art course, followed by the next one and the next one. I set up a studio in our basement, found an amazing community of artists, and oh my goodness what is happening?! I absolutely love painting these days, and it has been one of the things that kept my creativity flowing even when I was stepping away from my beloved *Oh She Glows* work. I'm the type of person who has to do something creative every day to fill my cup, so this was just what I needed. My kids also love to paint, so it's something creative we enjoy doing together (and I've made peace with the fact that some areas of our house are now permanently "decorated"!). Sometimes life just throws these really unexpected curveballs, and discovering a passion for painting has to be one of my life's favorites thus far.

Soon-to-be party of 5!

With my sweet Annie, 2019

Lake Minnewanka, Alberta

Calgary, 2024

My first 36 × 48-inch painting

While I was away, I received an email from my dear editor, Andrea, who wrote to me to catch up and to ask if I would be interested in writing another cookbook. I immediately thought, *OMG. This is wild . . . I am a mere shadow of my former workaholic self and can barely keep up with family life lately!* I did what every semi-panicked person would do: I immediately marked the email as unread and closed my laptop so I could temporarily live in denial (la la la la laaaaa). But I couldn't get the thought of doing another cookbook out of my mind. Creating is in my bones, and I thrive when working on stimulating projects. As any good Taurean would do, I thought about it long and hard for weeks and weeks before I finally made a decision: I spoke with family and friends. I brainstormed over two hundred solid new recipe ideas before I felt confident that I could even do it. My Right-Hand Gal and Head Recipe Tester, Nicole, was over the moon excited to join me, which was just the nudge and encouragement I needed.

Still, I was unsure. I was so unsure that I created a folder in Google Docs called "Imaginary Salad Cookbook," as I really didn't know if I could do it as a mom going through the trenches. Calling it "Imaginary" totally took the pressure off, and if I determined that life was just too hectic right now, I would still benefit from having a collection of new and family-favorite salad recipes we could make at home. I kept chipping away at it during Levi's naps and late at night. Then I started testing recipes. Oh, I had oodles of ideas! The ideas just poured out, as they tend to do after a long break. Nicole and I reached out to our dedicated group of recipe testers, who were also very much on board. A non-imaginary cookbook started to form very fast!

I asked Andrea, "What if I include a dessert chapter at the end of the salad cookbook to balance out all the veggies?" She loved it. I loved it. It was decided. Title in progress: *The Best Darn Salad Cookbook You've Ever Seen with an Entire Dessert Chapter at the End as the Cherry on Top.*

As I wrap up my manuscript at long last, a joyous yet bittersweet moment, I have to say that creating an entire book of plant-based salads has been my favorite project to date. If there was ever a Hype Girl for a salad and dessert cookbook it's me, because I have been sharing them with everyone and ranting and raving about each new creation (okay, maybe not ranting). I think because I love salads so much and recognize their immense potential, this book has been all the more fun to bring to life . . . as I said above, *recipe nerd alert*!

Thank you, my dear readers, for coming on this journey with me and for supporting what I do with so much love and enthusiasm. I can't say thank you enough to those of you who have supported my previous cookbooks (*The Oh She Glows Cookbook*, *Oh She Glows Every Day*, and *Oh She Glows for Dinner*) as well as this newest creation—never in my wildest dreams would I have imagined I'd have the privilege to embrace this career, and I'm eternally grateful to each and every one of you! I truly hope that you'll go wild for this new collection of recipes, share them with friends and family for years to come, sticky-note oodles of pages (one of my favorite things to see as a cookbook author), and delight in how satisfying, flavor-forward, and satiating healthy salads can taste while giving you a glow from the inside out like no other. I'm all about that glow from the inside out.

Cheers to having more salads and sweets in our lives!

♡ Angela

P.S. Nothing would make me happier than seeing the recipes you create from the book! If you feel like sharing, I'd absolutely love to see your photos—just tag them with #OSGSALADS and #OHSHEGLOWS so I don't miss them. Okay, let's get this salad glow-up started, shall we?

My salad wall!

tips and tricks to create crave-worthy salads that will impress everyone

Let's be real: whipping up memorable, hearty, and balanced-tasting plant-based salads doesn't come naturally to many of us. My salads of years ago were probably a bit sad (no, miserable . . . hey, we all have to start somewhere, right?). But over the years I've learned so many tips and tricks through good ol' fashioned trial and error, and I hope these will help you, too.

It's all about contrast. This is the trick that has helped me the most (and one that I learned from an art course, of all places). To build the best, most memorable salads, I'm always trying to enhance the various *contrasts*. We need contrasts in flavors, textures, ingredients, temperatures, cooking methods, colors, herbs and spices, and presentation to create the most enjoyable bowls. I know that can sound intimidating, but fear not, as I have done the work for you.

Whenever a dish is feeling a bit flat, it often needs more contrast as I mentioned above. Glow up your salads by adding the contrasts in the sections below.

Maximize Textures. For the most exciting and interesting salad-eating experience, I love to have every type of texture in a salad, including soft and creamy, hard and crunchy, chewy, tender, gooey, crispy, and juicy.

Here are some ingredient examples to help get the inspiration flowing:

- **Soft and Creamy:** chopped avocado, drizzle of tahini, my Vegan Feta Cheese (page 259) or Protein-Powered Cashew-Hemp Cheese (page 197), creamy dressings, soft beans like cannellini or lentils, and pesto.

- **Hard and Crunchy:** chopped almonds, peanuts, toasted pepitas, roasted chickpeas, vegan parmesans, croutons, and veggies like radishes, red onion, cabbage, and celery.

- **Chewy:** dried cranberries, grains such as farro and pearl couscous, pasta, soba noodles or rice, veggies like corn, cooked mushrooms, sun-dried tomatoes, edamame, and roasted brassicas.

- **Tender:** roasted vegetables like carrots, mushrooms, and sweet potatoes, steamed or boiled veggies like beets and potatoes, and baked tofu.

- **Gooey:** Crispy and Chewy Barbecue Tofu (page 187), candied roasted nuts like Rosemary, Maple, and Cayenne Roasted Pecans and Walnuts (page 209), or maple-glazed roasted veggies.

- **Crispy:** Shake-and-Bake Sesame-Crusted Tofu (page 195), Crispy Breaded Tofu Tenders (page 185), raw veggies like cucumber, bell pepper, and green onion.

- **Juicy:** fresh strawberries, apples, clementines and oranges, cherry or grape tomatoes, cucumber, radishes, and corn.

Include an Array of Flavors. On a similar note, I love to have every kind of flavor in each salad: tangy and sour, sweet, bitter, savory, umami, and salty. Some of these will be subtle background flavors, while others play a prominent role, depending on the recipe. They all have an important place in the overall flavor balance, so it's important to include each one.

Mix Temperatures. I absolutely adore a good cool-warm temperature contrast in a salad. Top crisp veggies and chilled lettuce with some fresh-out-of-the-oven roasted nuts and warm breaded tofu, farro, or roasted veggies, and the contrast of temperatures is downright heavenly.

Vary Cooking Methods. Roasting veggies provides a chewy texture and a caramelized flavor. Roasting or baking tofu makes it wonderfully firm and allows you to add so many varied spice and coating options, and roasting chickpeas creates a delightful crunch that we all love on a salad. Steaming veggies yields a soft mouthfeel with a more subtle flavor, while sautéing adds a buttery note and releases yet another different flavor profile.

Keep It Colorful. Presentation matters! Having a variety of gorgeous vibrant colors is important, though it tends to happen naturally when you're making plant-based salads. You won't be able to have every color in every dish, but at least one pop of color makes a salad come to life. Try adding a sprinkle of fresh herbs, bright red tomatoes, sunny carrots, shredded purple cabbage, diced red onion, sliced red radish, yellow or orange bell pepper, or even a lemon or lime wedge on the side.

Remove the Seeds. When using large tomatoes such as Roma, on-the-vine, or beefsteak, I remove the gelatinous tomato seeds, as too many of them in a salad can make the salad greens soggy over time. It's not necessary to do this with smaller tomatoes such as grape or cherry. I am also careful to remove the seeds from jalapeño peppers to prevent a heat overload in my salad.

Layer Dressing. Whenever possible, I love to coat the lettuce in a small amount of dressing before adding any other ingredients, which ensures you won't be left with dry lettuce at the bottom of the bowl. Every bite will be flavor-packed. Aw yeah!

Get Herby. Herbs and spices, both fresh and dried, such as basil, mint, cilantro, dill, parsley, and oregano, add a bright flavor punch to salads, dressings, pestos, and vegan parmesans. Dried spices like garlic powder, smoked paprika, chili powder, and cumin, to name just a few, also taste and look lovely sprinkled over warm salads.

Make It Ahead. Prep certain components ahead of time to make salads come together lightning fast. This is especially helpful when cooking for others or before a special occasion. Check out my "A-to-Z Guide to Recipes You Can Make Ahead and All My Tips!" (page 323), which lists make-ahead options for every single salad in this book. You'll never have to wonder how to fit something into your busy schedule again! I also provide storage information to let you know how long something will keep in the fridge or freezer.

Add Protein for Staying Power. Whether it's my beloved Crispy Breaded Tofu Tenders (page 185), boiled or roasted chickpeas, crispy Shake-and-Bake Sesame-Crusted Tofu (page 195), roasted cauliflower sprinkled with hemp hearts, The Crunch Nutty Protein Topper (page 211), or Vegan Feta Cheese (page 259), to name a few, adding protein ensures the salad won't leave you hungry.

Create Eye-Catching Salads. If you enjoy beautifully presented salads like I do, for individual portions, try using shallow pasta bowls instead of deep and narrow salad bowls. The wide shape of a pasta bowl allows all the ingredients to shine on full display. Of course, use whatever you have on hand and whatever you prefer!

Make It Once, Enjoy It Several Times. With my tried-and-true storage instructions, you can make these salads and confidently know how long they will keep in the fridge without compromising the quality. In many recipes, I provide reheating instructions, too. Make it once, enjoy it for days to come . . . not much makes me happier than having delicious leftovers waiting for me in the fridge. Especially if it's leftovers of my Triple-Layer Mocha Fudge Torte (page 297)!

Mix and Match. Speaking of fabulous leftovers, something I discovered as I tested oodles of recipes, and therefore had oodles of deliciousness stored in my fridge at any given moment, is that many of my salads and dressings can be mixed and matched. I find that using a different dressing than the one called for in a recipe, or integrating leftover roasted veggies or other salad leftovers, creates something entirely new! Get creative with the recipes, mix and match to your heart's content, and even try my wide array of salad dressings on some of your longtime favorite dishes. The combos are literally endless!

Use Healthy Fats. Healthy fats keep you feeling full for longer, have a wide array of health benefits, and keep that skin a-glowing! Healthy fats come from many varied sources in your salad, such as: avocado or olive oil in dressings (try my Apple Cider, Shallot, Maple, and Dijon Vinaigrette, page 220), nuts (such as my Rosemary, Maple, and Cayenne Roasted Pecans and Walnuts, page 209), hemp hearts (such as in my Addictive Smoky Roasted Cauli, Chickpeas, and Taters, page 200), pepitas, and tofu (like Crispy and Chewy Barbecue Tofu, page 187).

Use Flavor Boosters. Floral, umami-rich sun-dried tomatoes, fresh herbs (I love parsley, dill, mint, cilantro, and basil), assertive or lightly bitter-tasting produce like radishes, arugula, and onion, and pops of sweetness from dried cranberries or chopped apricots are all great, not to mention uber-easy, ways to boost flavor.

Practical Tips When Assembling. Wash and dry your produce before beginning the recipe, to keep things running smoothly. The prep time for the recipes in this book assumes produce has already been washed and dried. Ensuring your greens are nice and dry allows the dressing to cling to each leaf. I use a salad spinner for larger amounts of greens or, for a smaller amount, simply pat them dry with a kitchen towel.

Size Matters. Bite-size greens are more enjoyable to eat than huge mouthfuls of leaves (we've all been there, am I right?). Depending on the recipe, I sometimes suggest stemming the greens (such as removing any thick stems from baby spinach or arugula) to make eating easier and more pleasurable. (I'll never forget that time I was testing a recipe and almost choked on a huge baby spinach stem . . . good times!) Of course, it's always up to you whether you remove the thick stems or not, and sometimes I'll skip that step when I'm really pressed for time.

Perfect Proportions. As you may know, I love to really get into the details in my recipes to ensure that you are able to replicate these amazing bowls in your own kitchen. Often, I'll share how to construct the perfectly portioned bowl, such as by specifying how many cups or tablespoons of the ingredients or toppings to add to each individual bowl (for example, to each bowl, add 1½ cups lettuce, ½ cup roasted sweet potato, ⅓ cup cooked farro, ¼ cup chopped avocado, 3 tablespoons dressing, etc.). These amounts are derived for the best texture and flavor in proportion to one another. Some of you may well prefer to wing it and do your own thing, or to simply throw everything together in one big bowl, so feel free to ignore my suggested amounts if you wish! Another benefit of providing you with "individual bowl" amounts is that you may wish to make only a single serving at one time, rather than the typical 4 or more servings my recipes make. If you only want to make one single salad, simply zoom down to the end of the directions, where you will often find the exact amounts needed to make a single serving. Handy, eh?

Get Creative with Toppings. Garnishes or extra toppings are what can take salads over the top in deliciousness, from an 8 to a whopping 12/10! (Yes, some of my testers have rated my salads 12/10.) Some of my favorite fun toppers are roasted nuts, savory chickpeas, vegan parmesan, bright pestos, garlicky homemade croutons, crispy tortilla strips, and vegan feta or cashew cheese cubes.

The Finishing Touch. Combining all the components I listed above and finishing the salad with a pretty citrus wedge, a sprinkle of pepitas or sesame seeds, or a scattering of one of my homemade vegan cheeses takes the presentation to the next level.

Glowing HOUSE Vinaigrette

how to create irresistible salad dressings

In *Oh She Glows Salads,* I share the exact measurements that I use in each dressing recipe. Give them a whirl as written right off the bat—they've been taste-tested and given the seal of approval by me and my fantastic recipe testing team!

After the first trial, feel free to customize any dressings in the book to suit your own tastes. You may like your dressings tangier or sweeter or with less or more oil or salt, so play around with them to suit your taste buds. To help customize your dressings to perfection, see my guide on the following pages.

This cookbook has a wide array of wonderful dressings and vinaigrettes to try out. I carefully selected and matched each dressing to suit the flavor profile of each particular salad. However, feel free to experiment with different dressing pairings if you wish! Many of the dressings work well in several salads, so have fun experimenting and mix-and-matching different dressings in the recipes. We had a *very* hard time deciding which dressing to pick in some of the recipes because many work so well. So if you find one of these dressings that you like even better on one of the salads, by all means, you do you!

Common Salad Dressing Dilemmas

Lip-Puckering Tanginess Overload. Add a touch of sweetener (such as pure maple syrup or vegan honey), slowly, to taste. If your recipe calls for a nut or seed butter, try adding a teaspoon at a time and processing to combine, tasting between each addition.

Too Salty. You can help neutralize the salinity by adding a touch of oil, a teaspoon at a time to avoid changing the flavors too much. You may then need to add a bit more of the acid(s) called for to balance the dressing. Adding a tiny bit more lemon juice may also help in certain recipes that already call for lemon juice.

Sharp or Bitter. Sometimes a prominent flavor like tahini or a herb such as oregano in a dressing may taste more bitter than you prefer. Balance it out by adding a touch of pure maple syrup or an extra teaspoon of the oil called for in the recipe, tasting after each addition. A touch of salt can also help counteract bitterness.

Dull and Bland. Some people prefer a truly *bold* dressing on their salads that'll just about knock their taste buds over. If this is you, pack in more of a punch to suit your tastes by adding a little extra grated garlic, about ¼ teaspoon at a time, and/or an acid called for in the recipe, a teaspoon at a time, tasting after each addition. You may wish to season with a little extra salt and pepper, too.

Off-the-Charts Spicy. I love using spicy tones like old-fashioned Dijon mustard, sriracha, ginger, and garlic in my recipes. If you crave a more mellow dressing, try adding a little extra of the oil called for in the recipe, a teaspoon at a time, and/or a touch more sweetener, such as maple syrup or vegan honey, just a few drops at a time, tasting after each addition.

Too Sweet. Add more of the acids that are already used in the recipe, a teaspoon at a time, tasting between additions. Some examples of acids include lemon or lime juice and balsamic, white wine, red wine, seasoned rice, or apple cider vinegars.

Solidified Dressing. Some dressings, like my Perfect Balsamic-Maple Vinaigrette (page 218), will partially solidify or thicken when chilled. If you made a dressing in advance, let it sit on the counter to come to room temperature and soften before use, and shake to recombine, if needed.

A Note on Oils. Oils used in salad dressings aren't necessarily interchangeable, due to their different flavor profiles. I tested various oils in the dressings and vinaigrettes to find the ones that taste best in each recipe. If you select a different oil than the one listed, your dressing will likely have a very different flavor than what I intended. In this book, you'll find dressings made with extra-virgin olive oil, avocado oil, and untoasted and toasted sesame oils, to name a few. For recipes where I have found a good swap option, I list it for you in the Tips section.

a guide to greens

There is such a vast world of crisp, hydrating greens that make lovely bases for salads, so how do we choose from among them? I decided that this cookbook—brimming with colorful, tasty salads—would feature greens that are easy to find and familiar, with zero compromise on the texture and flavor. There is nothing worse than reading through an ingredient list and seeing fancy produce you just know you won't find at your local grocery store! I like to get fancy, too, but instead of using frilly greens like frisée and mâche, I select their more easily sourced counterparts to keep this cookbook as useful as possible. I sometimes suggest substitutions in a recipe if a different lettuce will work well, too. My goal is for you to get these delectable, nutritious, and satisfying salads in your belly, not to have you traveling from store to store looking for an elusive veggie!

Arugula, baby: Arugula's lightly bitter and pungent taste plays against sweet ingredients such as berries, sweet potatoes, or squash, like in my Butternut, Cranberry, and Rosemary-Maple Pecan and Walnut Arugula Salad (page 153). Due to its delicate nature, it will hold up in the fridge, dressed, for about a day. Its dainty texture is best suited to vinaigrettes and makes it suitable for mixing with heartier greens. It doesn't require chopping, being only a few inches long, but I like to remove any thick stems for a more enjoyable eating experience. Baby arugula is usually packaged in a clamshell container; select one that is several days away from its best-before date and with no soggy or yellowing leaves.

Butter Lettuce: This tender, soft leafy green may also be called Bibb or Boston lettuce. It's lovely in cold salads featuring crunchy ingredients where a mild-tasting tender green is called for so there isn't too much crunch, like in my Nourishing Warm Brunch Salad Bowls (page 113), and it suits a light vinaigrette. Butter lettuce is often sold as a whole head in a clamshell with the roots attached to help prolong freshness; choose one that is several days away from its best-before date and with crisp, dry leaves.

Iceberg Lettuce: Iceberg lettuce is a firm, crunchy lettuce with a mild, sweet flavor. I use it to add a light crunch and very subtle taste to salads where it combines well with more strongly flavored greens, like in my Roasted Chickpea and Parm Romaine Crunch Salad (page 91), where it complements romaine lettuce beautifully. Because of its large leaves, I always chop a head of iceberg before adding it to salads. Iceberg is sold as a whole head; choose firm, light green lettuce with no brown spots.

Kale, curly (and baby kale): This cruciferous green features firm, fibrous, frilly-edged leaves that are often green or purple and taste earthy, grassy, and slightly bitter. Kale can be eaten cooked, but in this book I have used it in cold salads like my Glow Girl Kale Slaw (page 39), where I pair it with a lightly sweet vinaigrette to play against its deep, earthy flavor. The trick to preparing this hearty green is to remove the stems, chop or shred the leaves finely, then massage it with the dressing and let it marinate. The acids in the dressing will break down the fibers, softening the kale and making it more pleasant to chew. Mature kale is sold in bunches with large leaves; choose one with crisp, deeply colored leaves. Tender baby kale is simply the immature version of the plant, and it doesn't need to be massaged. It works well with the stems removed, combined with other baby greens in salads. Baby kale is often sold in clamshell containers; choose one that is several days from its best-before date and with dry, dark green leaves.

Little Gem: With its tender, soft, medium green leaves and tiny size, you can think of Little Gem as a cute younger sibling of romaine. It has a sweet flavor and light crunch, making it perfect for both vinaigrettes and lighter creamy dressings. I love using it in my Sweet Potato and Edamame Salad with Roasted Almond Butter, Ginger, and Lime Dressing (page 143). Due to its fast rise in popularity, Little Gem can be found in most grocery stores and is usually packaged in a clamshell container; choose one that is several days away from its best-before date and with no soggy or browning leaves. If you don't spot it at your local store, baby romaine lettuce makes an excellent swap.

Mixed Spring Greens: This mix, also called mesclun, is usually made up of tender young greens such as baby versions of romaine, spinach, arugula, endive, chard, kale, or other lettuces, each 3 to 6 inches (8 to 15 cm) long. The colorful green and purple mixture always contains some sweet and some bitter or sharp-tasting leaves, making it a lovely mix to serve with a lightly sweet vinaigrette and sweet veggies like tomatoes and cucumbers, as I do in my Radiant Garden Side Salad (page 89). You'll find mixed spring greens in clamshell containers; choose one that is several days from its best-before date and with no soggy or discolored leaves.

Mixed Baby Greens: For some salads in this book, I either call for mixed baby greens or I call for a specific combo, such as baby spinach and arugula. I find the blend of delicate but different textures and tastes adds dimension to salads while keeping the greens uniform in size. No need for chopping with baby greens, which is such a time-saver, but I do prefer to remove any thick stems. Mixed baby greens are usually sold in clamshell containers; choose one that is several days from its best-before date and with no soggy or discolored leaves.

Romaine (and baby romaine) Lettuce: Romaine (and baby romaine) lettuce has tall, crisp, medium- to dark-green leaves with a central white rib. Hearty and crunchy, it suits most dressings, from the lightest vinaigrette to the heaviest, creamiest dressing; along with its sweet flavor, these qualities make it a popular salad base. I prefer to chop romaine lettuce into bite-size pieces for my salads, like The Ultimate Ranch Barbecue Tofu Cobb Salad (page 85). Baby romaine lettuce is a delicate, soft, sweet little version of its mature counterpart, with 6- to 8-inch (15 to 20 cm) leaves, and I love to use it in Dreamy Barbecue Tofu and Roasted Green Bean Salad (page 57). Romaine is sold as a single leafy head or a trio package of hearts (heads with some outer leaves removed), and baby romaine is sold in clamshell containers. For all, choose lettuce with no wilted leaves or brown spots, and for packages, choose one that is several days from its best-before date.

Spinach, baby: I love using this delicate green in salads, as it is so nutrient-dense, has a tender, slightly firm and chewy texture, and has a subtly sweet taste. I often remove thick stems to make the salad more pleasant to chew. This deep green leafy vegetable is wonderful in both warm and cold salads, particularly with a light vinaigrette, either on its own or with another green, like in my chilled Strawberry Arugula Salad with Feta and Rosemary-Maple Nuts (page 86). Baby spinach is usually sold in a clamshell container; choose one that is several days away from its best-before date and with no soggy or yellowing leaves.

kitchen tools and appliances

These are the tools and appliances that you'll find used throughout this book. Keep in mind that not all of them are necessary by any means; some of them just make cooking a bit easier!

Kitchen Tools

- Small and medium glass canning jars (1-cup/250 mL, 2-cup/500 mL, and 20-ounce/590 mL)
- Large (13 by 18-inch/33 by 45 cm) and extra-large (15 by 21-inch/38 by 53 cm) rimmed baking sheets
- Small and large skillets
- Cast-iron grill pan
- Pot with steamer insert or steamer appliance
- Baking pans (round and square cake pans, loaf pan, springform pan, and bundt pan)
- Kitchen scale
- Chef's knife
- Whisk
- Microplane rasp grater
- Citrus juicer
- Vegetable peeler
- Fine-mesh sieve
- Box grater
- Tofu press
- Silicone pastry brush

Appliances

- Food processor
- Mini food processor
- Blender (high-speed preferred)
- Handheld mixer
- Immersion blender

tips for cooking in the oh she glows kitchen

I thrive on giving you the most knowledge, tips, and tricks, and help to ensure you have success! For the recipe pros out there, you'll likely know much of what I talk about in this section, but I encourage you to read over these pages anyway, because many of the things I do are unique to my own kitchen and habits. They will help you obtain the best results.

Allergy and Preparation Labels

Near the top of each recipe, you'll find handy allergy and prep labels that will help you quickly identify the recipes that will work for your needs (just like the recipe ninja you are)! This allergy list is not meant to be exhaustive (for example, I don't know which brand of non-dairy milk or vegan Worcestershire sauce you may use, and every brand's ingredients will differ), so please be proactive and always check your ingredient labels if you are concerned.

Optional ingredients and optional sub-recipes are *not* included in the allergy and preparation labels, to prevent the allergy information being too lengthy.

Vegan: This recipe does not contain any animal products. All the recipes in this book are vegan.

Gluten-Free: This recipe is free of gluten. Be sure to use certified gluten-free ingredients for these recipes to ensure they are gluten-free if this is a concern for you.

Nut-Free: There are no nuts or nut products in this recipe. Please be aware that Health Canada does not classify coconut as a nut, thus my recipes that contain coconut are labeled nut-free. Please ensure that you read each recipe's ingredient list closely if you or someone you are cooking for has a coconut allergy.

Soy-Free: This recipe does not contain soy products such as tofu, edamame, tamari, or soy-based miso.

Grain-Free: This recipe does not contain grains. A grain is classified as a cultivated cereal crop or the fruit/seed of a cereal. Rice, oats, and wheat are examples of grains. Quinoa is a seed, but since many grain-free diets prohibit quinoa (counting it as a pseudo-cereal grain), I include it in the grain category.

Oil-Free: This recipe doesn't contain added oils (this includes vegan mayonnaise). However, it may still be rich in healthy fats, like those found in avocado, hemp hearts, and chia seeds, and naturally occurring oils such as those found in nut and seed butters.

Raw/No Bake: This recipe does not require cooking, although a few of these recipes may involve minimal heating of an ingredient, such as melting coconut oil, or toasting bread.

Advance Prep Required: One or more components in this recipe must be prepared in advance before you can proceed with the recipe. Examples of advance prep include soaking nuts or seeds, chilling a can of coconut milk or cream, pressing tofu, or preparing a sub-recipe in advance, such as one that requires chilling after preparation.

Kid-Friendly: This recipe received the thumbs-up from 60 percent or more of the children who tasted the recipe during the testing stage.

Freezer-Friendly: This recipe has been stored successfully in the freezer. In my storage tip with the recipe, I'll share how long it keeps in the freezer without losing texture or flavor, how to store it, and I'll often include reheating directions when helpful. Am I your recipe Guardian Angel? Why yes, yes, I just might be.

On the Glow: This recipe is particularly suited to being stored and transported, so it makes a wonderful lunch or on-the-go meal.

One Pot or One Bowl: This recipe requires just ONE pot or bowl (and in one case, One Pan) and minimal fuss.

Option: The word "option" often follows some labels. Whenever you see, for example, "nut-free option," it means I've provided a tip for turning the recipe into a nut-free recipe (such as by swapping cashews for pepitas in a salad). I only suggest substitutions if I've tested them and the recipe has been approved by my testing group, so you can be confident our suggestions will work well!

Prep Time and Total Time

The prep time and total time estimates are based on averages from my recipe testers along with my own experience. Yours may differ depending on how speedy you are in the kitchen.

Prep Time: Your active prep time in the kitchen (chopping, processing, blending, assembling, etc.) ends when you can "walk away" from the kitchen and let the dish cook (or chill). The prep time does *not* include sub-recipes or ingredients marked as "optional." It also does not include washing and drying produce.

Total Time: This is the total amount of time it takes to make the recipe from start to finish, including cooking time (but not including sub-recipes and ingredients marked as "optional"). Total time does *not* include soaking time, pressing time, or cooling time. Total times are based on averages, and they assume the cook is going at a steady pace without any breaks.

Ingredient List

Order of the Action Word: Pay close attention to the placement in the ingredient list of the action word (minced, chopped, diced, etc.), or you might end up with a quantity that's different from what's intended. For example, "1 cup minced fresh parsley leaves" means you mince the parsley before you measure 1 cup, but "1 cup fresh parsley leaves, minced" means you first measure 1 cup of whole parsley leaves, then turn them out and mince them.

Minced Versus Grated Garlic: When the ingredient list instructs you to "mince" garlic, this means to finely chop the clove with a sharp knife, whereas "grated" means to grate the clove on a Microplane rasp grater or on the smallest holes of a box grater. This distinction is important, as grated garlic is much more potent and intense-tasting, and some salad dressings can't handle the intensity of grated garlic.

Old-Fashioned Dijon Mustard Versus Smooth Dijon Mustard: When I use mustard in my dressing recipes, I most often call for old-fashioned Dijon, which is the coarse, grainy variety with visible mustard seeds. It is less pungent than smooth Dijon mustard, so it's important not to substitute smooth Dijon where old-fashioned Dijon is indicated. For more information, including alternate names for old-fashioned Dijon, see my "Pantry Staples" (page 342).

Adding "to taste": I know it can feel a bit daunting to read that you are to add an ingredient "to taste" when you've never made the recipe before. I will often suggest a range of amounts to help guide you, but I always encourage you to add to taste. Go slow, adding a bit at a time and tasting as you go.

Measuring Flour: I recommend that, for the best result, you weigh your flour whenever possible, and my recipes provide the exact flour weights. In recipes, flour is traditionally measured using the spoon-and-level method, where flour is spooned into the measuring cup and leveled off with a knife, scraping the excess off the top.

However, I like to keep things as speedy as possible, so I use my scoop-and-shake-until-level method. Simply stir the flour in the bag or container to aerate it, then scoop the flour into your measuring cup (using the measuring cup itself) and shake the cup gently, side to side, until the flour is level with the top of the cup. If you don't have a kitchen scale, which is the most accurate way to measure, please use the *scoop-and-shake-until-level* method.

Storage

Each recipe tells you how to store leftovers in the fridge and how long they'll last. If it's a freezer-friendly recipe, I'll let you know how to store it in the freezer and how long it'll keep for. Often I'll provide tips on reheating, too. Yes, we've tested them all to make your life easier!

Tips and Make-It Swaps

The asterisks in the ingredient list correspond with the asterisks, in the Tips. I do this so that when you read through the ingredient list, you won't miss important notes specific to an ingredient.

Occasionally, I've included a general tip or two with no asterisk and those appear at the end of the Tips. For example, I include ideas if you want to assemble one big salad instead of individual salads, and suggestions for using leftovers.

Make It Gluten-, Nut-, Soy-, or Grain-Free: I only provide swaps and suggestions if we have tested them successfully in our own test kitchens, so you never have to wonder if the recipe will be successful and as tasty as the original.

spring and summer

spring and summer

Recipes

grain salads

vegan • soy-free • kid-friendly • on the glow

Glow Up Pesto Dream Bowl

makes 4 (2½-cup) salads • prep time: 35 minutes • total time: 40 minutes

Close your eyes and picture warm breezes, sunshine on your face, the sounds of birds singing, and children playing on the lawn. That's exactly how this Glow Up Pesto Dream Bowl makes me feel. This dish came about when I gave a simple pesto pasta recipe a serious glow up, featuring more bright flavor, varied textures, a rainbow of colors, and a pesto that delights with every bite. It features crisp bell pepper, sweet cherry tomatoes, juicy cucumber, chewy farro, peppery basil, umami-rich sun-dried tomatoes, creamy beans, buttery pine nuts, and more. Adding a scoop of my zippy, peppery, and bright Ultra-Creamy Flavor Burst Basil Pesto (page 257) onto each serving creates a dreamy bowl you won't be able to stop eating!

6 cups water or vegetable broth

1 cup (184 g) uncooked pearled farro, rinsed and drained*

Fine sea salt and freshly ground black pepper

1 batch Ultra-Creamy Flavor Burst Basil Pesto (page 257)

1 pint (283 g) cherry or grape tomatoes, quartered (1¾ cups)

3 medium Persian (mini) cucumbers (220 g total), sliced (1½ cups)

1 large bell pepper (256 g), seeded and diced (1⅓ cups)**

½ cup (39 g) thinly sliced green onions (3 medium)

⅔ cup packed (20 g) fresh basil leaves, finely chopped

½ heaping cup (95 g) oil-packed sun-dried tomatoes, drained and chopped

1½ cups (240 g) cooked cannellini beans or chickpeas, drained and rinsed

4 lemon wedges

¼ cup (38 g) pine nuts***

1. In a medium pot, bring the water (or vegetable broth) to a boil over high heat. (If using water, add ¼ teaspoon fine sea salt.)
2. When the water comes to a boil, add the drained farro, reduce the heat to medium-high, and simmer, uncovered, for 30 to 31 minutes (or according to the package directions), until al dente. Drain the farro. Season to taste with salt and pepper, if desired, and let cool for a few minutes.
3. While the farro cooks, make the Ultra-Creamy Flavor Burst Basil Pesto.
4. Prepare the cherry tomatoes, cucumbers, bell pepper, green onions, basil, sun-dried tomatoes, and beans (or chickpeas), adding them to separate small bowls or simply arranging them in groupings on an extra-large cutting board.

recipe continues

storage

Store leftovers in an airtight container in the fridge for up to 3 days.

tips

* Garlic lovers can substitute my Easy Garlic-Infused Farro (page 268).

** You can use red, orange, or yellow bell pepper. Do not use green bell pepper. I usually opt for red bell pepper as it's the sweetest.

*** Untoasted or toasted pine nuts work well. For toasting instructions, see "Pantry Staples" (page 342).

If you'd like to assemble the entire salad in a single batch, to 1 large serving bowl, mix together the cooked and drained farro along with the prepared cherry tomatoes, cucumbers, bell pepper, green onions, basil, sun-dried tomatoes, and beans. To 4 large bowls, portion about 2 cups of the farro mixture into each. Top each bowl with ⅓ cup of pesto, 1 tablespoon of pine nuts, and season to taste with a sprinkle of salt and pepper. Garnish each serving with a lemon wedge.

5. Assemble: Gather 4 large bowls. To each bowl, add a generous ½ cup of cooked farro, ⅓ heaping cup of cherry tomatoes, ⅓ heaping cup of cucumber, ⅓ cup of bell pepper, 2 tablespoons of green onion, 2 tablespoons of basil, 2 tablespoons of sun-dried tomatoes, ⅓ generous cup of beans (or chickpeas), 1 lemon wedge (I love squeezing a pop of lemon juice over top!), ⅓ cup of pesto, and 1 tablespoon of pine nuts. Season to taste with salt and pepper. (To serve from one large bowl, see Tips.)

vegan • gluten-free option • nut-free option • soy-free option • advance prep required • kid-friendly • on the glow

Glow Girl Kale Slaw

makes 4 (1¾-cup) salads • prep time: 30 minutes • total time: 45 minutes

Every delicious, colorful ingredient in this fiber- and protein-rich kale slaw will make you glow from the inside out! Deep green kale, sweet carrots, zesty bell pepper, and crunchy red onion all come together in a beautiful, lively dish brimming with nutrients and flavor. Sticky Roasted Tamari-Maple Almonds (page 203) provide glow-promoting vitamin E and an umami-rich, addictive crunch to this summer slaw. An unexpected addition is the light-as-air ancient grain bulgur, which softens the chewy texture of kale and imparts a rich, nutty taste, not to mention fiber, iron, B vitamins, and protein. The flavors are all brought together by my tangy yet sweet Apple Cider, Shallot, Maple, and Dijon Vinaigrette (page 220) and a few spoonfuls of vegan mayo for creaminess. It's a dreamy picnic or potluck addition, as it's fully assembled in advance; I get rave reviews whenever I bring it along!

1 batch Sticky Roasted Tamari-Maple Almonds (page 203; optional)

½ cup (85 g) medium-grind (#2) uncooked bulgur (1½ cups cooked)*

1 cup water

⅓ cup + 2 tablespoons Apple Cider, Shallot, Maple, and Dijon Vinaigrette (page 220)

1 medium bunch curly kale (250 g), stemmed and finely chopped (6 cups)**

1 teaspoon celery seeds

1 cup (120 g) diced red onion (½ medium)***

1 medium red bell pepper (200 g), seeded and diced (1 cup)

3 medium carrots (230 g total), peeled and grated on the large holes of a box grater (1½ cups)

2 to 3 tablespoons Soy-Free Vegan Mayonnaise (page 265) or store-bought, to taste

Fine sea salt and freshly ground black pepper

2 to 3 teaspoons white wine vinegar, to taste (optional)

1. Make the Sticky Roasted Tamari-Maple Almonds (if using).

2. Cook the bulgur in advance so it has time to cool: In a small pot, stir together the bulgur and water. Bring to a boil over high heat, then reduce the heat to low, cover with a tight-fitting lid, and gently simmer for 11 to 13 minutes (or according to the package directions), until the water has been absorbed and the bulgur is tender. Drain any excess water, if needed. Transfer the cooked bulgur to a large shallow dish, spread it in a layer about 1 inch (2.5 cm) thick, and fluff it lightly with a fork. Refrigerate, uncovered, for at least 20 minutes until cool before using (if the bulgur is too hot, it will wilt the vegetables).

3. Meanwhile, make the Apple Cider, Shallot, Maple, and Dijon Vinaigrette.

4. Prepare the kale (see Tips) and place in a large bowl. Toss the kale with the vinaigrette and the celery seeds. Massage the dressing into the kale, squeezing it firmly between your hands, for about 30 seconds. Set aside to let the kale soften while you prepare the other veggies.

storage

Store leftovers in an airtight container in the fridge for up to 2 days. Revive the flavors by tossing with a tiny drizzle of vinaigrette.

tips

* I like Bob's Red Mill whole-grain red bulgur, which is a medium grind (#2 coarseness). Bulgur is extremely hot and dense once cooked, so I like to prepare it the day before so it has ample time to cool. After cooling, fluff it and break apart any clumps with a fork before using.

** I like to slice the stemmed kale into thin ribbons about 1 to 2 inches (2.5 to 5 cm) long.

*** If you are sensitive to the flavor of raw onion, consider reducing the amount to ⅔ or ¾ cup.

make it gluten-free

Use 1½ cups of cooked and gently cooled quinoa in place of the bulgur. Use gluten-free light tamari or coconut aminos (also called soy-sauce substitute or soy-free seasoning to make the Sticky Roasted Tamari-Maple Almonds (if using).

make it nut-free

Omit the Sticky Roasted Tamari-Maple Almonds.

make it soy-free

If using store-bought vegan mayo, be sure to select a soy-free variety. Use the coconut aminos option for the Sticky Roasted Tamari-Maple Almonds.

5. Toss the diced red onion into a small bowl. Cover with cold water and let sit for 5 minutes. Drain well.
6. Assemble: Prepare the bell pepper and carrots, then add them to the bowl with the kale and toss to combine.
7. Add the drained diced red onion and the cooled bulgur to the kale mixture and stir to combine.
8. Stir in the vegan mayonnaise until combined. Season to taste with salt and pepper (I like to use ¼ teaspoon salt, or a touch more). If you'd like the salad to be more tangy, add the white wine vinegar, 1 teaspoon at a time, tasting as you go.
9. Cover and refrigerate for at least 15 minutes so the flavors can meld before serving. If you're in a rush, simply serve immediately.
10. To serve, portion a generous 1¾ cups into each bowl and sprinkle 1 to 2 tablespoons of the Sticky Roasted Tamari-Maple Almonds on top (if using). (If you have extra Apple Cider, Shallot, Maple, and Dijon Vinaigrette on hand, drizzle more over top, if desired.)

vegan • gluten-free option • nut-free • advance prep required • kid-friendly

Backyard Barbecue Tofu and Jalapeño-Tomato Rice Salad

makes 4 (3½-cup) salads • prep time: 50 minutes • total time: 1 hour, plus pressing time

The explosive flavor of my Backyard Barbecue Tofu and Jalapeño-Rice Salad is guaranteed to impress! My Crispy and Chewy Barbecue Tofu (page 187) is tangy and chewy and has that traditional grilled barbecue taste, perfect for those fleeting summer days, while my Savory Jalapeño-Tomato Rice (page 270) is rich and smoky with a bit of attitude from the smoked paprika and gently cooked jalapeños. Bright and fresh Glow Up Garden Guacamole (page 283), with its zesty lime and cilantro, makes all the flavors shine, and the optional Lime and Sriracha Aioli (page 264) lends a creamy texture and extra kick of heat that brings it all together. The response I usually get to this salad is "I could eat this every single day!" I recommend making the complete recipe, as it's truly out of this world, but if you're ever short on time, here are my time-saving tips for this recipe: In the tofu recipe, use your favorite store-bought barbecue sauce instead of homemade; prepare the tofu, rice, and aioli the day before, then simply reheat the tofu and rice before serving; swap my Savory Jalapeño-Tomato Rice for plain cooked white rice, and you can even swap the Glow Up Garden Guacamole for simple sliced and seasoned avocado (see Tips). This salad pairs beautifully with a side of corn on the cob.

1 batch Crispy and Chewy Barbecue Tofu (page 187)

1 batch Lime and Sriracha Aioli (page 264; optional)

1 batch Savory Jalapeño-Tomato Rice (page 270)

2 medium red bell peppers (400 g total), seeded and sliced (3 cups)

2 teaspoons extra-virgin olive oil*

⅛ teaspoon fine sea salt

1 batch Glow Up Garden Guacamole (page 283)**

4 cups packed (128 g) chopped romaine hearts or iceberg lettuce (1 large heart or 1 small head)

1 cup (155 g) grape or cherry tomatoes, halved (or diced larger tomatoes)

Freshly ground black pepper

1. For the Crispy and Chewy Barbecue Tofu, press the tofu for at least 30 minutes. Preheat the oven to 400°F (200°C).

2. While the tofu presses, make the Lime and Sriracha Aioli (if using) and the Savory Jalapeño-Tomato Rice. Keep the cooked rice covered, off the heat.

3. While the rice cooks, prep the Crispy and Chewy Barbecue Tofu. Add it to one side of the baking sheet.

4. Just before baking the tofu, prepare the red peppers. Add them to the other side of the baking sheet and toss them with the olive oil and salt.

recipe continues

storage

Store the components in separate airtight containers in the fridge for up to 4 days.

tips

* You can use grapeseed oil instead of extra-virgin olive oil.

** The Glow Up Garden Guacamole can be swapped for 2 large ripe avocados (450 g total), pitted, peeled, and sliced. Drizzle with a squeeze of lemon juice and sprinkle with fine sea salt, then divide among the bowls.

make it gluten-free

Use gluten-free vegan Worcestershire sauce in the barbecue sauce, if using it for the Crispy and Chewy Barbecue Tofu.

5. Roast the tofu and veggies as directed in the tofu recipe. You can leave the sliced peppers on the pan for the full amount of time, as their charring adds a lot of flavor.

6. While the tofu and veggies roast, make the Glow Up Garden Guacamole (or prepare 2 large ripe avocados; see Tips).

7. Prepare the lettuce and tomatoes, arranging them in separate groupings on a large cutting board.

8. Assemble: Gather 4 large bowls. Add 1 packed cup of lettuce to each bowl, then layer on the toppings (I like to group the toppings as shown in the photo). For each bowl, add ½ heaping cup of guacamole (or sliced, seasoned avocado), a generous ¾ cup of Savory Jalapeño-Tomato Rice, scant ½ cup of tofu, ⅓ cup of roasted red pepper, and ¼ cup of tomatoes. Drizzle 1 to 2 tablespoons of Lime and Sriracha Aioli over top (if using). Season to taste with salt and pepper. Serve warm.

vegan • gluten-free option • nut-free • kid-friendly • on the glow

Sunflower, Ginger, and Lime Crunch Salad

makes 6 (2-cup) bowls • prep time: 35 minutes • total time: 35 minutes

Have you ever felt that a traditional peanut-based dish would be "missing something" if made nut-free? Well, not on my watch! This Thai-inspired Sunflower, Ginger, and Lime Crunch Salad is bursting with gingery, nutty, citrusy flavors. Toasty, chewy brown rice, crunchy red and green cabbage, sweet carrots, zippy bell pepper, cooling cucumber, citrusy cilantro, and crisp green onion come together to create an explosion of taste and texture. It's all drizzled liberally with my nutty, gingery, and bright Nut-Free Sunflower, Ginger, and Lime Dressing (page 224) and sprinkled with crunchy toasted sunflower seeds. We love serving it with Shake-and-Bake Sesame-Crusted Tofu (page 195) to amp up the protein. This recipe makes a generous 11 to 12 cups (plus more, if using the optional edamame), making it a lovely salad to have on hand for luscious leftovers . . . if you can stop your family from eating it all in one go!

1 cup (178 g) uncooked long-grain brown rice

2 cups water

Fine sea salt

1½ batches Nut-Free Sunflower, Ginger, and Lime Dressing (page 224, see Variation)*

2 cups (150 g) finely sliced green cabbage (2-inch/5 cm long strips)

1½ cups (120 g) finely sliced red cabbage (2-inch/5 cm long strips)

3 medium carrots (343 g total), peeled and julienned (2 cups)**

½ medium English cucumber, sliced into matchsticks (1¾ cups/203 g)

1 medium bell pepper (210 g), seeded and thinly sliced (1⅓ cups)***

⅔ cup packed (21 g) fresh cilantro leaves, chopped

Freshly ground black pepper

½ cup (39 g) thinly sliced green onions (3 medium)

¼ cup packed (7 g) fresh Thai basil leaves, minced (optional)

1 cup (123 g) frozen shelled edamame, thawed and drained (optional)

½ cup (75 g) toasted sunflower seeds****

1. Cook the rice: In a medium pot, stir together the rice and water. Bring to a boil over high heat, then reduce the heat to low, stir, cover with a tight-fitting lid, and gently simmer for 30 to 40 minutes, until chewy and soft (but not mushy) and the water has been absorbed. Drain. Season to taste with salt.

2. While the rice cooks, make the 1½ batches of Nut-Free Sunflower, Ginger, and Lime Dressing.

3. Prepare the green and red cabbage, carrots, cucumber, bell pepper, and cilantro, tossing them together in a large bowl as you go. Stir in the cooked rice (I prefer it warm). Season with salt and pepper to taste.

recipe continues

storage

Store undressed salad in an airtight container in the fridge for up to 5 days. If you enjoy this salad warm, gently heat leftovers in the microwave for about 25 seconds, until heated, before adding the dressing.

tips

* Change up this salad by using 1½ batches of my Roasted Almond Butter, Ginger, and Lime Dressing (page 222, see Variation) and Sticky Roasted Tamari-Maple Almonds (page 203) instead of the Nut-Free Sunflower, Ginger, and Lime Dressing and toasted sunflower seeds. The recipe will no longer be nut-free.

** Use a julienne peeler or a mandoline fitted with the julienne blade. Or simply grate the carrots on the large holes of a box grater.

*** You can use red, orange, or yellow bell pepper. Do not use green bell pepper. I usually opt for red bell pepper as it's the sweetest.

**** To toast raw sunflower seeds, see "Pantry Staples" (page 342).

Have leftover cabbage? Why not make my Summer Roll Salad with Pickled Carrots (page 101) or Sweet Potato and Edamame Salad with Roasted Almond Butter, Ginger, and Lime Dressing (page 143).

make it gluten-free

Use gluten-free light tamari in the Nut-Free Sunflower, Ginger, and Lime Dressing.

4. Prepare the green onion and Thai basil (if using) and sprinkle them, along with the edamame (if using), over the veggies in the bowl.

5. Using tongs, portion the salad into 6 large bowls (about 2 cups per serving). Drizzle with about ¼ cup of dressing, and sprinkle 1½ tablespoons of sunflower seeds over each bowl. Season to taste with salt and pepper.

vegan • gluten-free option • nut-free • advance prep required • on the glow

Toppled Taco Salad

makes 5 (3-cup) salads • prep time: 45 minutes • total time: 55 minutes, plus pressing time

This ferociously flavorful taco salad is fully loaded with so many colorful toppings, I bet you won't be able to stop dreaming about it! I assemble each serving with a bed of crisp romaine lettuce and avocado sprinkled with smoky cumin and chili powder. Then I add heaping scoops of my savory Cilantro-Jalapeño Rice (page 273), which brings comforting staying power. My spicy-sweet Taco Tofu Crumble (page 193), with its chewy, crispy texture, is layered on next, followed by creamy black beans, juicy tomato, crunchy bell pepper, and red onion. It's pulled together with bright cilantro and drizzles of my spicy, tangy Lime and Sriracha Aioli (page 264). I originally created this as a stacked salad—but since my salad tower quickly toppled over, it became even better.

- 1 batch Taco Tofu Crumble (page 193)
- 1 batch Lime and Sriracha Aioli (page 264)
- 1 batch Cilantro-Jalapeño Rice (page 273)
- 1 medium tomato (155 g), diced (¾ cup)
- ⅔ cup (80 g) diced red onion (½ medium)
- 1 small red bell pepper (180 g), seeded and diced (¾ cup)
- 1 medium head romaine lettuce (358 g), chopped (5 cups packed)
- ¾ cup packed (24 g) fresh cilantro leaves, chopped
- 3 large ripe avocados (675 g total), halved, pitted and peeled
- 1½ cups (270 g) cooked black beans, drained and rinsed
- Chili powder, to taste
- Ground cumin, to taste
- Fine sea salt and freshly ground black pepper
- Sriracha, to taste

1. For the Taco Tofu Crumble, press the tofu for at least 30 minutes. Preheat the oven to 400°F (200°C). Make the Lime and Sriracha Aioli and the Taco Tofu Crumble.
2. Once you add the tofu to the oven for the Taco Tofu Crumble, make the Cilantro-Jalapeño Rice.
3. While the tofu and rice cook, prepare the tomato, red onion, bell pepper, lettuce, cilantro, avocados, and black beans, placing them in small individual bowls. If you don't plan to group the toppings as shown in the photo, you can simply place all the prepared veggies and black beans in one bowl.
4. Assemble: Gather 5 large bowls. Place 1 packed cup of lettuce in each bowl and top with an avocado half, sliced like in the photo if desired, cut side up. Sprinkle the avocado with a pinch each of chili powder, cumin, and salt and pepper, all to taste. (You'll have half an avocado left over, so you can chop it up and scatter it over the assembled bowls if desired or simply refrigerate for another use.)
5. To each bowl, layer on ⅔ heaping cup of rice, ⅓ heaping cup of tofu, ¼ heaping cup of black beans, 2 heaping tablespoons of tomato, 2 tablespoons of red onion, 2 heaping tablespoons of bell pepper, and 2 tablespoons of cilantro, and drizzle on 3 tablespoons of aioli. Top with a drizzle of sriracha to taste.

storage

Store the components in separate airtight containers in the fridge for up to 4 days. Prepare the avocado just before serving.

make it gluten-free

Use gluten-free vegan Worcestershire sauce in the Taco Tofu Crumble (page 193).

vegan • gluten-free • nut-free • soy-free option • grain-free option • on the glow

Spring Fever Lentil and Quinoa Salad with Sriracha Honey-Mustard Dressing

makes 5 (3-cup) salads • prep time: 35 minutes • total time: 35 minutes

Leap into spring with my Spring Fever Lentil and Quinoa Salad with Sriracha Honey-Mustard Dressing! Nutty quinoa, creamy lentils, and chickpeas provide a protein-rich base for al dente asparagus, delicate baby salad greens, sweet cherry tomatoes, crisp cucumbers, crunchy radish, and salty roasted pepita seeds. We'll often stir in a perfectly ripe avocado—I love the soft texture it adds, not to mention the healthy fats. A generous drizzle of sweet and spicy Sriracha Honey-Mustard Dressing (page 242) pulls it all together with a flavor as glorious as that first day of spring. A friend recently told me, "I could seriously eat this salad every day for the rest of my life," and I'd have to agree! If you are short on time or ingredients, this salad still tastes great even without the asparagus, peas, and quinoa; feel free to customize it however you like.

1¾ cups (242 g) cooked and cooled white quinoa*

Double batch Sriracha Honey-Mustard Dressing (page 242, see Variation)

1 large bunch asparagus (496 g)**

1 cup (135 g) frozen peas

Fine sea salt and freshly ground black pepper

½ cup (60 g) diced red onion (1 small)

5 ounces (142 g) mixed baby greens***

1 pint (283 g) cherry tomatoes, halved (1¾ cups)

3 medium Persian (mini) cucumbers (209 g total), thinly sliced (1½ cups)****

1½ cups (250 g) cooked brown lentils, drained and rinsed

1½ cups (228 g) cooked chickpeas, drained and rinsed

4 medium radishes (80 g), thinly sliced (½ cup)

1 medium ripe avocado (175 g), pitted, peeled, and chopped (¾ cup; optional)

⅓ cup (45 g) salted roasted pepitas (optional)

Sriracha, for serving (optional)

1. Cook the quinoa (see Tips) and make the double batch of Sriracha Honey-Mustard Dressing.

2. In a large pot, bring a few of inches of water to a boil over high heat and place a steamer basket on top. Break the woody ends off the asparagus and discard. Chop the asparagus into 1- to 1½-inch (2.5 to 4 cm) pieces (you should have about 3¼ generous cups). Place the asparagus in the steamer, cover, and steam for 4 to 8 minutes, until al dente. During the last minute or two of cooking, add the frozen peas to the asparagus and continue to steam until the peas are warmed through. Remove the steamer from the pot and rinse the vegetables under cold running water for 10 to 15 seconds to stop the cooking process. Season to taste with a pinch each of salt and pepper, and toss to coat.

recipe continues

storage

Store undressed salad in an airtight container in the fridge for up to 2 days.

tips

* To cook the quinoa: In a medium pot, stir together ½ cup uncooked white quinoa and ¾ cup plus 2 tablespoons water. Bring to a boil over high heat, then reduce the heat to low, cover with a tight-fitting lid, and simmer for 12 to 14 minutes, until the water has been absorbed and the quinoa is fluffy. Remove from the heat, fluff with a fork, and let sit, uncovered, to cool. This makes 1¾ cups.

** Select thin asparagus spears if possible, as they are more delicate-tasting and cook faster.

*** Baby romaine lettuce or mixed spring greens also work well.

**** Feel free to use English cucumber instead of Persian (mini) cucumbers.

make it soy-free

Use a soy-free mayonnaise when making the Sriracha Honey-Mustard Dressing.

make it grain-free

Omit the quinoa.

3. Meanwhile, toss the diced red onion into a small bowl. Cover with cold water and let sit for 5 minutes. Drain well.

4. Assemble: Add the baby greens to a large salad bowl. Prepare the tomatoes, cucumbers, lentils, chickpeas, and radishes, adding them to the salad bowl as you go. Add the steamed asparagus and peas, drained diced red onion, and cooled quinoa, and toss the salad. Gently fold in the avocado (if using).

5. Portion the salad into 5 large bowls (about 3 generous cups per serving). Top each bowl with 3 to 4 tablespoons of dressing and 1 tablespoon of pepitas (if using). If you'd like a tangy pop like I do, drizzle on a bit of sriracha to taste.

vegan • gluten-free • soy-free option • advance prep required • kid-friendly • on the glow

Spicy Chipotle Corn Salad

makes 4 (generous 2-cup) salads • prep time: 45 minutes • total time: 50 minutes

Sweet-tasting corn, juicy tomatoes, assertive red onion, bring-the-heat jalapeño, bright and citrusy cilantro, and nutty wild rice come together to create a sweet and spicy salad you won't want to stop eating! Creamy avocado adds a rich, unifying element to the dish, and the velvety, tangy, smoky dressing enhances all the flavors. We love it warm, room temperature, and even chilled. Stir in some black beans to boost the protein and make it a meal. I'll sometimes spoon some of this flavorful salad into a wrap for an instant burrito, and it's also lovely scooped up with tortilla chips. If you have my Vegan Feta Cheese (page 259) in the fridge or freezer, it is unbelievable on this salad, adding a burst of creamy tanginess that plays so nicely with the sweet corn and gently spicy dressing. Yes, please!

1 batch Creamy Chipotle Dressing (page 237)

6 cups water

½ cup (92 g) uncooked wild rice blend (1½ cups cooked)*

8 husked small/medium sweet corncobs (3.5 pounds/1.5 kg total)**

⅔ cup (80 g) diced red onion (1 small)

1 pint (283 g) grape or cherry tomatoes, halved (1¾ cups)

1 medium jalapeño pepper (40 g), seeded and minced (3 scant tablespoons)

½ cup packed (17 g) fresh cilantro leaves, minced

2 medium ripe avocados (350 g total), pitted, peeled, and diced (1½ cups)

Fine sea salt and freshly ground black pepper

For serving

Chipotle powder

Lime wedges

1. Make the Creamy Chipotle Dressing.
2. Cook the wild rice: Pour the water into a medium pot and bring to a boil over high heat. Add the rice, then reduce the heat to medium-high, stir, and simmer, uncovered, for 30 to 40 minutes, until the rice is chewy and soft (but not mushy). Drain well.
3. While the rice cooks, bring a tall, large stockpot of water to a boil over high heat. Husk the corn, then carefully add it to the pot and boil, uncovered, for 4 to 6 minutes, until bright yellow and tender, then turn off the heat. Using metal tongs, transfer the corn to a plate or colander until cool enough to handle, about 5 minutes.
4. While the rice and corn cook, add the diced red onion to a small bowl. Cover with cold water and let sit for 5 minutes. Drain well.

recipe continues

storage

This salad is best served fresh, but you can store leftover salad and dressing in separate airtight containers in the fridge for up to 2 days. Drain the salad in a colander, revive the flavors with a squeeze of lime, and drizzle with the dressing.

tips

* To reduce the cooking time a bit and to help the recipe flow, I cook the wild rice like pasta, boiling it in plenty of water and uncovered. Be sure to keep an eye on the rice while cooking, as different wild rice blends may have different cooking times.

** This recipe works well using frozen corn kernels if fresh sweet corn isn't available. It'll also save you about 15 minutes of prep work! Simply substitute 4 cups (560 g) of frozen corn kernels for the 8 cobs of fresh corn; use a large pot of water, cook for the time given in the recipe, and drain well.

make it soy-free

If using store-bought vegan mayo in the dressing, be sure to select a soy-free variety.

5. Prepare the tomatoes, jalapeño, cilantro, and avocados, adding them to a large salad bowl as you go. Add the drained diced red onion to the bowl when it's ready.

6. When the corn is cool enough to handle, using a chef's knife, slice in a downward motion over a cutting board until all the kernels are removed from each cob (you should have 4 to 5 cups of kernels). Add the kernels and the cooked rice (no need to cool it) to the bowl with the veggies and stir to combine. Season to taste with salt and pepper.

7. Assemble: Gather 4 large bowls. Add 2 generous cups of salad to each bowl. Drizzle 2 to 3 tablespoons of dressing over each salad and serve immediately. Set out the chipotle powder and lime wedges on the table, should anyone want their salad to be spicier or tangier.

vegan • gluten-free option • nut-free option • grain-free option • advance prep required • kid-friendly

Dreamy Barbecue Tofu and Roasted Green Bean Salad

makes 4 (4-cup) salads • prep time: 40 minutes • total time: 65 minutes, plus pressing and soaking time

This vibrant roasted salad is such a dreamboat. The textures are so satisfying, the flavors are beyond delicious, and it is a filling, comforting yet fresh dish that makes it feel like summer. I love the tangy and sweet Crispy and Chewy Barbecue Tofu (page 187) that gives it staying power, and the flavor of the barbecue sauce in each bite is heavenly. This salad features lightly charred green beans and the tofu served over a bed of delicate greens dressed with my silky-smooth Creamy Cashew, Garlic, and Lemon Dressing (page 240). This hearty bowl is topped with juicy tomatoes, crisp green onion, crunchy pepitas, and delicate sesame seeds. Nutty, warm brown rice makes it even more satiating and comforting. You'll quickly see why everyone raves about its chewy, crunchy texture and zingy, sweet, and lightly spicy flavor from the first bite! Be sure to allow yourself a bit of time to press the two blocks of tofu and to soak the cashews (for the dressing) beforehand.

1 batch Creamy Cashew, Garlic, and Lemon Dressing (page 240)

1 cup (178 g) uncooked long-grain brown rice

2 cups water

Double Batch Crispy and Chewy Barbecue Tofu (page 190)

12 ounces (340 g) fresh green beans, trimmed and halved crosswise (3⅓ cups)

1 teaspoon grapeseed oil

Fine sea salt and freshly ground black pepper

1 pint (283 g) cherry or grape tomatoes, halved (1¾ cups)

¾ heaping cup (62 g) thinly sliced green onions (3 large)

5 ounces (142 g) baby romaine or chopped butter lettuce (6 cups)*

8 teaspoons sesame seeds

4 tablespoons (34 g) salted roasted pepitas

1. Make the Creamy Cashew, Garlic, and Lemon Dressing in advance. Set the dressing out on the counter to soften before starting to make the salad.

2. Cook the Rice: In a medium pot, stir together the brown rice and water. Bring to a boil over high heat, then reduce the heat to low, stir, cover with a tight-fitting lid, and gently simmer for 30 to 40 minutes, until chewy and soft (but not mushy) and all the water has been absorbed. Season to taste with salt. There's no need to cool the rice before using—it's lovely warm.

3. Position the racks in the upper and lower thirds of the oven.

recipe continues

storage

Store the rice and green beans, salad veggies (tomatoes, romaine, green onions), tofu, and the dressing in separate airtight containers in the fridge for up to 3 days. Reheat the rice and beans in a covered pan, along with a splash of water, over medium heat for 5 to 6 minutes. Reheat the tofu, if desired.

tips

* Mixed baby greens or chopped romaine work well too.

Don't have any lettuce on hand? Simply leave it out and turn this into a delectable tofu, green bean, and rice bowl.

make it gluten-free

Use gluten-free vegan Worcestershire sauce in the barbecue sauce, if making it for the Crispy and Chewy Barbecue Sauce.

make it nut-free

Use Velvety Sunflower Garlic Dressing (page 227) instead of the Creamy Cashew, Garlic, and Lemon Dressing.

make it grain-free

Omit the rice.

4. While the rice cooks, prep the Double Batch Crispy and Chewy Barbecue Tofu, from step 1 to the end of step 5. Note that this includes making the Sweet and Tangy No-Chop Barbecue Sauce (alternatively, you can use store-bought barbecue sauce). Don't bake the tofu yet. Set aside the bag that was used to shake the tofu.

5. Line a second large rimmed baking sheet with parchment paper. Prepare the green beans, adding them to the reserved tofu bag along with the grapeseed oil and ¼ teaspoon of salt. Secure the bag and shake until the beans are coated. Spread the beans in an even layer on the prepared baking sheet.

6. Bake the tofu on the bottom rack and the green beans on the top rack for 20 to 30 minutes, until the green beans are tender and lightly charred and the tofu is slightly firm, flipping both halfway through baking and rotating the pans from upper to lower and back to front.

7. Meanwhile, prepare the tomatoes and green onions.

8. Assemble: Gather 4 large bowls. Add 1½ cups of baby romaine to each bowl. Top each with a generous tablespoon of dressing. Then add a generous ½ cup of warm rice to each bowl over the lettuce.

9. When the tofu and beans are ready, add ½ cup of the green beans to each bowl. Using tongs, toss the tofu with ⅔ cup of warmed barbecue sauce directly on the pan until coated. Top the rice in each bowl with 1 cup of tofu and a scant ½ cup of tomatoes.

10. Sprinkle each salad with 2 to 3 tablespoons of green onions, 2 teaspoons of sesame seeds, and 1 tablespoon of pepitas. Spoon on another 2 to 3 tablespoons of dressing. Add a sprinkle of salt and a few cranks of freshly ground black pepper, if desired. Serve warm.

vegan • gluten-free option • nut-free • soy-free option • advance prep required • kid-friendly

Mile-High Warm Portobello Fajita Salad

makes 4 (3-cup) salads • prep time: 50 minutes • total time: 1 hour

This salad came to life when I had leftovers from the most delicious fajita night and a craving for a meal-worthy salad. Thick-sliced portobellos are sautéed with sweet bell peppers and red onion (so colorful!) in a smoky fajita spice mix while fluffy white rice cooks away in a pot. We love the way the dressing, tortilla strips, and Glow Up Garden Guacamole (page 283) all give this dish incredible *ka-pow,* but you can add your own faves too; try sliced green onion, pickled jalapeños, sriracha, or cilantro leaves. To boost the protein, I love to add cooked black beans. Be sure to check out my make-ahead tips in my "A-to-Z Guide to Recipes You Can Make Ahead and All My Tips!" (page 323), as this is a good recipe to take advantage of make-ahead steps.

Dressing and Toppings

1 batch Lime and Sriracha Aioli (page 264)

1 batch Crispy Tortilla Strips (page 254; optional)*

1 batch Glow Up Garden Guacamole (page 283)**

Rice

1 cup (180 g) uncooked long-grain white rice

2 cups water

½ scant teaspoon fine sea salt, or to taste

1 to 2 tablespoons vegan buttery spread, to taste

Fajita Mixture

4 large portobello mushrooms (475 g total)

3 tablespoons extra-virgin olive oil

1½ scant cups (115 g) thinly sliced red onion (½ medium)

2 medium bell peppers (425 g total), seeded and thinly sliced (3 scant cups)***

1½ teaspoons chili powder

1½ teaspoons ground cumin

1½ teaspoons garlic powder

1½ teaspoons dried oregano

2 to 3 tablespoons tomato paste, to taste

Fine sea salt and freshly ground black pepper

1 medium head romaine lettuce (400 g), chopped (4 cups packed)

1. Make the Lime and Sriracha Aioli and the Crispy Tortilla Strips (if using) in advance (see Tips).

2. Make the Glow Up Garden Guacamole.

3. Cook the Rice: In a medium pot, stir together the rice, water, and salt. Bring to a boil over high heat, then reduce the heat to low, stir, cover with a tight-fitting lid, and simmer for 15 to 25 minutes (checking at the 15-minute mark), until the water has been absorbed and the rice is tender. Remove from the heat and fluff with a fork. Add the butter to taste, cover with the lid, and let sit off the heat until melted. Stir to combine. Keep covered until ready to serve. Season to taste with more salt, if desired.

recipe continues

storage

Store the rice, cooked veggies, and lettuce in separate airtight containers in the fridge for up to 4 days.

tips

* If you aren't making the optional Crispy Tortilla Strips, I recommend serving the salads with something equally crunchy, such as corn or cassava chips.

** In a time crunch? Swap the Glow Up Garden Guacamole for 2 large ripe avocados (450 g total, pitted, peeled, and sliced or chopped), divided among the salads. Season the avocado with a sprinkle of salt.

*** You can use red, orange, or yellow bell peppers. Do not use green bell peppers.

make it gluten-free

Use gluten-free tortillas to make the Crispy Tortilla Strips or serve with corn tortilla chips.

make it soy-free

Use soy-free vegan butter.

4. While the rice cooks, make the Fajita Mixture: Remove the stems from the portobello mushrooms. With a small spoon, scrape out the black gills inside the cap and discard them. Wipe the mushrooms clean with a damp paper towel, then slice into ¼- to ½-inch (5 mm to 1 cm) thick slices (you should have about 5 cups). Heat the olive oil in a large, deep skillet or pot over medium-low heat. Add the mushroom slices and sprinkle with a pinch of salt. Cook over medium-low heat for 4 to 5 minutes, stirring occasionally, while you prepare the red onion and bell peppers.

5. Stir the red onion and bell peppers into the mushrooms, then increase the heat to medium. Stir in the chili powder, cumin, garlic powder, oregano, and the tomato paste (to taste). Cook, uncovered, for 10 to 15 minutes, stirring occasionally, adding a splash of water and reducing the heat if necessary to prevent sticking, until the vegetables are just tender and the liquid from the mushrooms has evaporated. Season to taste with salt and pepper.

6. While the veggies cook, prepare the lettuce.

7. Assemble: Gather 4 large bowls. Add 1 packed cup of chopped lettuce to each bowl and drizzle with 1½ to 2 tablespoons of aioli. Top each bowl of dressed lettuce with a generous ½ cup of warm rice, ¾ cup of warm mushroom mixture, and ½ cup of guacamole. Garnish with ¼ cup of tortilla strips (if using). Drizzle each salad with another 1½ to 2 tablespoons of aioli before serving. Serve warm.

vegan • gluten-free • nut-free • soy-free option • advance prep required • kid-friendly • on the glow

Parsley, Sun-Dried Tomato, and Feta Quinoa Salad

makes 6 (1½-cup) salads • prep time: 35 minutes • total time: 35 minutes, plus pressing time

While this quinoa salad is incredible for gatherings, potlucks, and parties, it sure is great for an everyday meal, too! With piquant and umami-rich sun-dried tomatoes, green and peppery fresh parsley, sharp red onion, and velvety, lively Vegan Feta Cheese (page 259), this salad is colorful, bright, and tasty. The feta, nutty quinoa base, and chewy chickpeas make for a protein-packed salad with staying power. My tangy and zesty Light and Floral Lemony Garlic Vinaigrette (page 238) is the perfect pairing, bringing a lightly sweet yet vibrant tone to the dish. Enjoy it at room temperature or chilled straight from the fridge for the easiest leftovers. Whip up the cheese and quinoa in advance, and this comes together quickly.

1½ cups (175 g) diced Vegan Feta Cheese (page 259)*

3 cups (414 g) cooked and cooled white quinoa**

1 batch Light and Floral Lemony Garlic Vinaigrette (page 238)

½ large English cucumber, diced (2 cups/264 g)***

½ cup (60 g) diced red onion (½ small)****

¾ cup packed (26 g) fresh flat-leaf parsley leaves, minced

¾ cup (120 g) oil-packed sun-dried tomatoes, drained and chopped

1½ cups (228 g) cooked chickpeas, drained and rinsed

Fine sea salt and freshly ground black pepper

1. Make the Vegan Feta Cheese up to 3 days ahead and cook the quinoa in advance. Cool the quinoa.
2. Make the Light and Floral Lemony Garlic Vinaigrette.
3. Prepare the cucumber, red onion, parsley, sun-dried tomatoes, and chickpeas, adding them to a large serving bowl as you go.
4. Assemble: Add the cooled quinoa to the bowl. Shake the vinaigrette to recombine, then toss the salad with ½ cup of the vinaigrette. Sprinkle the feta on top, and gently toss again just to combine. Season to taste with salt and pepper.

recipe continues

storage

Store leftovers in an airtight container in the fridge for up to 4 days. To revive the flavors, drizzle a bit of leftover dressing on top.

tips

* To make this recipe come together fast, I use Vegan Feta Cheese that I've made in advance and stored in the freezer. Just be sure to pop it in the fridge the day before to ensure it has enough time to thaw.

** To cook the quinoa: In a medium pot, stir together 1 cup uncooked quinoa and 1¾ cups water. Bring to a boil over high heat, then reduce the heat to low, cover with a tight-fitting lid, and simmer for 12 to 14 minutes, until the water has been absorbed and the quinoa is fluffy. Remove from the heat and fluff with a fork. Transfer the quinoa to a large shallow dish and refrigerate, uncovered, for 15 to 25 minutes, stirring a couple of times, to cool until it's no longer warm. (Overly warm quinoa will soften the feta.) This makes 3 cups.

*** Persian (mini) cucumbers work well, too.

**** If you are sensitive to the flavor of raw onion, soak the diced red onion in a bowl of cold water for about 5 minutes, then drain well.

make it soy-free

Swap the feta for my Protein-Powered Cashew-Hemp Cheese (page 197). Note that the recipe will no longer be nut-free.

vegan • gluten-free • soy-free • grain-free option • raw/no bake option • kid-friendly • on the glow

Zucchini and Carrot Ribbon Pesto Salad

makes 5 (2-cup) salads • prep time: 35 minutes • total time: 35 minutes

Perfect for scorching summer days, my Zucchini and Carrot Ribbon Pesto Salad is a delightfully cooling and playful salad. Sweet, crunchy carrot and mellow zucchini ribbons are pretty and simple to make (fun to eat, too), pairing them with protein-rich chickpeas and leftover quinoa amps up the fiber and protein, and I feel great serving it up as a hearty yet light summer meal. I stir in dollops of my texture-rich and umami-packed Sun-Dried Tomato, Walnut, and Basil Pesto (page 258), which I love to keep on hand in the freezer for speedy weeknight meals. A sprinkle of one of my fave parms, Oregano, Basil, and Lemon Zest Parmesan (page 280), offers up a subtle sweetness from the lemon zest and a hint of peppery goodness from the fresh herbs.

1 batch Oregano, Basil, and Lemon Zest Parmesan (page 280)

1 batch Sun-Dried Tomato, Walnut, and Basil Pesto (page 258)*

2½ cups (345 g) cooked and cooled white quinoa (optional)**

3 medium zucchini (558 g total)

3 medium carrots (215 g total), peeled

1 pint (283 g) grape tomatoes, halved (1¾ cups)

1½ cups (228 g) cooked chickpeas, drained and rinsed

Fine sea salt and freshly ground black pepper

5 lemon wedges

1. Make the Oregano, Basil, and Lemon Zest Parmesan. Transfer to a covered bowl.
2. Make the Sun-Dried Tomato, Walnut, and Basil Pesto. Make and cool the quinoa (if using).
3. Using a vegetable peeler (I use a Y-peeler), peel long ribbons of zucchini (I like to save the first green peel for another use, such as a smoothie), adding them to a large serving bowl as you go (you should have 5½ cups). Once I get about a third to half of the way through peeling a zucchini, I flip it and start peeling the other side. You'll be left with pieces that you can no longer peel. You can save these for another use, such as a stir-fry or a smoothie. Repeat this process to peel the carrots into ribbons (you should have 2½ cups).
4. Prepare the tomatoes, then add them and the drained chickpeas to the bowl with the zucchini and carrots. Toss to combine.

recipe continues

storage

This salad is best served fresh, but you can store leftover parmesan, pesto, and salad in separate airtight containers in the fridge for up to 24 hours. Drain off the salad juices before serving, then stir in a bit more pesto, a squeeze of lemon, and a dash of salt and pepper to revive the flavors.

tips

* My Ultra-Creamy Flavor Burst Basil Pesto (page 257) is also delicious in this salad.

** This salad works with or without quinoa, but I prefer including it when possible. If you don't have quinoa on hand, cooked long-grain white or brown rice is a great swap.

To make the quinoa (if you don't have leftovers): In a small pot, stir together ⅔ cup uncooked quinoa and 1⅓ cups water. Bring to a boil over high heat, then reduce the heat to low, cover with a tight-fitting lid, and simmer for 12 to 14 minutes, until the water has been absorbed and the quinoa is fluffy. Remove from the heat, fluff with a fork, and let sit, uncovered, until cool. This makes 2½ cups.

make it grain-free

Omit the optional quinoa.

make it raw/no bake

Omit the optional quinoa.

5. Add ¾ cup of the pesto to the salad and using 2 large spoons, gently mix to combine. Season to taste with salt and pepper.
6. Assemble: Gather 5 large bowls. To each bowl, add ½ cup of cooked quinoa (if using) and a generous 1½ cups of pesto salad mixture (be sure to scoop up the tomatoes and chickpeas from the bottom of the bowl!), and top with a generous ¼ cup of parmesan, 2 tablespoons of additional pesto, a sprinkle each of salt and pepper, and a lemon wedge. Serve immediately, as the salad will release water as it sits.

vegan • gluten-free • nut-free option • soy-free • advance prep required • on the glow

Busy Bee Big Salad

makes 1 large (5-cup) salad • prep time: 7 minutes (when using pre-made quinoa and cheese)
total time: 7 minutes (when using pre-made quinoa and cheese)

Much like Elaine in *Seinfeld*, I love a BIG salad. My stomach is like a bottomless pit when it comes to them (anyone else?). I love to keep a batch of cooked quinoa, homemade salad dressing, and Protein-Powered Cashew-Hemp Cheese (page 197) in the fridge or freezer, which makes this salad a breeze to throw together and also one of my *don't have to think about it* go-tos. It never disappoints, and I can sneak in a healthy meal even if I'm standing at the counter eating it most days . . . and I often am, with my kids running around me! I've listed the ingredients I try to have handy, but you can customize this dish using your own favorites. (It's the best way to finish up delicious leftovers, too.) You'll also get a nice flavor and protein boost by including my Crispy and Chewy Barbecue Tofu (page 187), Shake-and-Bake Sesame-Crusted Tofu (page 195), Garlic-Cayenne Roasted Chickpeas (page 202), Garlic Lovers' Cashew Parmesan (page 281), or Rosemary, Maple, and Cayenne Roasted Pecans and Walnuts (page 209). Be sure to see my Tips for the dressings we always enjoy on this salad . . . with so many to choose from, you'll never get bored!

1 cup (140 g) cooked and cooled white quinoa*

⅓ cup (33 g) cubed Protein-Powered Cashew-Hemp Cheese (page 197)

2 to 3 cups packed (64 to 96 g) chopped romaine lettuce (1 to 2 small hearts)

½ cup (73 g) grape or cherry tomatoes

½ cup (69 g) thinly sliced English cucumber

⅓ cup (47 g) pitted, peeled, and chopped ripe avocado (½ small)

1 tablespoon hemp hearts or salted roasted pepitas

3 to 4 tablespoons dressing of choice**

1. Cook the quinoa and make the Protein-Powered Cashew-Hemp Cheese in advance.
2. Prepare the romaine, tomatoes, cucumber, and avocado, adding them to a large bowl as you go.
3. Assemble: Add the cooked quinoa, cashew-hemp cheese, and hemp hearts or pepitas to the bowl. Drizzle on your favorite dressing, and enjoy your BIG salad. (Okay, okay, or share it if you must!)

recipe continues

storage

Store undressed salad in an airtight container in the fridge for up to 2 days.

tips

* In the cooler months, I like to warm leftover cooked quinoa before adding it to my salad. If I'm warming the quinoa, I add the cheese last so it doesn't melt.

To make the quinoa (if you don't have leftovers): In a small pot, stir together ⅔ cup of uncooked quinoa and 1⅓ cups of water. Bring to a boil over high heat, then reduce the heat to low, cover with a tight-fitting lid, and simmer for 12 to 14 minutes, until the water has been absorbed and the quinoa is fluffy. Remove from the heat and fluff with a fork. Let sit, uncovered, until cool (makes 2½ cups; leftovers can be enjoyed the next day or two).

** You can use a dressing you already have on hand or try my Perfect Balsamic-Maple Vinaigrette (page 218), 6-Ingredient Shake-and-Glow Vinaigrette (page 235), Apple Cider, Shallot, Maple, and Dijon Vinaigrette (page 220), Immunity-Boosting Tahini Dressing (page 229), Cold Moon Orange Vinaigrette (page 217), Velvety Cashew Garlic Dressing (page 226), or Velvety Sunflower Garlic Dressing (page 227).

make it nut-free

Swap the Protein-Powered Cashew-Hemp Cheese for Vegan Feta Cheese (page 259). Note that the recipe will no longer be soy-free.

vegan • gluten-free • nut-free • soy-free option • advance prep required • kid-friendly • on the glow

Sunny Day Charred Corn and Feta Salad

makes 5 (generous 1½-cup) salads • prep time: 45 minutes • total time: 55 minutes, plus pressing time

A bright summery day is the perfect time to enjoy this Sunny Day Charred Corn and Feta Salad. This dish even looks like a sunny day, with its beautiful golden hue from sweet corn kernels. I lightly oil cobs of corn and sprinkle them generously with chili powder and ground cumin, then grill (either outdoors on the barbecue or simply on my indoor grill pan) until lightly charred. The char adds a smoky element that just shouts summer! Next, slice the kernels off the cobs and toss them with red onion, citrusy cilantro, and cubes of my tangy Vegan Feta Cheese (page 259). We top it all off with my addictive and creamy Lime and Sriracha Aioli (page 264). If you are a sriracha lover, drizzle some extra over your serving for the most delightful kick. Enjoy this versatile dish warm, chilled, or at room temperature (chef's choice!).

- 1⅔ cups (210 g) cubed Vegan Feta Cheese (page 259)
- 8 husked medium sweet corncobs (4 pounds/1.8 kg total)
- 1 to 2 tablespoons pure avocado oil*
- 1 teaspoon chili powder
- 1 teaspoon ground cumin
- Fine sea salt and freshly ground black pepper
- 1 batch Lime and Sriracha Aioli (page 264)
- ¾ cup packed (24 g) fresh cilantro leaves, chopped**
- ½ heaping cup (70 g) diced red onion (½ small)

1. Make the Vegan Feta Cheese up to 5 days in advance and refrigerate until ready to serve.
2. Preheat an outdoor grill to medium-high heat (375°F to 400°F/190°C to 200°C) for 15 to 20 minutes. Alternatively, if cooking indoors, preheat a grill pan over medium heat for about 5 minutes.
3. Brush the avocado oil over all the husked corn. Sprinkle each cob with a dusting of chili powder and cumin, and season to taste with salt and pepper. If using an outdoor grill, cook the corn near the middle of the grill, as the back may be too hot and they might char too quickly. Grill the corn for 15 to 30 minutes, with the lid closed, turning every 5 minutes and checking for doneness, until tender and lightly charred. If any cobs finish cooking early, remove them from the grill. If using an indoor grill pan, grill the corn for 15 to 20 minutes, turning every 5 minutes, until tender and lightly charred.

recipe continues

storage

Store undressed salad in an airtight container in the fridge for up to 2 days.

tips

* You can use grapeseed oil or extra-virgin olive oil instead of avocado oil.

** If you aren't a cilantro fan, you can use fresh flat-leaf parsley instead.

My Cilantro, Lime, Cumin, and Jalapeño Dressing (page 236) is a great swap for the Lime and Sriracha Aioli.

We love to sprinkle a bit more chili powder and ground cumin over the salad just before serving.

make it soy-free

Use a soy-free variety of vegan mayonnaise for the aioli. Omit the Vegan Feta Cheese and use my Protein-Powered Cashew-Hemp Cheese (page 197) instead. Note that the recipe will no longer be nut-free.

4. While the corn grills, make the Lime and Sriracha Aioli.
5. Prepare the cilantro and red onion.
6. Toss the diced red onion into a small bowl. Cover with cold water and let sit for 5 minutes. Drain well.
7. Remove the corn from the grill and let cool for 3 to 5 minutes. When the corn is cool enough to handle, using a chef's knife, slice in a downward motion over a cutting board until all the kernels are removed from each cob (you should have 5 to 6 cups of kernels). Transfer to a large shallow serving bowl.
8. Assemble: To the bowl with the corn, add the drained diced red onion and chopped cilantro. Toss to combine. Season to taste with salt and pepper. Portion into 5 bowls (about 1¼ cups per bowl) and top each salad with ⅓ cup of feta. (Add the feta just before serving so the warm corn doesn't melt it.) Drizzle 2 to 3 tablespoons of the aioli over each salad.

vegan • nut-free option • advance prep required

Herby Couscous, Sun-Dried Tomato, and Chickpea Salad

makes 4 (2⅓-cup) salads • prep time: 45 minutes • total time: 45 minutes, plus pressing time

One of my favorite comforting carbs, pearl couscous, makes a delightful appearance in my Herby Couscous, Sun-Dried Tomato, and Chickpea Salad. Prepared using my Lemon and Garlic Pearl Couscous (page 266), it adds a buttery soft and chewy texture that complements the crisp greens, creamy, zesty Vegan Feta Cheese (page 259), and crunchy pine nuts. My Herby Lemon and White Wine Vinaigrette (page 231) has a light lemon flavor and floral notes of oregano and basil. It pulls the incredible flavors from the peppery fresh herbs, juicy tomatoes, umami-rich sun-dried tomatoes, crunchy red onion, and buttery chickpeas together into a tangy, tart, and sweet salad that is sure to impress.

1⅓ cups (167 g) cubed Vegan Feta Cheese (page 259)
1 batch Lemon and Garlic Pearl Couscous (page 266)
1 batch Herby Lemon and White Wine Vinaigrette (page 231)
½ cup (60 g) diced red onion (½ small)
⅔ cup (107 g) oil-packed sun-dried tomatoes, drained and chopped
½ cup packed (15 g) fresh basil leaves, finely chopped
½ cup packed (17 g) fresh flat-leaf parsley leaves, finely chopped
1 cup (155 g) grape tomatoes, chopped
1½ cups (228 g) cooked chickpeas, drained and rinsed
6 cups (224 g) lettuce of choice, chopped if needed
¼ cup (38 g) toasted pine nuts*
Fine sea salt and freshly ground black pepper

1. Make the Vegan Feta Cheese up to 4 days in advance.
2. Make the Lemon and Garlic Pearl Couscous and the Herby Lemon and White Wine Vinaigrette.
3. Toss the diced red onion into a small bowl. Cover with cold water and let sit for 5 minutes. Drain well.
4. Meanwhile, prepare the sun-dried tomatoes, basil, parsley, and grape tomatoes, adding them to a large bowl as you go. Add the drained diced red onion to the bowl when ready.
5. Once the couscous has cooled, stir it into the bowl of vegetables, along with the cooked chickpeas.
6. Assemble: Gather 4 large bowls. To each bowl, add 1½ cups of lettuce and toss with ½ tablespoon of vinaigrette until coated. Top each bowl of dressed lettuce with a generous ½ cup of the vegetable couscous mixture, 1 tablespoon of toasted pine nuts, ⅓ cup of feta, and 2 to 3 tablespoons of vinaigrette. Season to taste with salt and pepper.

storage

Store the components and vinaigrette in separate airtight containers in the fridge for up to 3 days.

tip

* To toast the pine nuts, see "Pantry Staples" (page 342).

make it nut-free

Omit the pine nuts.

spring and summer

Recipes

bean, lentil, and tofu salads

vegan • nut-free option • advance prep required • on the glow

Breaded Tofu Tender Salad with Barbecue Apple Cider Vinaigrette

makes 4 (5-cup) salads • prep time: 45 minutes • total time: 1 hour and 10 minutes, plus pressing time

There are days when I find myself craving all the tastes of a summer dinner without the desire to actually fire up the barbecue, and that's exactly how this salad was born. There's something so spirit-lifting about the scents and flavors of summer . . . sunscreen, beach air, and, of course, smoky barbecue. My Crispy Breaded Tofu Tenders (page 185) add such a fun crunch to this dish that no one can resist, and they make it both hearty and filling. A generous drizzle of my smoky, sweet, and tangy Barbecue Apple Cider Vinaigrette (page 243) coats everything in barbecue goodness! Juicy sweet tomatoes, refreshing cucumber, red onion, and velvety avocado round out the perfect veggie combo. Year-round, I love to serve up this cheerful, family-sized salad to family and friends with a little garnish of sriracha and a lemon wedge on the side for a spicy and zesty kick to remind us that summer will indeed return again, even when that's hard to imagine . . .

1 batch Crispy Breaded Tofu Tenders (page 185)

1 batch Barbecue Apple Cider Vinaigrette (page 243)

½ heaping cup (52 g) red onion thinly sliced into half-moons (½ small)

1 large head romaine lettuce (450 g), chopped (8 cups packed)

1 pint (283 g) grape or cherry tomatoes, halved (1¾ cups)

2 medium ripe avocados (350 g total), pitted, peeled, and sliced or chopped (1⅓ cups)

3 medium Persian (mini) cucumbers (200 g total), sliced (1⅓ cups)*

6 tablespoons (51 g) barbecue-flavored roasted peanuts**

Sea salt and freshly ground black pepper

Sriracha, for garnish (optional)

4 lemon wedges (optional)

1. Press the tofu for the Crispy Breaded Tofu Tenders for at least 30 minutes. After pressing, prepare the tofu tenders recipe.

2. While the tofu bakes, make the Barbecue Apple Cider Vinaigrette.

3. Toss the sliced red onion into a small bowl. Cover with cold water and let sit for 5 minutes. Drain well.

4. Meanwhile, prepare the romaine, tomatoes, avocados, and cucumbers. Place the romaine in a large bowl and place the tomatoes, avocado, and cucumber into separate small bowls.

recipe continues

storage

Store undressed salad in an airtight container in the fridge for up to 3 days.

tips

* English cucumber works well in place of Persian (mini) cucumbers.

** Barbecue-flavored roasted peanuts are often found in the bulk food section of the grocery store, or in the regular nut and seed section.

make it nut-free

Swap the peanuts for salted roasted pepitas.

5. Assemble: Gather 4 large bowls. To each bowl, add 2 cups of romaine, 4 tofu tenders (I like to halve mine lengthwise before adding), a generous ⅓ cup of tomatoes, ⅓ cup of chopped avocado, ⅓ cup of sliced cucumbers, 2 heaping tablespoons of drained sliced red onion, and 1½ tablespoons of peanuts. Drizzle 3 to 4 tablespoons of dressing on top. Season to taste with salt and pepper. Add a drizzle of sriracha for a spicy kick and a lemon wedge on the side, if desired.

vegan • gluten-free option • nut-free • raw/no bake • advance prep required • kid-friendly
on the glow • one bowl

High-Protein No-Egg Egg Salad

makes 8 (½-cup salad) sandwiches • prep time: 25 minutes • total time: 25 minutes, plus pressing time

Meet one of my go-to spring and summer (and, really, anytime of the year) easy meals! It's a bit of an addiction in this house. My High-Protein No-Egg Egg Salad is tangy from the mayo, lemon juice, and dill pickles, crisp with salad greens, celery, and green onions, and a little spicy and sweet thanks to sriracha. A garnish of sweet paprika, savory garlic powder, and Herbamare (herbed sea salt) take it over the top. I include black salt in the recipe, as its natural sulfuric flavor adds a genuine "eggy" taste. My unique twist is the addition of sauerkraut—it lends juicy, briny, and crunchy elements, not to mention gut-boosting prowess. Our favorite way to serve this salad is in a toasted sandwich with sliced dill pickle (an absolute must), lettuce, and a drizzle of sriracha. It's also lovely served with hummus spread over toasted bread, lettuce, and juicy sliced tomatoes. Picnic, anyone?

1 (12-ounce/350 g) block extra-firm tofu, pressed*

2 medium celery ribs (122 g total), diced (¾ cup)

½ cup (39 g) thinly sliced green onions (3 medium)

½ medium bell pepper (166 g), seeded and diced (½ cup)**

½ cup (72 g) drained sauerkraut, coarsely chopped

⅓ cup packed (13 g) fresh dill, finely chopped

½ cup + 2 tablespoons Soy-Free Vegan Mayonnaise (page 265) or store-bought, plus more if needed

2 to 3 teaspoons yellow mustard, to taste (I use 3 teaspoons)

2 to 3 teaspoons fresh lemon juice, to taste

¼ to ½ teaspoon black salt (kala namak), to taste (optional, but recommended)

½ to 1 teaspoon garlic powder, to taste, plus more for garnish

½ teaspoon sweet paprika, plus more for garnish

¼ teaspoon ground turmeric

Herbamare or fine sea salt and freshly ground black pepper

1. Press the tofu for at least 30 minutes (see page 357).
2. While the tofu is pressing, prepare the celery, green onions, bell pepper, sauerkraut, and dill, adding them to a large bowl as you go.
3. Using your hands, crumble the pressed tofu into pieces of various sizes into the bowl. I like a mix of ½- to ¾-inch (1 to 2 cm) pieces with some smaller mashed bits. Stir to combine with the veggies.
4. Stir in the vegan mayonnaise, mustard, and lemon juice until thoroughly combined. (If you'd like the salad creamier, feel free to add another tablespoon of mayonnaise.) Stir in the black salt (if using), garlic powder, paprika, and turmeric. Season to taste with Herbamare (or fine sea salt) and lots of black pepper. (I go wild with the pepper, as this salad can withstand a lot!) Taste the mixture; add a bit more lemon juice and mustard if you'd like more tanginess and bite. (Makes about 4 packed cups salad.)

recipe continues

For serving

1 loaf sandwich bread, sliced

2 medium ripe avocados (350 g total), pitted and peeled

3 to 4 medium dill pickles (102 to 136 g), thinly sliced

8 handfuls (200 g) chopped romaine lettuce (1 large head)

Sriracha, to taste (optional)

storage

Store leftover salad in an airtight container in the fridge for up to 4 days. To revive the flavors, stir in a bit of mayonnaise, lemon juice, mustard, salt, black pepper, garlic powder, and paprika to taste.

tips

* It's important to use extra-firm tofu and to press it as directed; otherwise, the salad may be watery.

** You can use red, orange, or yellow bell pepper. Do not use green bell pepper. I usually opt for red bell pepper as it's the sweetest.

make it gluten-free

Use gluten-free bread and ensure that the rest of your ingredients are gluten-free.

5. Assemble: Toast the sliced bread. For each sandwich, quickly mash 2 to 3 tablespoons of avocado onto a slice of toasted bread. Top the mashed avocado with sliced dill pickles and a layer of romaine. Spoon a generous ⅓ cup to ½ cup of the salad mixture on top of the lettuce and press it down gently and evenly. Garnish with a generous sprinkle each of black pepper, Herbamare (or fine sea salt), paprika, and garlic powder. For a pop of heat, add a drizzle of sriracha, if desired. Place the second piece of toasted bread on top. Slice in half and serve immediately.

vegan • gluten-free option • nut-free • grain-free • advance prep required • kid-friendly

The Ultimate Ranch Barbecue Tofu Cobb Salad

makes 4 (4½-cup) salads • prep time: 40 minutes • total time: 50 minutes, plus pressing time

Eating plant-based doesn't mean missing out on deluxe Cobb salads . . . no sirree. This meal-worthy mouthwatering salad is crispy, chewy, creamy, tangy, sweet, and filling. With crisp romaine lettuce as its base, and topped with sweet cherry or grape tomatoes, crisp cucumbers, sharp green onions, and mild avocado, this salad is already on its way to being fabulous. Add my smoky, sweet Double Batch Crispy and Chewy Barbecue Tofu (page 190), and now it's brimming with texture and flavor. And I'm not done yet! I created a creamy and bright Ranch Buttermilk Dressing (page 232), which is super-fast to whisk together. Drizzle it over your Cobb salad with a little added barbecue sauce drizzled over top, too, for an irresistible flavor experience that will blow your mind (and taste buds).

- 1⅓ cups (148 g) crumbled Vegan Feta Cheese (page 259; optional, but recommended)
- 1 batch Ranch Buttermilk Dressing (page 232)
- Double Batch Crispy and Chewy Barbecue Tofu (page 190)
- 8 cups packed (256 g) chopped romaine lettuce (3 medium hearts)
- 3 medium Persian (mini) cucumbers (200 g total), sliced (1⅓ cups)*
- 1 pint (283 g) cherry or grape tomatoes, sliced (1¾ cups)
- 1 large ripe avocado (225 g), pitted, peeled, and chopped (1 cup)
- ¾ cup (59 g) thinly sliced green onions (3 large)

1. If using, make the Vegan Feta Cheese up to 3 days in advance. Make the Ranch Buttermilk Dressing at least 30 minutes or up to 2 days in advance to allow the flavors to develop.
2. Press the tofu for the Double Batch Crispy and Chewy Barbecue Tofu for at least 30 minutes. After pressing, make the barbecue tofu.
3. As soon as the tofu is in the oven, prepare the romaine and place 2 cups of lettuce in each of 4 large bowls. Prepare the cucumbers, tomatoes, avocado, and green onions, placing them in separate piles on a cutting board or in separate small bowls.
4. Assemble: To each bowl, add the veggies in rows on top of the romaine (as shown the photo, if desired): a scant ½ cup of tomatoes, ⅓ cup of cucumber, ¼ cup of avocado, 3 tablespoons of green onions, ⅓ cup of crumbled feta (if using), and, ⅔ cup of warm tofu. Drizzle 3 to 4 tablespoons of dressing on top of each salad. If you're feeling really wild, drizzle a touch of leftover barbecue sauce on top for an extra-saucy delight (my fave)!

storage

Store undressed salads in separate airtight containers in the fridge for up to 4 days. Remove and reheat the tofu, if desired.

tip

* You can swap Persian (mini) cucumbers for thinly sliced English cucumber (about ½ large).

make it gluten-free

Use gluten-free vegan Worcestershire sauce in the barbecue sauce, if making it for the Crispy and Chewy Barbecue Tofu.

vegan • gluten-free • grain-free • advance prep required • kid-friendly • on the glow

Strawberry Arugula Salad with Feta and Rosemary-Maple Nuts

makes 4 (2½-cup) salads • prep time: 35 minutes • total time: 40 minutes, plus pressing time

1 heaping cup (135 g) crumbled Vegan Feta Cheese (page 259)

1 batch Perfect Balsamic-Maple Vinaigrette (page 218)

1 batch Rosemary, Maple, and Cayenne Roasted Pecans and Walnuts (page 209)

5 ounces (142 g) baby spinach and arugula mix, thick stems removed (6 cups)

1 pound (454 g) fresh strawberries, hulled and sliced (2½ heaping cups)

If you are craving the fresh tastes and floral scents of the spring and summer months, dig into my Strawberry Arugula Salad! Sweet, juicy strawberries are the star of the show, and their irresistible flavor is brought out by the sweet and zippy Perfect Balsamic-Maple Vinaigrette (page 218) and enhanced by the lightly bitter arugula. This salad is made extra-special and explosively flavorful by my tangy and salty oregano-topped Vegan Feta Cheese (page 259) and herby, spicy, sugared, and crunchy Rosemary, Maple, and Cayenne Roasted Pecans and Walnuts (page 209). It truly has all the flavors and textures. Not to mention, it's gorgeous! The fresh rosemary in the roasted nuts pairs unexpectedly well with the spring- and summer-themed flavors. Feel free to add a sprinkle of sesame seeds for a really pretty effect!

1. Make the Vegan Feta Cheese and Perfect Balsamic-Maple Vinaigrette up to 5 days in advance. The roasted nuts can also be made in advance, if desired; however, they are lovely served warm on this salad and take less than 10 minutes to prep!
2. If making a fresh batch of roasted nuts, preheat the oven to 325°F (160°C) and line a large rimmed baking sheet with parchment paper.
3. Make the Rosemary, Maple, and Cayenne Roasted Pecans and Walnuts.
4. While the nuts roast, prepare the spinach-arugula mix and strawberries.
5. Assemble: Gather 4 large bowls. Add about 1½ cups of greens to each bowl and toss with ½ tablespoon of dressing until coated. Top each bowl with ¼ cup of crumbled feta, ⅓ cup of roasted nuts, a generous ½ cup of sliced strawberries, and about another 1½ tablespoons of vinaigrette. Serve immediately.

storage

This salad is best served fresh, but you can store leftovers in an airtight container in the fridge for up to 2 days.

tip

Have leftover Rosemary, Maple, and Cayenne Roasted Pecans and Walnuts? Use them to top my Nourishing Warm Brunch Salad Bowls (page 113) or Butternut, Cranberry, and Rosemary-Maple Pecan and Walnut Arugula Salad (page 153).

vegan • gluten-free option • nut-free option • soy-free • grain-free option • raw/no bake option
kid-friendly • on the glow

Radiant Garden Side Salad

makes 12 (1-cup) salads • prep time: 20 minutes • total time: 20 minutes (when using pre-made cheese and croutons)

I have this salad in my back pocket for those meals that need a last-minute crisp, nutritious veggie side dish. It uses ingredients I tend to have handy, like crunchy cucumber, juicy red tomatoes, creamy avocado, and spring greens mix; you can change up the ingredients based on what you have in stock. I love to switch it up with seasonal ingredients, such as adding sweet caramelized roasted squash or sweet potatoes in winter, sautéed asparagus and sweet peas in spring, and a roasted brassica or two in the fall. This light, crisp green salad rockets to the next level with the addition of (totally optional, but recommended) Easy Rustic Double Garlic Croutons (page 252) and tangy Protein-Powered Cashew-Hemp Cheese (page 197) or Vegan Feta Cheese (page 259). Li'l pops of sweetness from dried cranberries and saltiness from roasted pepitas add chewy, crunchy texture and fun. In warmer months, try adding berries, like sliced strawberries or blueberries. Sliced radishes are also a great addition.

1 cup (100 g) cubed Protein-Powered Cashew-Hemp Cheese (page 197; optional)*

1 batch Easy Rustic Double Garlic Croutons (page 252; optional)

1 batch Herby Lemon and White Wine Vinaigrette (page 231) or dressing of choice**

5 ounces (142 g) mixed spring greens (7 cups)***

½ cup (60 g) diced red onion (½ small)****

½ large English cucumber, thinly sliced into half-moons (2 cups/242 g)

2 cups (320 g) chopped tomatoes of choice

1 large ripe avocado (225 g), pitted, peeled, and chopped (1 cup)

⅓ cup (49 g) sweetened dried cranberries

6 tablespoons (51 g) salted roasted pepitas*****

1. If using, make the Protein-Powered Cashew-Hemp Cheese (store in the refrigerator until ready to use) and the Easy Rustic Double Garlic Croutons in advance.
2. Make the Herby Lemon and White Wine Vinaigrette (or dressing of choice).
3. To a large serving bowl, add the mixed spring greens.
4. Prepare the red onion, cucumber, tomatoes, and avocado, scattering them on top of the greens as you go. Toss just briefly to combine. Sprinkle the dried cranberries and pepitas on top (or add them to individual servings).

recipe continues

storage

Store leftovers in an airtight container in the fridge for up to 3 days.

make it gluten- and grain-free

Omit the optional Easy Rustic Double Garlic Croutons.

make it nut-free

Use my Vegan Feta Cheese (page 259) instead of Protein-Powered Cashew-Hemp Cheese. Note that the recipe will no longer be soy-free.

make it raw/no bake

Omit the optional Easy Rustic Double Garlic Croutons and Protein-Powered Cashew-Hemp Cheese.

5. Assemble: Portion 1 cup of salad into bowls, being sure to scoop up the dried cranberries and pepitas from the bottom of the serving bowl. (If adding them to individual servings, sprinkle about ½ tablespoon each of the cranberries and pepitas over each salad.) Top each salad with 3 to 4 teaspoons of vinaigrette to taste, 3 to 5 cubes of cashew-hemp cheese (if using), and 3 or 4 croutons (if using).

tips

* Vegan Feta Cheese (page 259) is a great swap for the cashew-hemp cheese. Note that the recipe will no longer be soy-free.

** Other great dressing options: Perfect Balsamic-Maple Vinaigrette (page 218), 6-Ingredient Shake-and-Glow Vinaigrette (page 235), or Apple Cider, Shallot, Maple, and Dijon Vinaigrette (page 220).

*** You can swap the spring greens mix for 7 cups of chopped romaine lettuce.

**** If you are sensitive to the flavor of raw onion, swap for thinly sliced green onion or soak the diced red onion in cold water for 5 minutes, then drain well.

***** Change up the pepitas with any kind of seed or nut you enjoy.

vegan • gluten-free • soy-free • grain-free • advance prep required • kid-friendly • on the glow

Roasted Chickpea and Parm Romaine Crunch Salad

makes 4 (3-cup) salads • prep time: 35 minutes • total time: 50 minutes

This mouthwatering salad is a satisfying, nourishing dish that's packed with hydrating romaine and iceberg lettuce. My crunchy, bursting-with-flavor Garlic Lovers' Cashew Parmesan (page 281) and Garlic-Cayenne Roasted Chickpeas (page 202) provide sweet, nutty, and spicy flavors as well as protein and staying power; serving it with the crunchy chickpeas transforms this flavorful side salad into a satisfying meal, but rest assured, it's delicious without the chickpeas, too! Velvety avocado adds a lovely texture and healthy fats, and there is added freshness from the zippy green onions and beautiful red, gently spicy radishes. Tossed with Velvety Cashew Garlic Dressing (page 226), with its smooth, creamy texture and tangy, garlicky taste, it's a salad you won't be able to stop eating. If you don't need this dish to be gluten-free, try it topped with my savory Easy Rustic Double Garlic Croutons (page 252) or my ultra-buttery Garlic-Infused Olive Oil Crostini (page 249). Chopped tomatoes are also a delicious addition.

1 batch Velvety Cashew Garlic Dressing (page 226)

1 batch Garlic Lovers' Cashew Parmesan (page 281)

1 batch Garlic-Cayenne Roasted Chickpeas (page 202; optional)*

1 medium head romaine lettuce (358 g), chopped (5 cups packed)

1 medium head iceberg lettuce (528 g), chopped (5 cups packed)

2 medium ripe avocados (350 g total), pitted, peeled, and diced (1½ cups)

¾ cup (59 g) thinly sliced green onions (3 large)

5 medium radishes (116 g total), halved and thinly sliced (⅔ cup)

Herbamare or fine sea salt and freshly ground black pepper

1. Make the Velvety Cashew Garlic Dressing and Garlic Lovers' Cashew Parmesan up to 1 day in advance. Set the dressing on the counter for a couple of hours to soften before you begin the recipe.

2. Make the Garlic-Cayenne Roasted Chickpeas (if using).

3. Meanwhile, prepare the romaine and iceberg lettuce. Gather 4 large bowls. Place about 2½ cups of mixed lettuces into each bowl. Prepare the avocados, green onions, and radishes.

recipe continues

storage

Store undressed salad in an airtight container in the fridge for up to 2 days. Just before serving, add the dressing, then sprinkle with Herbamare (or salt) and pepper and a squeeze of lemon to revive the flavors.

tips

* If you are looking for a hearty meal-size salad, I suggest including the roasted chickpeas. However, if you'd like this as a side salad, you can leave out the chickpeas. It's delicious either way!

If you are serving this salad to a crowd, feel free to gently toss all the ingredients (except the chickpeas and parmesan) together in a large bowl, starting with a generous ¾ cup of dressing. Taste and add up to an additional generous ¼ cup of dressing, if desired, until it's as creamy as you like it. Sprinkle on the roasted chickpeas and parmesan. Serve leftover dressing on the side, if desired.

4. Assemble: Over each bowl of lettuce, scatter a generous ⅓ cup of avocado, 3 tablespoons of green onion, 2 to 3 tablespoons of sliced radishes, ¼ cup of roasted chickpeas (if using), 3 tablespoons of parmesan, and a drizzle or dollop of 3 to 5 tablespoons of dressing. Sprinkle each salad with a bit of Herbamare (or salt) and pepper to taste, to help all the flavors pop.

vegan • gluten-free • nut-free • soy-free • grain-free • raw/no bake • advance prep required • on the glow

Easy Breezy Deconstructed Guacamole Salad

makes 4 (1-cup) servings • prep time: 25 minutes • total time: 25 minutes, plus pickling time

This light-as-air sweet and spicy salad appears regularly on our table, as it is so quick to make and downright refreshing. Adults and kids alike have fun scooping up big bites with pita chips or tortilla chips, and it's wonderful served in lettuce cups. I change it up based on what we are looking for that day. A little crunch? I top it with my Easy Rustic Double Garlic Croutons (page 252). A protein boost? I toss in cooked chickpeas. I often make the Quick-Pickled Spicy Lime Red Onions (page 276, see Variations) up to a week in advance to save some time the day I make this salad.

1 batch Quick-Pickled Spicy Lime Red Onions (page 276, see Variations)

1 batch 6-Ingredient Shake-and-Glow Vinaigrette, Lime Variation (page 235)*

1 pint (283 g) grape or cherry tomatoes, halved (1¾ cups)

2 medium ripe avocados (350 g total), pitted, peeled, and chopped (1½ cups)

½ cup packed (17 g) fresh cilantro leaves, coarsely chopped

1 medium jalapeño pepper (40 g), seeded and minced (¼ cup; optional)

Herbamare or fine sea salt and freshly ground black pepper

Ground cumin, for garnish (optional, but recommended)

1. Make the Quick-Pickled Spicy Lime Red Onions and the 6-Ingredient Shake-and-Glow Vinaigrette, Lime Variation. Both can be made up 5 days in advance, if desired.
2. Prepare the tomatoes, avocados, cilantro, and jalapeño (if using), adding them to a large bowl as you go.
3. Assemble: Add 1 cup of drained pickled red onions to the bowl. Gently toss until just combined. Drizzle on ¼ cup of vinaigrette and toss again. Season to taste with Herbamare (or sea salt), black pepper, and cumin (if using). Portion the salad into bowls or onto small plates as a side salad. Serve with leftover dressing on the side for more drizzling action.

Single Serving Variation

Want to make just a single serving? Use ¼ cup drained pickled onion, scant ½ cup halved tomatoes, generous ⅓ cup chopped avocado, 1 to 2 tablespoons coarsely chopped cilantro, and 1 tablespoon seeded and minced jalapeño (if using). Drizzle on 1 to 2 tablespoons of dressing, then season to taste with Herbamare (or salt), black pepper, and cumin (if using).

storage

This salad is best enjoyed the same day.

tips

* You can change up the dressing by using my Cilantro, Lime, Cumin, and Jalapeño Dressing (page 236) instead.

This recipe can easily be doubled if you'd like more servings.

Boost the protein by adding 1 cup cooked and drained chickpeas. Feel free to add a bit more dressing, as needed.

spring and summer

Recipes

pasta and potato salads

vegan • gluten-free option • nut-free option • kid-friendly • on the glow

Edamame and Pistachio Soba Noodle Spinach Salad

makes 4 (generous 2-cup) salads • prep time: 25 minutes • total time: 30 minutes

This protein-packed noodle salad tossed with an umami-rich Toasted Sesame, Tamari, and Garlic Dressing (page 219) clocks in at over 15 grams of protein per serving! The abundance of protein, along with the carbohydrates from the soba noodles, gives this salad mega staying power. And let's take a minute for the flavor of this dish. This one has been in high demand ever since I first brought it to a family picnic (it travels like a dream!). It's crunchy and bright from the red bell pepper, and salty and nutty from the earthy soba noodles and the surprising addition of chopped pistachios. It also has a bit of a bite from the crisp green onions and little pops of crunch and toasty flavor from the sesame seeds. It's ready in less than 30 minutes, can be served warm or cold, makes flavorful leftovers, and can easily be transported *on the glow*. What more could you ask for?

1 cup (123 g) frozen shelled edamame

1 batch Toasted Sesame, Tamari, and Garlic Dressing (page 219)

5 cups water

1 medium red bell pepper (200 g), seeded and diced (1 cup)

¾ cup (59 g) thinly sliced green onions (3 large)

⅓ cup (47 g) raw or roasted pistachios, finely chopped*

½ cup packed (17 g) fresh cilantro leaves, coarsely chopped

6.4 ounces (180 g) dried soba noodles

2 cups packed (57 g) baby spinach, thick stems removed, chopped

Fine sea salt and freshly ground black pepper

4 teaspoons toasted sesame seeds**

4 lime wedges

1. Thaw the edamame and drain well.
2. Make the Toasted Sesame, Tamari, and Garlic Dressing.
3. Bring the water to a boil in a medium pot.
4. Meanwhile, prepare the bell pepper, green onions, pistachios, and cilantro, adding them to separate small bowls or arranging them in groupings on a large cutting board as you go.
5. When the water comes to a boil, add the soba noodles, reduce the heat to medium-high, stir, and simmer, uncovered, according to the package directions (most soba noodles cook in 3 to 5 minutes), until al dente. Be sure not to overcook the noodles or they will be mushy in your salad. Drain the noodles and rinse under cold running water for at least 1 minute to stop the cooking process and prevent the noodles from sticking. Drain very well.

recipe continues

storage

Store undressed salads and the dressing in separate airtight containers in the fridge for up to 3 days. If desired, reheat in the microwave just until warmed. Top with the leftover dressing.

tips

* I prefer the flavor of toasted and lightly salted pistachios, but raw pistachios work, too.

** To toast the sesame seeds, see "Pantry Staples" (page 342).

make it gluten-free

Use gluten-free soba noodles, and use gluten-free light tamari in the Toasted Sesame, Tamari, and Garlic Dressing.

make it nut-free

Omit the pistachios and top with salted roasted pepitas instead.

6. Prepare the spinach and place it in a large microwave-safe bowl.
7. Add the noodles to the spinach and toss until combined. If you'd like to serve this salad warm (like we do!), microwave the noodles and spinach on high for 30 to 90 seconds, stirring every 30 seconds, until warm. Otherwise, if you'd like to serve it room temperature or chilled, simply proceed with the recipe.
8. Toss the noodles and spinach with a scant ½ cup of dressing (reserving the rest for serving) until combined. Season to taste with salt and pepper.
9. Assemble: Using tongs, evenly divide the noodles and spinach among 4 bowls (about 1 cup per serving). To each bowl, add ¼ cup of diced bell pepper, a scant ¼ cup of edamame, 3 tablespoons of sliced green onion, 2 tablespoons of chopped cilantro, 1½ tablespoons of chopped pistachios, and 1 teaspoon of sesame seeds. (Or you can simply toss everything together in one serving bowl.) Drizzle 2 teaspoons of the reserved dressing over each salad and serve with a lime wedge on the side.

vegan • gluten-free option • nut-free option • grain-free option • advance prep required
kid-friendly • on the glow

Summer Roll Salad with Pickled Carrots

makes 5 (2¼-cup) salads • prep time: 35 minutes • total time: 35 minutes

I love the crunchy textures and flavors of summer rolls, but I rarely seem to find the time to make them. So I came up with this fun and tasty solution: meet my Summer Roll Salad with Pickled Carrots! Instead of a rice wrap, I use vermicelli or brown rice spaghetti and top it with crisp and bright red cabbage and bell pepper, crunchy sliced almonds, chewy edamame, and creamy avocado (see Tips). Ooh la la! I adore adding my tangy and sweet Quick-Pickled Carrots (page 276, see Variations); they are so quick and simple to make, but if you are super time-crunched, raw julienned and chopped carrots work great, too! Drizzle on my deeply flavored nutty, zesty Roasted Almond Butter, Ginger, and Lime Dressing (page 222) or my Nut-Free Sunflower, Ginger, and Lime Dressing (page 224) for the most dream-worthy, decadent-tasting, yet healthy summer roll salads.

- 1 batch Quick-Pickled Carrots (page 276, see Variations)*
- 1½ batches Roasted Almond Butter, Ginger, and Lime Dressing (page 222, see Variation) or 1½ batches Nut-Free Sunflower, Ginger, and Lime Dressing (page 224, see Variation)
- 8 ounces (225 g) dried rice vermicelli noodles or brown rice spaghetti noodles
- 4 cups (224 g) thinly sliced romaine lettuce (2 to 3 small hearts)
- 1 cup (80 g) thinly sliced red cabbage
- 1 small red bell pepper (180 g), thinly sliced (1¼ cups)
- ½ cup lightly packed (11 g) fresh cilantro leaves, minced
- ¼ cup packed (8 g) fresh mint leaves, minced
- 1¼ cups (164 g) frozen shelled edamame, thawed and drained
- Fine sea salt and freshly ground black pepper
- ⅓ cup (40 g) toasted sliced almonds**
- 5 teaspoons sesame seeds

1. Make the Quick-Pickled Carrots at least 30 minutes or up to a day in advance.
2. Make the 1½ batches of Roasted Almond Butter, Ginger, and Lime Dressing or 1½ Batches Nut-Free Sunflower, Ginger, and Lime Dressing.
3. Bring a medium pot of water to a boil. Cook the noodles according to the package directions. Drain and immediately rinse thoroughly under cold running water. Drain well.
4. Meanwhile, prepare the romaine, cabbage, bell pepper, cilantro, mint, and edamame, adding them to an extra-large salad bowl as you go.
5. Thoroughly drain the pickled carrots, then add them to the salad bowl.

recipe continues

storage

Store undressed salad in an airtight container for up to 4 days.

tips

* The Quick-Pickled Carrots can be swapped for 1½ cups peeled and julienned carrots (you can coarsely chop any long strands). I use a julienne peeler.

** To toast sliced almonds, see "Pantry Staples" (page 342).

Chopped ripe avocado is lovely in this salad, too. I like adding ¼ cup per bowl.

If you prefer a warm noodle salad, simply microwave each salad (before adding the dressing) for 15 to 40 seconds, then top with the dressing and serve.

make it gluten-free

Use gluten-free light tamari in the Roasted Almond Butter, Ginger, and Lime Dressing or Nut-Free Sunflower, Ginger, and Lime Dressing.

make it nut-free

Use Nut-Free Sunflower, Ginger, and Lime Dressing (page 224). Omit the sliced almonds and use toasted sunflower seeds instead.

make it grain-free

Use grain-free edamame spaghetti noodles.

6. Coarsely chop the cooked noodles, then add them to the bowl. Toss briefly to combine the ingredients. Season to taste with salt and pepper. (The salad will be quite bland before seasoning, so adding a bit of salt and pepper before portioning into bowls is helpful.)

7. Assemble: Gather 5 large bowls. Portion the salad into the bowls, topping each salad generously with 3 to 4 tablespoons of the dressing, 1 tablespoon of almonds, and 1 teaspoon of sesame seeds.

vegan • gluten-free option • nut-free option • soy-free • kid-friendly • on the glow

Minty Sesame, Lime, and Ginger Noodle Salad

makes 4 (scant 2-cup) salads • prep time: 25 minutes • total time: 25 minutes

Like a cool breeze on a humid day or a dip in the pool when it's a scorcher, my Minty Sesame, Lime, and Ginger Noodle Salad is light and refreshing and the ideal summer salad. Soba noodles and chickpeas make sure your appetite is satiated and add healthy protein and fiber to the dish. It has a cooling sensation from the mint, with a cleansing grassy tone from the parsley. Also, you'll discover the floral, hydrating cucumber, a mild bite from the red onion, chewy yet creamy chickpeas, and savory, salty chopped pistachios, not to mention a lovely sweet tang from the Sesame, Lime, and Ginger Dressing (page 228). We love serving it al fresco to friends and family, and everyone always comments on how rejuvenating it is.

- 5 cups water
- 1 batch Sesame, Lime, and Ginger Dressing (page 228)
- 6.4 ounces (180 g) dried soba noodles
- ⅔ cup (80 g) diced red onion (½ medium)
- ½ cup packed (16 g) fresh mint leaves, minced
- ¼ cup packed (9 g) fresh flat-leaf parsley leaves, minced
- 3 medium Persian (mini) cucumbers (220 g total), thinly sliced (1½ cups)*
- 1½ cups (228 g) cooked chickpeas, drained and rinsed
- Fine sea salt and freshly ground black pepper
- ½ cup (70 g) salted roasted pistachios, coarsely chopped
- 4 teaspoons sesame seeds
- 4 lime wedges (optional)

1. In a medium pot, bring the water to a boil.
2. Meanwhile, make the Sesame, Lime, and Ginger Dressing.
3. When the water comes to a boil, add the soba noodles, reduce the heat to medium-high, stir, and cook according to the package directions (most soba noodles cook in 3 to 5 minutes), until al dente. Be sure not to overcook the noodles or they will be mushy in your salad. Drain the noodles and rinse under cold running water for at least 1 minute to stop the cooking process and prevent the noodles from sticking. Drain well.
4. Meanwhile, toss the diced red onion into a small bowl. Cover with cold water and let sit for 5 minutes. Drain well.
5. Add the noodles to a large bowl.
6. Prepare the mint, parsley, cucumbers, and cooked chickpeas, adding them to the noodle bowl as you go. Add the drained diced red onion to the bowl and toss to combine.
7. Set aside 2 tablespoons of the dressing in a small bowl. Using tongs, toss the remaining dressing with the noodle mixture until coated. Season to taste with salt and pepper.

recipe continues

storage

This salad is best served fresh, but you can store it in an airtight container in the fridge for up to 24 hours.

tip

* You can swap Persian (mini) cucumbers for English cucumbers.

make it gluten-free

Use gluten-free soba noodles.

make it nut-free

Swap the pistachios for a scant ¼ cup of toasted sunflower seeds.

8. Assemble: Gather 4 large bowls. Portion the noodle salad into the bowls (about 1¾ cups per bowl), being sure to scoop up any toppings that have fallen to the bottom of the bowl. Top each salad with 2 tablespoons of pistachios and 1 teaspoon of sesame seeds, and drizzle on ½ tablespoon of the reserved dressing. Season to taste with more salt and pepper and a squeeze of lime, if desired. Serve at room temperature or cold.

vegan • gluten-free option • nut-free • soy-free option • grain-free option • advance prep required • on the glow

On the Glow Pasta Salad

makes 4 (2½-cup) salads • prep time: 35 minutes • total time: 35 minutes, plus pressing time

Are you ready to have the most delectable pasta salad packed and ready to eat (or *ready to glow*) at a moment's notice? Sign me up! I know I tend to eat healthier during the day when I can grab something out of the fridge for what I like to call a "glow up lunch." If I'm headed out for the day, my lunch has more nutrition and is more flavorful when I bring my own instead of buying it (making it a money saver, too). This salad is a dream lunch or dinner, featuring your favorite pasta of choice, crunchy, colorful bell pepper, juicy cherry or grape tomatoes, aromatic dill and parsley, and my sweet and tangy Creamy ACV, Shallot, Maple, and Dijon Vinaigrette (page 233). Layering it into jars is a simple step that'll give you four effortless, packable meals. What could be better? If you plan to serve the salad all at once to a group, feel free to toss all the salad components and dressing together in a large salad bowl, reserving the Vegan Feta Cheese (page 259) for garnish. (I keep my Vegan Feta Cheese handy in the freezer so it's simple to add.) A big thank you to Fayette Nyehn for inspiring the method for this packable salad!

1⅓ cups (167 g) cubed Vegan Feta Cheese (page 259)

1 batch Creamy ACV, Shallot, Maple, and Dijon Vinaigrette (page 233)

8 ounces (3¼ cups/225 g) dried rotini pasta*

1 pint (283 g) cherry or grape tomatoes, halved (1¾ cups)

1 large bell pepper (225 g), seeded and diced (1 cup)**

½ cup (39 g) thinly sliced green onions (3 medium)

1½ cups (240 g) cooked white beans of choice or chickpeas, drained and rinsed (optional)

½ cup packed (19 g) fresh dill, minced

½ cup packed (17 g) fresh flat-leaf parsley leaves, minced

Fine sea salt and freshly ground black pepper

1. Make the Vegan Feta Cheese at least a few hours or up to 4 days in advance.

2. Make the Creamy ACV, Shallot, Maple, and Dijon Vinaigrette.

3. Bring a large pot of water to a boil. Cook the pasta according to the package directions, until tender. Drain and rinse under cold running water.

4. Meanwhile, gather 4 (16- to 20-ounce/500 to 590 mL) mason jars or jars with lids.

5. Prepare the tomatoes, bell pepper, green onions, beans (or chickpeas), dill, and parsley, placing them in separate small bowls as you go.

recipe continues

storage

Store in jars or airtight containers in the fridge for up to 3 days.

tips

* You can swap the rotini pasta for 4 cups of your favorite cooked short-cut pasta (such as fusilli or penne).

** You can use red, orange, or yellow bell pepper, although I prefer orange for this recipe as it creates an extra-colorful salad. Do not use green bell pepper.

make it gluten- and grain-free

Use 4 cups of your favorite cooked legume pasta. Note that gluten-free and grain-free pastas may not store well in the fridge, so I recommend you test the shelf life of your chosen pasta before using it in this salad.

make it soy-free

Swap the Vegan Feta Cheese for my Protein-Powered Cashew-Hemp Cheese (page 197). Note, the recipe will no longer be nut-free. If using store-bought vegan mayo in the dressing, be sure to select a soy-free variety.

6. Assemble: For each jar, layer the ingredients in the following order: ¼ cup of dressing (give it a shake before adding), ⅓ heaping cup of halved tomatoes, 2 tablespoons of green onions, ⅓ heaping cup of cooked beans, 1½ tablespoons of minced dill, 1½ tablespoons of minced parsley, ¼ cup of diced bell pepper, 1 cup of cooked pasta, and ⅓ cup of cubed vegan feta cheese.
7. Screw on the lids and refrigerate until ready to enjoy. When ready to serve, tip the contents of a jar into a large shallow bowl. Toss to combine, and season to taste with salt and pepper.

vegan • gluten-free option • soy-free • grain-free option • advance prep required • on the glow

Sun-Kissed On the Glow Pasta Salad

makes 4 (2½-cup) salads • prep time: 30 minutes • total time: 30 minutes

This pasta salad features sun-kissed summer-sweet cucumber and cherry tomatoes, peppery basil, chickpeas, rich and sweet-tart sun-dried tomatoes, and penne pasta. You can choose between my garlicky Garlic Lovers' Cashew Parmesan (page 281) or Oregano, Basil, and Lemon Zest Parmesan (page 280) for a crunchy, nutty addition. I like to add a handful of buttery toasted pine nuts if I have them on hand. My bright and punchy Ultra-Creamy Flavor Burst Basil Pesto (page 257) coats this salad in a nutty, garlicky goodness and brings out all the cheery flavors. Prepping the ingredients and layering them into jars is a fun process, and when you are ready to eat, simply tip a jar over your bowl and scoop out the delicious contents before mixing it all up. Of course, this salad is just as delicious served in a big salad bowl, too! Toss all the salad components and pesto together in the bowl, reserving the parmesan and pine nuts for garnish. Give this pasta salad a new twist by mixing in a handful of chopped romaine just before serving for extra crispness and hydration.

1 batch Ultra-Creamy Flavor Burst Basil Pesto (page 257)

1 batch Garlic Lovers' Cashew Parmesan (page 281) or Oregano, Basil, and Lemon Zest Parmesan (page 280)

9 ounces (2½ heaping cups/258 g) dried penne pasta*

½ large English cucumber, quartered lengthwise and thinly sliced (1⅓ cups/176 g)

1 pint (283 g) cherry or grape tomatoes, quartered (1¾ cups)

⅔ cup packed (20 g) fresh basil leaves, finely chopped

1½ cups (228 g) cooked chickpeas or cannellini beans, drained and rinsed (see Tips)

1 cup (160 g) oil-packed sun-dried tomatoes, drained and chopped

¼ cup (38 g) toasted pine nuts (optional)**

Fine sea salt and freshly ground black pepper

1. Make the Ultra-Creamy Flavor Burst Basil Pesto and Garlic Lovers' Cashew Parmesan or Oregano, Basil, and Lemon Zest Parmesan in advance.
2. Bring a large pot of water to a boil. Cook the pasta according to the package directions, until tender. Drain and rinse under cold running water.
3. Meanwhile, gather 4 (20-ounce/590 mL) mason jars or jars with lids (see Tips).
4. Prepare the cucumber, cherry tomatoes, basil, chickpeas (or cannellini beans), and sun-dried tomatoes, placing them in separate small bowls as you go.

recipe continues

storage

Store in jars or airtight containers in the fridge for up to 3 days.

tips

* 9 ounces (258 g) of dried penne should make a bit more than the 4 cups needed.

** To toast the pine nuts, see "Pantry Staples" (page 342).

Don't have 20-ounce (590 mL) jars? You can use 16-ounce (500 mL) jars instead; simply omit the chickpeas or beans to use less space and gently push down on the ingredients to pack them in.

make it gluten- and/or grain-free

Use gluten-free pasta or grain-free pasta. Note that gluten-free and grain-free pastas may not store well in the fridge, so I recommend you test the shelf life of your chosen pasta before using it in this salad.

5. Assemble: For each jar, layer the ingredients in the following order: ¼ to ⅓ cup of pesto (use ¼ cup for a very light coating and ⅓ cup for a creamier salad), 1 cup of cooked pasta (you will have a little left over), scant ¼ cup of sun-dried tomatoes, scant ⅓ cup of cucumber, scant ½ cup of cherry tomatoes, ⅓ heaping cup of chickpeas, 2 tablespoons of finely chopped basil, 1 tablespoon of pine nuts (if using), and ¼ to ⅓ cup of parmesan. (You can leave the parmesan and pine nuts out of the jar and sprinkle on top of the salad just before serving, if you prefer them as a garnish rather than mixed in. It's delicious either way.)

6. Screw on the lids and refrigerate until ready to enjoy. When ready to serve, tip the contents of a jar into a large bowl and scoop them all out. Toss to combine, and season to taste with salt and pepper.

vegan • gluten-free • nut-free option • soy-free • grain-free • advance prep required • kid-friendly • on the glow

Nourishing Warm Brunch Salad Bowls

makes 4 (3½-cup) salads • prep time: 40 minutes • total time: 1 hour 10 minutes

This brunch-worthy salad bowl is a dazzling combo of juicy citrus fruit and sweet strawberries with crisp green lettuce, herby and garlicky roasted yellow and sweet potatoes, summery grape or cherry tomatoes, and creamy, satisfying avocado. The savory ingredients are drizzled with my zippy Apple Cider, Shallot, Maple, and Dijon Vinaigrette (page 220), which pulls together all the salad's varied flavors and adds a kick of its own! I couldn't just leave it there, though. Whether your brunch is a lazy-day, PJ-wearing family affair or you're dressing up and having guests over, it should still be something special, so I dress up these bowls even further by scattering on top my sweet and savory Rosemary, Maple, and Cayenne Roasted Pecans and Walnuts (page 209) for added crunch and even more flavor complexity. My roasted seasoned yellow and sweet potatoes also make a fantastic topper on just about any salad, so feel free to roast a batch anytime you need a warm and cozy accompaniment to a salad.

- 1 batch Rosemary, Maple, and Cayenne Roasted Pecans and Walnuts (page 209)
- 1 pound (454 g) sweet potatoes
- 1 pound (454 g) Yukon Gold, new, or fingerling potatoes
- 2 tablespoons extra-virgin olive oil
- 2 teaspoons Italian seasoning blend
- 1½ teaspoons garlic powder
- Fine sea salt and freshly ground black pepper
- 1 batch Apple Cider, Shallot, Maple, and Dijon Vinaigrette (page 220)
- 5 ounces (142 g) baby romaine or chopped Little Gem or butter lettuce (7 cups)
- 1 heaping cup (168 g) grape or cherry tomatoes, sliced
- 12 medium fresh strawberries (279 g), hulled and sliced (1½ heaping cups)
- 2 large clementines or 1 medium navel orange (224 g total), sliced into rounds (optional)
- 1 large ripe avocado (225 g), pitted and peeled

1. Make the Rosemary, Maple, and Cayenne Roasted Pecans and Walnuts in advance.
2. Preheat the oven to 425°F (220°C) and line an extra-large rimmed baking sheet (or 2 large baking sheets) with parchment paper.
3. Peel the sweet potatoes and chop them into ¾-inch (2 cm) cubes (you should have 3½ cups). Chop the yellow potatoes into 1-inch (2.5 cm) cubes (you should have 2¾ cups). Place all the potatoes on the prepared baking sheet and toss with the olive oil, Italian seasoning, garlic powder, a generous pinch of salt, and several cranks of freshly ground black pepper until coated. Spread the potatoes into an even layer.
4. Roast the potatoes, uncovered, for 28 to 35 minutes, until fork tender and golden around the edges, flipping once halfway through baking.

recipe continues

storage

Store undressed salad in an airtight container in the fridge for up to 2 days. I recommend slicing the avocado just before assembling the salad, to keep it fresh.

make it nut-free

Omit the nuts and top with toasted pepitas.

5. Meanwhile, make the Apple Cider, Shallot, Maple, and Dijon Vinaigrette.

6. Assemble: Gather 4 large bowls. Divide the lettuce among the bowls (about 1½ cups per bowl). Prepare the tomatoes, strawberries, and clementines or navel oranges (if using). Top each bowl with about ¼ cup of sliced tomatoes, 2 to 3 sliced strawberries, and 2 clementine (or navel orange) rounds, arranging them in groupings as shown in the photo, if desired.

7. When the potatoes are ready, slice the avocado (you should have 1⅓ cups; I like to slice the avocado just before serving so it's fresh).

8. Spoon about 1 cup of potatoes into each bowl. Divide the sliced avocado among the bowls and drizzle the savory items (not the fruit) with about 3 tablespoons of vinaigrette. Scatter about 2 tablespoons of roasted nuts over each bowl. Sprinkle the potatoes with a bit more salt, if desired. Serve warm.

CRYPTIC CROSSWORD

fall
and
winter

fall and winter

grain salads

vegan • gluten-free option • soy-free • grain-free option • raw/no bake option • on the glow

Fall Crunch Farro Kale Salad

makes 11 (1-cup) salads with farro • prep time: 35 minutes • total time: 35 minutes

I wanted to create the most perfect kale salad that would work at any kind of gathering or potluck, or simply as a delectable (and often spotlight-stealing!) side salad for just about any kind of meal. After a lot of work perfecting this one, I can say: *mission accomplished*. This is one of my newest favorite ways to enjoy kale, and it's a salad I turn to again and again whenever I'm invited to a potluck (you know I *always* volunteer to bring a plant-based salad!) or hosting a gathering at home. I start by getting my Easy Garlic-Infused Farro (page 268) simmering away on the stovetop; farro adds a delightful heartiness and chewiness to this salad, but it's optional, as the salad works well even without it. Next, I stem the kale leaves and finely chop them before marinating them in a crowd-pleasing garlic, apple cider vinegar, and maple dressing. I add crunchy sliced celery and top it all with my show-stealing crunchy and garlicky nutty protein topper and a scattering of sweet and tangy dried cranberries.

1 batch Easy Garlic-Infused Farro (page 268; optional)

1 batch The Crunch Nutty Protein Topper (page 211)

1 extra-large bunch or 2 small bunches curly kale (300 g total)

1 batch Glowing House Vinaigrette (page 230)

2 large celery ribs (136 g total), thinly sliced (1 cup)

Fine sea salt and freshly ground black pepper

½ cup (73 g) sweetened dried cranberries

1. Make the Easy Garlic-Infused Farro (if using). When done, remove from the heat and gently cool for a few minutes before adding to the salad.
2. Make The Crunch Nutty Protein Topper.
3. While the farro cooks, remove the stems from the kale and discard. Finely chop the leaves into 1-inch (2.5 cm) long strands or smaller (you should have about 8 packed cups). Transfer to a large bowl.
4. Make the Glowing House Vinaigrette. Shake the dressing to recombine, then pour ½ cup of vinaigrette over the kale and massage it into the leaves for 30 seconds or so, until fully coated. Reserve the rest of the vinaigrette for later.

recipe continues

storage

This salad is best served fresh, or within 4 to 6 hours of making it. However, leftovers can be stored in an airtight container in the fridge for up to 2 days. Revive the salad by drizzling on leftover Glowing House Vinaigrette.

make it gluten- and grain-free and raw/no bake

Omit the optional farro.

5. Assemble: Add the sliced celery to the kale and toss to combine.
6. If using farro, add the cooled farro to the kale mixture and toss to combine. Shake the vinaigrette to recombine, then pour another ¼ cup over the salad and toss well until combined. Season to taste with salt and pepper.
7. Sprinkle on 2 cups of The Crunch Nutty Protein Topper (you'll have some left over for another use) and scatter the dried cranberries over the salad. Portion into bowls or onto plates and serve the remaining nutty protein topper and vinaigrette on the side for extra scattering and drizzling deliciousness.

vegan • gluten-free option • nut-free • kid-friendly • on the glow

Sweater Weather Toasted Sesame, Tamari, and Garlic Kale Salad

makes 4 (3-cup) salads • prep time: 45 minutes • total time: 55 minutes

Finely shredded kale and fluffy quinoa are paired with one of my favorite sweet, savory, and umami-rich dressings, Toasted Sesame, Tamari, and Garlic Dressing (page 219), ensuring that every little piece of kale and quinoa tastes phenomenal. I love loading up this delectable kale and quinoa base with my garlicky and spicy Garlic-Cayenne Roasted Chickpeas (202), caramelized roasted sweet potatoes, a sprinkle of zesty diced sweet bell pepper, mild green onions, and salty pepitas for that crunch we all love. It's important to chop the sweet potatoes into pieces no larger than about 1 inch (2.5 cm) to ensure they cook in about the same amount of time as the roasted chickpeas, so avoid using big chunks of potato. This is a great recipe to take advantage of my make-ahead tips (page 323), so be sure to check those out to save you prep time on the day of. I often like to make the quinoa up to a couple of days in advance and make the dressing and prep the kale one day in advance to expedite the salad on the day I'm serving it.

1½ batches Toasted Sesame, Tamari, and Garlic Dressing (page 219, see Variation)

Roasted Chickpeas and Sweet Potatoes

1 batch Garlic-Cayenne Roasted Chickpeas (page 202)*

3 to 4 medium sweet potatoes (1.8 pounds/825 g total)

2 tablespoons extra-virgin olive oil

½ teaspoon fine sea salt

Freshly ground black pepper

Quinoa

¾ cup (138 g) uncooked white quinoa**

1⅓ cups vegetable broth or water

Kale and Raw Veggies

1 extra-large bunch or 2 small bunches curly kale (300 g total)

2 teaspoons extra-virgin olive oil

½ cup (69 g) diced red bell pepper (½ small)

¼ cup (20 g) thinly sliced green onions (2 small)

¼ cup (34 g) salted roasted pepitas

2 teaspoons sesame seeds

1. Make the 1½ batches of Toasted Sesame, Tamari, and Garlic Dressing up to 1 day in advance.
2. Position the racks in the upper and lower thirds of the oven and preheat the oven to 375°F (190°C). Line 2 large rimmed baking sheets with parchment paper.
3. Prepare the Garlic-Cayenne Roasted Chickpeas, spreading them on one of the prepared baking sheets, but don't roast them yet. Set aside the filled pan.
4. Peel the sweet potatoes and chop them into 1-inch (2.5 cm) cubes (you should have 6 scant cups). Place the sweet potatoes on the second prepared baking sheet, drizzle with the 2 tablespoons of olive oil, and toss until thoroughly coated. Spread into an even layer and season with the salt and several cranks of freshly ground black pepper.

recipe continues

storage

Store leftovers in an airtight container in the fridge for up to 4 days. If you'd like it served warm, reheat the salad in a covered oiled skillet over medium heat for 2 to 3 minutes. Drizzle to taste with more dressing.

tips

* If you prefer to skip the spicy heat from this salad, simply omit the cayenne called for in the roasted chickpea recipe for a more neutral flavor.

** You'll need 2 cups of cooked quinoa if you are using pre-cooked or leftover quinoa.

make it gluten-free

Use a gluten-free light tamari to make the Toasted Sesame, Tamari, and Garlic Dressing.

5. Roast both the chickpeas and potatoes, uncovered, for 15 minutes. Toss the chickpeas and potatoes, then rotate the pans from upper to lower and back to front. Continue roasting for another 10 to 27 minutes, until the potatoes are fork-tender and the chickpeas are golden. (I roast the chickpeas for about 34 minutes total and the potatoes for 37 minutes total.) If the chickpeas finish cooking first, remove them from the oven and continue cooking the potatoes until done. Cool the chickpeas and potatoes on the pans for a few minutes.
6. Meanwhile, Cook the Quinoa: In a medium pot, stir together the quinoa and broth (or water). Bring to a boil over high heat, then reduce the heat to low, cover with a tight-fitting lid, and simmer for 12 to 14 minutes, until the liquid has been absorbed and the quinoa is fluffy. Remove from the heat, fluff with a fork, and let sit, uncovered, until cooled slightly.
7. Meanwhile, remove the stems from the kale and discard. Finely chop the leaves into 1-inch (2.5 cm) long strands or smaller (you should have about 7 cups). Transfer the kale to a large salad bowl and drizzle with the 2 teaspoons of olive oil. Massage the oil into the kale with your hands, squeezing the kale to help soften it. Let sit for a few minutes. Prepare the bell pepper and green onions.
8. When the quinoa has cooled slightly, stir it into the kale. Toss with ½ cup of the dressing until well combined. Let sit for a few minutes to soften slightly.
9. Assemble: Gather 4 large bowls. Add 1¾ cups of the kale-quinoa mixture to each bowl and top with 1 scant cup of roasted sweet potatoes, ¼ cup of roasted chickpeas, 2 tablespoons of diced bell pepper, 1 tablespoon of green onions, 1 tablespoon of pepitas, ½ teaspoon of sesame seeds, and 2 tablespoons of dressing. Season to taste with salt and pepper. Enjoy warm.

vegan • gluten-free option • nut-free option • advance prep required • freezer-friendly • on the glow

Super Green Bean, Rice, and Avocado Salad

makes 5 (2½-cup) salads • prep time: 45 minutes • total time: 50 minutes

My Super Green Bean, Rice, and Avocado Salad is a flavor explosion! Velvety avocado, garlicky tamari green beans, and crispy, sweet carrots create a robust bowl (or stack) along with my comforting Cilantro-Jalapeño Rice (page 273). It's all topped with my brightly flavored Lime, Cumin, and Red Pepper Parmesan (page 278), which adds a bit of crunch and brings a nutty, spicy, zesty flavor. I drizzle this dish with my sweet and gingery Sesame, Lime, and Ginger Dressing (page 228), which brings it all together. You can serve this salad stacked or simply as a humble bowl, depending on your mood. If you want to try stacking it, I've provided directions on the next page.

1 batch Sesame, Lime, and Ginger Dressing (page 228)

1 batch Lime, Cumin, and Red Pepper Parmesan (page 278)

1 batch Cilantro-Jalapeño Rice (page 273)

2 medium carrots (190 g total), peeled and julienned (1¼ cups)*

½ heaping cup (41 g) thinly sliced green onions (3 medium)

3 large ripe avocados (675 g total), pitted, peeled, and cubed (2½ cups)

Garlicky Tamari Green Beans

5 cups water

12 ounces (340 g) fresh green beans, trimmed and chopped into 1½-inch (4 cm) pieces (3 cups)

2 teaspoons light tamari**

¼ teaspoon garlic powder, or to taste

Fine sea salt

1 tablespoon sesame seeds

1. Make the Sesame, Lime, and Ginger Dressing and the Lime, Cumin, and Red Pepper Parmesan in advance.
2. Make the Cilantro-Jalapeño Rice.
3. While the rice cooks, in a medium pot, bring the water for the green beans to a boil over high heat.
4. Meanwhile, prepare the green beans, carrots, green onions, and avocados, adding them to separate small bowls or simply arranging them in groupings on a large cutting board.
5. When the water comes to a boil, add the green beans and boil for 2 to 3 minutes, until just tender (you'll want a tiny bit of crunch left). Drain well, then return the beans to the pot over medium-low heat. Stir in the tamari and season to taste with garlic powder and salt. Stir in the sesame seeds. Remove from the heat and cover to keep warm. Reheat if necessary just before serving.

recipe continues

storage

Store the components (except the avocado; I suggest preparing it just before serving) in separate airtight containers in the fridge for up to 4 days. Freeze the rice, green beans, and parmesan separately for up to 1 month. Reheat the rice and beans in a covered pot, over medium-low heat, with a little veggie broth to moisten, or simply microwave the rice, green beans, carrots, and green onions in 15-second increments until warmed, then top with chopped avocado, dressing, and parmesan.

tips

* If you have a spiralizer, you can spiralize the carrots for a pretty twist (literally!).

** It's important to use light tamari (not regular full-sodium tamari) or the bean mixture will be too salty.

make it gluten-free

Use gluten-free light tamari.

make it nut-free

Omit the parmesan and top each bowl with 2 teaspoons of chopped toasted pepitas instead.

6. Assemble: Gather 5 large bowls. To each bowl, add ½ cup of cubed avocado, a generous ¾ cup of warm rice, ½ cup of warm green beans, ¼ cup of julienned carrot, and 1½ tablespoons of sliced green onions. Sprinkle each salad with 2 tablespoons of the parmesan and drizzle 2 tablespoons of the dressing on top. Serve warm.

Make a Stacked Salad

To make a stacked salad, grab a large food-stacking ring, or cut off the bottom of a large (16-ounce/473 mL) paper or plastic cup, trimming about 1½ inches (4 cm) from the bottom. Place the ring or the widest end of the cup on a plate. While holding the ring or cup in place with one hand, spoon ½ cup of avocado cubes into the cup and press down with a spoon to lightly pack them into the bottom. Spoon ¾ heaping cup of warm rice on top of the avocado and gently push down with a spoon to pack it in. Add ½ cup of warm green beans on top of the rice and again push down with a spoon. Roughly chop ¼ cup of julienned carrot into about 1-inch pieces, then add them on top of the beans. Finally, add 1½ tablespoons of green onions. Slowly and carefully lift the ring or cup straight up. Voilà! Sprinkle on the parmesan and dressing and serve immediately. The salads will tumble as soon as the fork makes contact (if not before!), but they sure are a pretty and fun way of displaying the salad.

vegan • gluten-free • nut-free option • soy-free • kid-friendly • on the glow

Stuffed Butternut Squash Wild Rice Salad

makes 10 (¾-cup rice, plus sliced squash) salads • prep time: 45 minutes • total time: 1 hour 15 minutes

This cozy salad is the epitome of autumn with its burnished-orange roasted butternut squash, pops of dark red cranberries, and the tiniest pops of green from the tart Granny Smith apple. I used nutty wild rice to add wonderful chewiness to the creamy squash, tart cranberries, sweet apricots, and creamy chickpeas, and we all love the light crunch from the celery and pecans. If you are serving this dish to celebrate the arrival of fall or at your holiday table, I suggest pairing it with my sweet and citrusy Cold Moon Orange Vinaigrette (page 217). Its orange and apple taste shines in this salad, and you'll get that "first time this season putting on a cozy sweater" feeling. Other times of year, and especially if serving the wild rice salad without the squash (you can totally do this; the rice is delicious all on its own), we drizzle it liberally with my Luxurious ACV and Dijon Dressing (page 221); I like to use 2 teaspoons of pure maple syrup in the Luxurious dressing to enhance the sweetness of the salad. My Perfect Balsamic-Maple Vinaigrette (page 218) works wonderfully, too. For extra-special occasions, I like to leave out the pecans and instead scatter each serving with chopped Rosemary, Maple, and Cayenne Roasted Pecans and Walnuts (page 209).

Roasted Butternut Squash

1 large butternut squash (2½ pounds/1.2 kg)

1 tablespoon extra-virgin olive oil, divided

Fine sea salt and freshly ground black pepper

Wild Rice Salad

Double batch Cold Moon Orange Vinaigrette (page 217, see Variation)

1 cup (190 g) uncooked wild rice blend (3 cups cooked)

2 cups water

1¼ cups (150 g) diced red or yellow onion (½ large)

1 tablespoon olive oil

Fine sea salt

4 ounces (113 g) cremini mushrooms, chopped (2 scant cups)

2 large celery ribs (136 g total), thinly sliced (1 scant cup)

½ medium Granny Smith apple (90 g), diced (¾ scant cup)

1½ cups (228 g) cooked chickpeas, drained and rinsed

⅓ cup (72 g) dried apricots, chopped

⅓ cup (49 g) sweetened dried cranberries, chopped

½ cup (58 g) toasted or raw pecan halves, chopped

Freshly ground black pepper

1. Make the double batch of Cold Moon Orange Vinaigrette.
2. Preheat the oven to 400°F (200°C) and line a large rimmed baking sheet with parchment paper.
3. Peel the squash (if you don't mind eating the edible peel, feel free to leave it on!), trim the ends, then halve the squash lengthwise. Scoop out and discard the seeds. Brush the cut side of each squash half with ½ tablespoon of the olive oil and sprinkle with a generous ¼ teaspoon each of salt and pepper. Place the halves, seasoned side down, on the prepared baking sheet and roast, uncovered, for 45 to 55 minutes, until a fork easily slides in when pierced.

recipe continues

storage

Store leftovers in an airtight container in the fridge for up to 4 days.

make it nut-free

Omit the pecans.

4. While the squash roasts, cook the wild rice: In a medium pot, stir together the rice and water. Bring to a boil over high heat, then reduce the heat to low, cover with a tight-fitting lid, and simmer for 35 to 50 minutes (or follow the package directions), until the water has been absorbed and the rice is soft, tender, and slightly chewy. Turn off the heat and steam, covered, for 10 minutes or so.
5. Dice the onion. In a large skillet, heat the 1 tablespoon olive oil over low heat for a minute. Add the onion and a pinch of salt, stir, and cook over medium-low to medium heat for 7 to 8 minutes, stirring occasionally, until the onion is soft and translucent. Meanwhile, prepare the mushrooms and celery, adding them to the skillet once the onions are ready. Continue cooking, uncovered, stirring occasionally, for 10 minutes or until the vegetables have softened.
6. Dice the apple and stir it into the vegetable mixture. Cook for another 2 to 4 minutes, until the apple is slightly softened but still has some crispness to it.
7. Stir in the cooked rice and continue cooking over low heat.
8. Prepare the chickpeas, dried apricots, cranberries, and pecans, adding them to the skillet as you go. Stir to combine, and season to taste with salt and pepper (I add about ½ teaspoon of salt). Ensure the mixture is heated through before serving.
9. Assemble: Place the roasted squash halves cut side up on an extra-large platter. Drizzle 1 to 2 tablespoons of dressing over each half, then season with a sprinkling of salt and pepper. Spoon half of the wild rice salad onto each squash half, pressing down lightly if desired. To serve, slice the squash into 1-inch (2.5 cm) thick slices and transfer each slice to a plate or shallow bowl, scooping any tumbling warm rice salad (about ¾ cup) back on top of each slice. Drizzle each serving with about 3 tablespoons of vinaigrette, and sprinkle with salt and pepper. Serve warm with any leftover vinaigrette on the side.

vegan • gluten-free • soy-free • grain-free • kid-friendly • on the glow

Cuddle Up Warm Pesto Dream Bowl

makes 4 (scant 3-cup) bowls • prep time: 40 minutes • total time: 55 minutes

When fall arrives early and the temps drop, I start to crave the sweet and robust flavor of roasted veggies and can't resist creating a cozy bowlful to snuggle up with. On the other hand, I'm not always (okay, ever!) ready to say goodbye to summer. What's a lover of hot weather to do? My solution is to add those bright, herby, zesty tastes of summer to my dish by topping it with Ultra-Creamy Flavor Burst Basil Pesto (page 257). My Cuddle Up Warm Pesto Dream Bowl was born of this summer-gives-way-to-fall-but-I'm-not-ready dilemma. The flavors *are* dreamy—the sweetness of the roasted carrots plays perfectly with the lemony, peppery basil pesto. The tender red onion and bell pepper, lightly bitter arugula, and umami-rich sun-dried tomatoes add depth of flavor and chewy texture to the dish, and it's all mellowed out by the creamy new potatoes. Sometimes, we love to squeeze a lemon wedge over our bowls to add a tangy pop. If you'd like to bulk up your bowl even further, try adding cooked beans (such as cannellini beans or chickpeas) or farro for more heft.

Roasted Veggies

1 pound (454 g) baby or new potatoes

5 medium carrots (513 g total)

3½ tablespoons extra-virgin olive oil, divided

1 scant teaspoon fine sea salt, divided

Freshly ground black pepper

2 large bell peppers (450 g total), seeded and chopped (2½ cups)*

1 large bunch broccoli (570 g), cut into 1-inch (2.5 cm) florets (4 cups)**

1 medium red onion (172 g), peeled and cut into 1-inch (2.5 cm) chunks (1 cup)

For assembly

1 batch Ultra-Creamy Flavor Burst Basil Pesto (page 257)

2 cups packed (60 g) baby arugula, coarsely chopped***

⅓ cup packed (11 g) fresh basil leaves, finely chopped

½ cup (39 g) thinly sliced green onions (3 medium)

⅓ cup (53 g) oil-packed sun-dried tomatoes, drained and chopped

¼ cup (38 g) pine nuts or salted roasted pepitas

4 lemon wedges

1. Position the racks in the upper and lower thirds of the oven and preheat to 400°F (200°C). Line 2 extra-large rimmed baking sheets with parchment paper.

2. Halve the potatoes or quarter them if large, adding them to one of the prepared baking sheets as you go (you should have 3½ cups). Peel the carrots and cut them into ½-inch (1 cm) rounds, adding them to the potatoes as you go (you should have 3 scant cups). Toss with 1½ tablespoons of the olive oil, a scant ½ teaspoon of the salt, and several cranks of freshly ground black pepper. Set a timer for 10 minutes and start roasting the vegetables, uncovered.

recipe continues

storage

Store the roasted and raw veggies in separate airtight containers in the fridge for up to 4 days. Reheat the cooked vegetables before assembling.

tips

* You can use red, orange, or yellow bell peppers. Do not use green bell peppers.

** For a fun twist, swap the broccoli for cauliflower and add some cooked farro to your bowl.

*** I like to remove any long or thick stems from the arugula before chopping.

This salad is extra delicious served with my Protein-Powered Cashew-Hemp Cheese (page 197).

Have leftover arugula? Why not use it in my Strawberry Arugula Salad with Feta and Rosemary-Maple Nuts (page 86) or Butternut, Cranberry, and Rosemary-Maple Pecan and Walnut Arugula Salad (page 153).

3. Meanwhile, prepare the bell peppers, broccoli, and red onion, adding them to the second baking sheet as you go. Toss with the remaining 2 tablespoons olive oil, the remaining scant ½ teaspoon salt, and several cranks of freshly ground black pepper. When the 10-minute timer goes off, slide the second pan of vegetables into the oven. Continue roasting both pans of vegetables for 10 minutes, then flip the veggies, rotate the pans from upper to lower and back to front, and continue roasting for another 10 to 25 minutes, until tender and golden.
4. While the veggies roast, make the Ultra-Creamy Flavor Burst Basil Pesto.
5. Prepare the arugula, basil, green onions, and sun-dried tomatoes.
6. Assemble: Gather 4 large bowls. When the veggies are finished roasting, add about ¾ cup of pepper-broccoli mixture and 1 generous cup of potato-carrot mixture to each bowl. Place ½ cup of arugula on one side of each bowl. Top each bowl with 1 generous tablespoon of finely chopped basil, 2 tablespoons of sliced green onions, 1 generous tablespoon of chopped sun-dried tomatoes, 1 tablespoon of pine nuts or pepitas, and ¼ to ⅓ cup of pesto. Season to taste with salt and pepper. Serve with a lemon wedge on the side to squeeze over your bowl, for a tangy pop!

vegan • gluten-free option • nut-free • soy-free option • on the glow

Harvest Roasted Carrot and Herb Salad

makes 4 (generous 3-cup) salads • prep time: 30 minutes • total time: 50 minutes

Simple, rustic, unassuming, and bursting with incredible flavor! If you think a roasted carrot salad sounds a bit dull, then hold on to your taste buds because earthy and sweet caramelized roasted carrots pair beautifully with my flavor-bursting Barbecue Apple Cider Vinaigrette (page 243)—a match made in heaven! The vinaigrette adds a sweet, spicy, summery brightness that is the remedy to any cold, dreary day. To boost the protein, I love making my Garlic-Cayenne Roasted Chickpeas (page 202) to serve in this salad; simply roast them on a separate large rimmed baking sheet for around the same amount of time as the carrots, rotating the pans halfway through cooking, watching closely, and pulling them out of the oven early, if needed. It's also tasty served with my Crispy Breaded Tofu Tenders (page 185). Feel free to change up this salad, roasting up all of your favorite on-hand veggies (sweet potato, brussels sprouts, cauliflower, parsnips, and broccoli are a few ideas). If you have a few cups of leftover roasted veggies already in the fridge, it's easy to reheat them and use them on the salad in place of the carrots.

7 medium carrots (788 g total)

2 tablespoons extra-virgin olive oil

½ teaspoon fine sea salt

Freshly ground black pepper

1 cup (185 g) uncooked white quinoa*

1¾ cups water

1 batch Barbecue Apple Cider Vinaigrette (page 243)

6 cups packed (296 g) chopped romaine hearts (3 medium)

⅓ cup packed (12 g) fresh flat-leaf parsley leaves, chopped

⅓ cup packed (12 g) fresh cilantro leaves, chopped**

6 tablespoons (51 g total) salted roasted pepitas

1. Preheat the oven to 400°F (200°C) and line an extra-large rimmed baking sheet with parchment paper.
2. Peel the carrots and trim the ends. Halve the carrots lengthwise, then cut them into 3-inch (8 cm) long by ½-inch (1 cm) thick wedges (you should have about 5 heaping cups).
3. Place the carrots on the prepared baking sheet and toss with the olive oil. Spread into an even layer and sprinkle with the salt and several cranks of freshly ground black pepper.
4. Roast the carrots for 15 minutes, then flip the carrots and rotate the pan. Continue roasting for another 15 to 20 minutes, until fork-tender and charred (I roast for 35 minutes total).

recipe continues

storage

Store undressed salad in an airtight container in the fridge for up to 2 days. Reheat the carrots in a 400°F (200°C) oven for 3 to 5 minutes, until warmed through, then return them to the salad and top with the dressing and pepitas.

tips

* To change up the grain, try swapping the quinoa for my Easy Garlic-Infused Farro (page 268). The salad will not be gluten-free, however.

** If you aren't a cilantro fan, feel free to omit it and simply use more fresh parsley if desired.

This salad is extra gorgeous when topped with a sprinkle of sesame seeds. (Bonus points because they also add calcium!)

make it gluten- and soy-free

If making my Sweet and Tangy No-Chop Barbecue Sauce, which is an optional ingredient in my Barbecue Apple Cider Vinaigrette, use gluten- and soy-free vegan Worcestershire sauce, or simply select a gluten- and soy-free store-bought barbecue sauce, if needed.

5. Meanwhile, cook the quinoa: In a medium pot, stir together the quinoa and water. Bring to a boil over high heat, then reduce the heat to low, cover with a tight-fitting lid, and simmer for 12 to 14 minutes, until the water has been absorbed and the quinoa is fluffy. Remove from the heat, fluff with a fork, and let sit, uncovered, to gently cool. Season to taste with salt.
6. Prepare the Barbecue Apple Cider Vinaigrette.
7. Prepare the romaine, parsley, and cilantro.
8. Assemble: Gather 4 large bowls. To each bowl, add 1½ packed cups of romaine. Top each with a generous ½ cup of warm quinoa, then drizzle 1 tablespoon of dressing over top. Top each bowl with about ⅔ to ¾ cup of warm roasted carrots, 1 heaping tablespoon of cilantro, 1 heaping tablespoon of parsley, 1½ tablespoons of pepitas, and another 1 to 2 tablespoons, to taste, of vinaigrette.

fall and winter

Recipes

bean, lentil, and tofu salads

vegan • gluten-free • nut-free • soy-free • grain-free • kid-friendly • on the glow

Warm and Cozy Roasted Mediterranean Lentil Salad

makes 4 (1¾-cup) salads • prep time: 35 minutes • total time: 1 hour 5 minutes

This dish is ideal for those quintessential crisp fall or winter nights, or enjoyed on a cool and rainy spring or summer day. Warm your belly and your spirit by digging into my Warm and Cozy Roasted Mediterranean Lentil Salad. I love how the mild zucchini, sweet grape tomatoes, and zippy bell peppers transform during roasting into a slightly caramelized, rich, and warming salad, which contrasts so deliciously with the invigorating Zesty Lemon, Dill, and Oregano Dressing (page 239). It's also tasty when served with my Immunity-Boosting Tahini Dressing (page 229) or Velvety Cashew Garlic Dressing (page 226) for a delectable creamy twist! Serve it with toasted pita bread for scooping or piled high on my Garlic-Infused Olive Oil Crostini (page 249). I also love topping my bowls with cubes of my tangy Vegan Feta Cheese (page 259). For a traditional salad feel and added crunch, try serving it on top of dressed baby romaine lettuce.

- 4 medium yellow potatoes (1½ pounds/690 g total), peeled
- 1 large or 2 small zucchini (290 g total)
- 2 medium red bell peppers (400 g total), seeded
- 1 pint (283 g) grape tomatoes
- 3 tablespoons extra-virgin olive oil
- Fine sea salt and freshly ground black pepper
- 1 batch Zesty Lemon, Dill, and Oregano Dressing (page 239)
- 1½ cups (250 g) cooked brown lentils, drained and rinsed*
- ½ cup packed (19 g) fresh dill, minced
- ½ cup packed (15 g) fresh basil leaves, finely chopped
- ½ cup (80 g) oil-packed sun-dried tomatoes, drained and finely chopped

1. Position the racks in the upper and lower thirds of the oven and preheat to 400°F (200°C). Line 2 large rimmed baking sheets with parchment paper.
2. Chop the peeled potatoes, zucchini, and bell peppers into ¾-inch (2 cm) pieces, adding them to the 2 prepared baking sheets as you go (you should have 4 cups potatoes, 2 cups zucchini, and 3 heaping cups bell peppers). Cut the grape tomatoes in half, adding them to the baking sheets (you should have 1¾ cups).
3. Sprinkle each sheet of veggies with half of the olive oil and toss until thoroughly coated. Season generously with salt and pepper. Spread in an even layer.

recipe continues

storage

Store the salad and dressing in separate airtight containers in the fridge for up to 3 days. Revive the flavors with a squeeze of lemon juice, more dressing, and a sprinkle of salt. If you like the salad warm, heat individual bowls in the microwave until warm.

tip

* Using canned or freshly cooked lentils? See "Pantry Staples" (page 342).

4. Roast the veggies, uncovered, for 30 to 40 minutes, until fork-tender and golden, flipping the veggies and rotating the pans from upper to lower and back to front halfway through roasting.
5. Meanwhile, make the Zesty Lemon, Dill, and Oregano Dressing.
6. Prepare the lentils, dill, basil, and sun-dried tomatoes, adding them to a large bowl as you go. When the veggies are finished roasting, add them to the bowl and toss until well combined. Season to taste with salt and pepper.
7. Assemble: Gather 4 large bowls. Divide the salad among the bowls (about 1¾ cups per bowl). Drizzle 3 generous tablespoons of dressing on top of each salad. Serve warm.

vegan • gluten-free option • nut-free option • grain-free • advance prep required • kid-friendly • on the glow

Sweet Potato and Edamame Salad with Roasted Almond Butter, Ginger, and Lime Dressing

makes 4 (generous 3½-cup) salads • prep time: 35 minutes • total time: 50 minutes

This is a colorful, fresh and crisp, and deeply flavorful eat-it-all-year-round salad. It's roasty and sweet from the caramelized sweet potatoes, juicy from the grated carrot, energizing from the red cabbage and edamame, citrusy from the cilantro, and creamy and tangy from my Roasted Almond Butter, Ginger, and Lime Dressing (page 222, see Tips for a modified nut-free version). And let's talk about the hint of crunch and umami flavor from my sliced Sticky Roasted Tamari-Maple Almonds (page 203). They are a sweet and savory addition, caramelizing into little candied bundles while toasting that are simply lovely on this salad. Try serving this salad with my Shake-and-Bake Sesame-Crusted Tofu (page 195), as it adds a crunchy, chewy texture and the sesame flavor pairs beautifully with the salad.

- 1 batch Sticky Roasted Tamari-Maple Almonds, Sliced Version (page 203)
- 2 to 3 medium sweet potatoes (1½ pounds/692 g total)
- 1½ tablespoons extra-virgin olive oil
- ½ teaspoon fine sea salt
- Freshly ground black pepper
- 1 batch Roasted Almond Butter, Ginger, and Lime Dressing (page 222)
- 1 cup (80 g) thinly sliced red cabbage
- 1½ cups (185 g) frozen shelled edamame, thawed and drained
- 3 medium carrots (280 g total), peeled and grated on the large holes of a box grater (2 cups)
- 1 cup packed (34 g) fresh cilantro leaves, coarsely chopped
- 5 ounces (142 g) baby romaine or chopped Little Gem lettuce*
- 4 lime wedges

1. Make the sliced version of the Sticky Roasted Tamari-Maple Almonds in advance.
2. Preheat the oven to 400°F (200°C) and line a large rimmed baking sheet with parchment paper.
3. Peel the sweet potatoes, then chop into 1-inch (2.5 cm) cubes, adding them to the prepared baking sheet as you go (you should have 4½ cups). Toss with the olive oil to coat and spread in an even layer. Sprinkle with the salt and several cranks of freshly ground black pepper. Roast, uncovered, for 30 to 40 minutes, until tender and lightly browned in some spots, flipping once halfway through roasting.

recipe continues

storage

Store undressed salad in an airtight container in the fridge for up to 4 days. Reheat the sweet potatoes in a 400°F (200°C) oven for 6 to 8 minutes, until warmed through, then return them to the salad and add the dressing.

tip

* Swap the baby romaine or Little Gem lettuce for 1 large head of romaine lettuce, chopped, if desired.

make it gluten-free

Use gluten-free light tamari in the Roasted Almond Butter, Ginger, and Lime Dressing and Sticky Roasted Tamari-Maple Almonds.

make it nut-free

Use Nut-Free Sunflower, Ginger, and Lime Dressing (page 224) and omit the roasted almonds.

4. Meanwhile, make the Roasted Almond Butter, Ginger, and Lime Dressing.
5. Prepare the cabbage, edamame, carrots, cilantro, and romaine.
6. Assemble: Gather 4 large bowls. Divide the lettuce among the bowls (about 1½ cups per salad). To each bowl, add ¼ cup of cabbage, a generous ⅓ cup of edamame, ½ cup of carrot, ¼ cup of cilantro, a generous ½ cup of roasted sweet potato, and 2 generous tablespoons of roasted almonds, arranged in groupings as shown in the photo, if desired. Drizzle 3 to 4 tablespoons of dressing over each bowl and serve with a lime wedge on the side. Serve warm.

vegan • gluten-free • nut-free option • soy-free option • grain-free • kid-friendly • on the glow

Cozy Potato, Zucchini, and Cannellini Bean Salad with Luxurious ACV and Dijon Dressing

makes 4 (generous 2-cup) salads • prep time: 30 minutes • total time: 40 minutes

Move over, traditional boring potato salad, and make room for my Cozy Potato, Zucchini, and Cannellini Bean Salad with Luxurious ACV and Dijon Dressing! You really can't go wrong with this warm and delectable salad that features crispy potatoes with caramelized bottoms, roasted zucchini, sweet grape tomatoes, crunchy green onion, and aromatic fresh dill. Ooh la la. Top it with chopped walnuts for crunch or make it nut-free by sprinkling on toasted pepitas. Cannellini beans add extra fiber and protein, not to mention staying power. My Luxurious ACV and Dijon Dressing (page 221) is a velvety *wow* salad dressing featuring a base of creamy mayo and sweet apple cider vinegar that adds such a lovely tang to the salad. Sprinkling a little garlic powder and Italian seasoning over each bowl before serving is magical and takes it to the next level. This salad moves quickly, so I recommend having all the ingredients ready at hand to keep it running smoothly.

3 medium Yukon Gold or 8 medium fingerling potatoes (1.2 pounds/543 g total)

2 large zucchini (516 g total)

2 tablespoons extra-virgin olive oil, divided

2 teaspoons Italian seasoning blend, divided, plus more for serving

1½ teaspoons garlic powder, divided, plus more for serving

Fine sea salt and freshly ground black pepper

1 batch Luxurious ACV and Dijon Dressing (page 221)

1 pint (283 g) grape tomatoes, sliced (1¾ cups)

⅓ cup packed (13 g) fresh dill, minced

½ cup (39 g) thinly sliced green onions (3 medium)

½ heaping cup (68 g) raw walnut halves, chopped*

1½ cups (240 g) cooked cannellini beans, drained and rinsed

1. Position the racks in the upper and lower thirds of the oven and preheat to 425°F (220°C). Line 2 large rimmed baking sheets with parchment paper.
2. Chop the potatoes into ¾-inch (2 cm) cubes, adding them to a prepared baking sheet as you go (you should have 3¾ cups). Toss the potatoes with 1 tablespoon of the olive oil, 1 teaspoon of the Italian seasoning, ¾ teaspoon of the garlic powder, a pinch of salt, and several cranks of freshly ground black pepper until coated.
3. Roast the potatoes, uncovered, for 5 minutes.

recipe continues

storage

Store undressed salad in an airtight container in the fridge for up to 2 days.

tip

* If desired, toast the walnuts for a rich, toasty flavor.

make it nut-free

Swap the walnuts for toasted pepitas.

make it soy-free

If using store-bought vegan mayo in the Luxurious ACV and Dijon Dressing, be sure to select a soy-free variety.

4. While the potatoes roast, cut the zucchini in half lengthwise, then slice into ¼- to ½-inch (5 mm to 1 cm) thick half-moons, adding them to the second baking sheet as you go (you should have 4 cups). Toss the zucchini with the remaining 1 tablespoon olive oil, the remaining 1 teaspoon Italian seasoning, the remaining ¾ teaspoon garlic powder, a pinch of salt, and several cranks of freshly ground black pepper until coated.
5. Once the potatoes have been roasting for 5 minutes, add the zucchini to the oven and continue roasting both pans, uncovered, for 10 minutes, then flip the potatoes and zucchini and roast for another 10 minutes, until tender and golden on the bottom.
6. Meanwhile, make the Luxurious ACV and Dijon Dressing.
7. Prepare the tomatoes and add them to a large bowl. Set aside. Prepare the dill, green onions, and walnuts.
8. After 20 minutes of roasting, remove the zucchini pan from the oven. Add the cannellini beans to the pan, spreading them into an even layer, and sprinkle with a bit of salt. Rotate the pans from upper to lower and back to front, and roast the zucchini-bean mixture and the potatoes for another 3 to 5 minutes, until the beans are warmed through.
9. Transfer the roasted potatoes, zucchini, and beans into the bowl with the tomatoes and gently toss. Add the minced dill and gently toss again.
10. Assemble: Gather 4 large bowls. Divide the roasted veggie and bean mixture among the bowls (about 2 cups per bowl). Top each with 2 tablespoons of green onions, 2 tablespoons of walnuts, 2 to 3 tablespoons of dressing, and a sprinkle of garlic powder, Italian seasoning, and salt and pepper, if desired. Alternatively, you can serve the salad in a large serving bowl with the dressing on the side. Serve warm.

vegan • gluten-free option • nut-free • grain-free option • kid-friendly • on the glow

Magnificent Miso Salad

makes 4 (2½-cup) salads • prep time: 25 minutes • total time: 45 minutes

Roasted sweet potatoes, caramelized and chewy, top a bed of delicate baby greens tossed in my umami-rich and tangy Miso, Maple, and Ginger Dressing (page 241). Red onion adds a little bite, cilantro brightens, and the little nutty pops of sesame seeds and roasted pepitas are always so fun to eat. Depending on what I have on hand, I will toss on some grated carrot, cucumber slices, or sweet bell peppers (or all three, my favorite way). *Chef's kiss.* When I'm serving this salad as a meal, I love to add soft and fluffy white rice or top it with seasoned cubes of my Shake-and-Bake Sesame-Crusted Tofu (page 195). For a stick-to-your-bones kind of meal, we include both! Load up your bowl as much as you like or leave it as a simple salad of crisp greens with caramelized sweet potatoes, red onions, and tangy miso dressing. This delightful combination of ingredients is inspired by Gwyneth Paltrow's Kale and Sweet Potato Salad with Miso from *The Clean Plate.*

1 batch Shake-and-Bake Sesame-Crusted Tofu (page 195) or 2 cups (275 g) cooked long-grain white or brown rice (optional)*

3 to 4 medium sweet potatoes (1.8 pounds/820 g total)

2 tablespoons extra-virgin olive oil

½ teaspoon fine sea salt

1 batch Miso, Maple, and Ginger Dressing (page 241)

½ cup (60 g) diced red onion (½ small)

½ cup packed (17 g) fresh cilantro leaves, chopped

1 cup grated peeled carrot (82 g), sliced cucumber, or diced bell pepper (optional)**

5 ounces (142 g) mixed baby greens (6 cups)***

4 teaspoons sesame seeds

8 teaspoons salted roasted pepitas

1. Prepare the Shake-and-Bake Sesame-Crusted Tofu or cooked rice (if using).
2. Preheat the oven to 400°F (200°C) and line an extra-large rimmed baking sheet with parchment paper.
3. Peel the sweet potatoes, then chop into ¾-inch (2 cm) cubes (you should have 5⅓ cups), adding them to the prepared baking sheet as you go. Toss the potatoes with the olive oil until coated. Spread into an even layer and sprinkle with the salt.
4. Roast, uncovered, for 30 to 40 minutes, until the potatoes are tender and golden on the bottom, flipping once halfway through baking.
5. Meanwhile, make the Miso, Maple, and Ginger Dressing.

recipe continues

storage

Store the warm and cold components in separate airtight containers in the fridge for up to 4 days (cool the warm components before storing). Reheat the sweet potatoes and tofu (if using) in a 400°F (200°C) oven for 6 to 8 minutes, until warmed through. Reheat the rice (if using) on the stovetop with a splash of water or broth, covered, over low heat, stirring occasionally until hot and fluffy. Transfer warmed components to the salad and add the dressing.

tips

* ½ cup uncooked rice makes about 2 cups cooked. Feel free to use both cooked rice and the sesame tofu, if desired. If you're making the Shake-and-Bake Sesame-Crusted Tofu at the same time, I recommend adding the sweet potato to the oven 10 to 15 minutes before adding the tofu so they finish baking around the same time.

** You can use red, orange, or yellow bell pepper. Do not use green bell pepper. I usually opt for red bell pepper as it's the sweetest.

*** Green leaf lettuce works well, too.

make it gluten-free

Use gluten-free tamari in the Miso, Maple, and Ginger Dressing.

make it grain-free

Serve with the Shake-and-Bake Sesame-Crusted Tofu option.

6. Toss the diced red onion into a small bowl. Cover with cold water and let sit for 5 minutes. Drain well.
7. While the red onion soaks, prepare the cilantro and carrot, cucumber, and/or bell pepper (if using), adding them to separate small bowls or simply arranging them in groupings on an extra-large cutting board.
8. Assemble: Gather 4 large bowls. To each bowl, add 1½ cups of mixed greens, tossed with 1 tablespoon of the dressing. Add ½ cup of tofu or warm cooked rice (if using), ¾ cup of roasted sweet potatoes, 2 tablespoons of drained diced red onion, 2 tablespoons of cilantro, ¼ cup of carrot, cucumber, or bell peppers (if using), 1 teaspoon of sesame seeds, and 2 teaspoons of salted roasted pepitas. Drizzle each bowl with an additional 2 to 3 tablespoons of dressing, to taste. Serve warm.

vegan • gluten-free • soy-free • grain-free • on the glow

Butternut, Cranberry, and Rosemary-Maple Pecan and Walnut Arugula Salad

makes 6 (1-cup) salads • prep time: 35 minutes • total time: 1 hour 40 minutes

This salad is the very epitome of autumn, as it features the glorious colors of red, orange, green, and brown and the scent and sweet flavors of roasting squash, spicy cinnamon, fresh savory rosemary, and zippy apple cider vinegar. It'll surely help you say goodbye to summer and embrace the cooler temperatures. Peppery arugula is tossed in my Glowing House Vinaigrette (page 230) and topped with creamy caramelized butternut squash, tart and sweet dried cranberries, and a handful of my lightly spicy Rosemary, Maple, and Cayenne Roasted Pecans and Walnuts (page 209) for the perfect sweet, nutty crunch. This gorgeous salad definitely impresses! Serve it as a side salad (you'll have about six 1-cup portions) or serve it as a main for two or three people. Make a hearty meal by serving my Crispy and Chewy Barbecue Tofu (page 187) alongside.

1 batch Rosemary, Maple, and Cayenne Roasted Pecans and Walnuts (page 209)

1 large butternut squash (2.2 pounds/1 kg)

2 tablespoons pure maple syrup

1 tablespoon extra-virgin olive oil

¾ teaspoon fine sea salt

Freshly ground black pepper

1 batch Glowing House Vinaigrette (page 230)*

5 ounces (142 g) baby arugula (7 cups)**

½ scant cup (59 g) sweetened dried cranberries

Cinnamon, to taste

1. Make the Rosemary, Maple, and Cayenne Roasted Pecans and Walnuts.
2. Preheat the oven to 400°F (200°C) and line an extra-large rimmed baking sheet (or 2 large baking sheets) with parchment paper.
3. Peel the squash, then trim both ends. Halve the squash lengthwise. Scoop out and discard the seeds. Chop the squash into ¾-inch (2 cm) cubes, adding them to the prepared baking sheet as you go (you should have 6½ to 7 cups).
4. Drizzle the maple syrup and olive oil over the squash and toss well to coat. Spread the squash into an even layer with a little space between the cubes. Sprinkle with the salt and several cranks of freshly ground black pepper.

recipe continues

storage

Store leftover dressed salad in an airtight container in the fridge for up to 2 days.

tips

* My Apple Cider, Shallot, Maple, and Dijon Vinaigrette (page 220) works well as a swap for the Glowing House Vinaigrette.

** You may prefer to remove and discard any long or thick arugula stems before using.

For spice lovers, try garnishing your salad with a sprinkle of cayenne pepper along with cinnamon.

5. Roast the squash, uncovered, for 20 minutes. Flip, and continue cooking for another 15 to 30 minutes, until tender and golden brown on the bottom. Cool for a few minutes on the pan.
6. Meanwhile, make the Glowing House Vinaigrette.
7. Assemble: Once the squash is finished cooking, to a large salad bowl add the arugula and 2 tablespoons of vinaigrette. Using your hands, toss until well combined. This will be a very light coating of vinaigrette—you want to avoid adding too much dressing, as it can wilt the arugula.
8. Spoon on all the warm roasted squash, the dried cranberries, and 1 generous cup of roasted nuts (or simply add them to taste if you don't want the salad to be as sweet). Gently toss to combine.
9. Gather 6 small bowls. Divide the salad among the bowls (about 1 cup per bowl) and drizzle each bowl with a scant 1½ tablespoons of vinaigrette (or to taste). Sprinkle with a bit of salt, pepper, and cinnamon, all to taste. Serve warm.

vegan • gluten-free option • grain-free option • advance prep required • kid-friendly • on the glow

Roasted Vegetable Medley with Sun-Dried Tomato, Walnut, and Basil Whipped Feta

makes 4 (2⅓-cup) salads • prep time: 40 minutes • total time: 65 minutes, plus pressing time

This satiating Roasted Vegetable Medley with Sun-Dried Tomato, Walnut, and Basil Whipped Feta salad is a flavor, color, and nutrient explosion! My Sun-Dried Tomato, Walnut, and Basil Whipped Feta Spread (page 247), with its peppery fresh basil, tart lemon juice, protein-packed tofu, and tangy sun-dried tomato, provides the creamy base for roasted and caramelized sweet and smoky veggies piled on top. We drizzle a spoonful or two of my Perfect Balsamic-Maple Vinaigrette (page 218) over top to pull all the flavors together. Believe me when I tell you, you are going to love this unique dish! I recommend making up a batch of buttery Garlic-Infused Olive Oil Crostini (page 249) for scooping up the whipped feta and providing a delightful crunchy contrast, but your favorite store-bought crackers are a great choice, too.

1 batch Garlic-Infused Olive Oil Crostini (page 249; optional)

1 batch Sun-Dried Tomato, Walnut, and Basil Whipped Feta Spread (page 247)

3 medium unpeeled yellow potatoes (1 pound/454 g total)

2 large carrots (252 g total)

2 tablespoons extra-virgin olive oil, divided

½ teaspoon fine sea salt, divided

Freshly ground black pepper

1 medium head cauliflower (1.4 pounds/650 g)

2 large red bell peppers (450 g total)

2 medium zucchini (387 g total)

1 batch Perfect Balsamic-Maple Vinaigrette (page 218; optional)

1. Make the Garlic-Infused Olive Oil Crostini (if using) in advance. Press the tofu for the Sun-Dried Tomato, Walnut, and Basil Whipped Feta Spread for at least 30 minutes.
2. Position the racks in the upper and lower thirds of the oven and preheat to 400°F (200°C). Line 2 extra-large rimmed baking sheets with parchment paper.
3. Cut the unpeeled potatoes into ½-inch (1 cm) thick wedges, adding them to one of the prepared baking sheets as you go (you should have 3 cups). Peel the carrots and cut on a diagonal into ½-inch (1 cm) thick ovals, adding them to the potatoes as you go (you should have a scant 2 cups). Toss the veggies with 1 tablespoon of the olive oil. Spread out into an even layer, then sprinkle ¼ teaspoon of the salt and lots of freshly ground black pepper over top.

recipe continues

storage

Store the cooled roasted veggies in an airtight container, or the assembled salads on covered plates, in the fridge for up to 3 days. Reheat the roasted veggies on a baking sheet lined with parchment paper in a 400°F (200°C) oven for 10 minutes. Spoon the warmed veggies over the whipped feta, season to taste with salt and pepper, and garnish with sun-dried tomatoes, basil, walnuts, and a drizzle of vinaigrette.

make it gluten- and grain-free

Omit the optional Garlic-Infused Olive Oil Crostini.

4. Cut the cauliflower into ¾-inch (2 cm) florets (you should have 3 cups). Remove the seeds from the bell peppers, then chop into 1-inch (2.5 cm) pieces (you should have 3 cups). Cut the zucchini in half lengthwise and slice the halves into ½-inch (1 cm) thick half-moons (you should have 3 cups). Add the cauliflower, bell peppers, and zucchini to the second baking sheet as you go. Toss the veggies with the remaining 1 tablespoon olive oil. Spread into an even layer, then sprinkle the remaining ¼ teaspoon salt and lots of freshly ground black pepper over top.
5. Roast both pans of veggies, uncovered, for 35 to 45 minutes, until fork-tender and golden brown around the edges, flipping once and rotating the pans from upper to lower and back to front halfway through cooking. (I cook the cauliflower, bell pepper, and zucchini mixture for about 40 minutes and the potato and carrot mixture for about 45 minutes so the potatoes can brown a bit more.)
6. Meanwhile, make the Sun-Dried Tomato, Walnut, and Basil Whipped Feta Spread, but instead of roasting the walnuts as directed, toast them in a dry pan over medium heat for 4 to 6 minutes, until fragrant and lightly golden. Leave the whipped feta in the processor bowl and place it, uncovered, in the fridge to chill for 15 to 20 minutes.
7. Make the Perfect Balsamic-Maple Vinaigrette (if using).
8. Assemble: Gather 4 large bowls or salad plates. Spoon a scant ⅔ cup of whipped feta into each bowl or plate and spread it into a circle, about 7 inches (18 cm) wide, or as wide as your dish allows.
9. When the veggies are finished roasting, spoon about 2 cups of mixed roasted veggies on top of each portion of whipped feta, and season to taste with salt and pepper. Scatter the reserved sun-dried tomatoes, basil, and walnuts from the feta recipe evenly over each bowl or plate. Drizzle each salad with 1 tablespoon or so of Perfect Balsamic-Maple Vinaigrette (if using). Serve warm with crostini on the side (if using).

vegan • gluten-free • nut-free • soy-free • grain-free • advance prep required • kid-friendly

Smoky Seasoned Roasted Cauliflower and Potato Salad

makes 5 (4½-cup) salads • prep time: 40 minutes • total time: 50 minutes

Hello, beautiful summer harvest, I'd like to introduce you to the golden days of autumn. The last of the sweet grape tomatoes, crisp cucumber, and green onions are in their full glory during the final half of the summer, while cruciferous, crunchy cauliflower and creamy potatoes are just getting ready for their first harvest of the year. It's a partnership made in heaven! I smash up the seasons by roasting the cauliflower and potatoes in a savory, smoky dusting of both sweet and smoked paprika, and garlic powder, then I toss in some chickpeas for the easiest roasted chickpeas you've ever made. Their roasty, caramelized goodness tops a fresh green romaine salad and is drizzled with my rich and decadent Velvety Sunflower Garlic Dressing (page 227). Each bowl is sprinkled with deliciously salty roasted pepitas for the perfect amount of crunch with each bite. Lemon lovers: try this with a lemon wedge served on the side for a juicy pop of lemon flavor.

1 batch Velvety Sunflower Garlic Dressing (page 227)

1 batch Addictive Smoky Roasted Cauli, Chickpeas, and Taters (page 200)

1 large head romaine lettuce (450 g), chopped (7½ cups packed)

1 pint (283 g) grape tomatoes, halved (1¾ cups)

½ large English cucumber (202 g), thinly sliced into half-moons (1⅔ cups/202 g)

⅔ cup (52 g) thinly sliced green onions (4 medium)

⅓ cup (45 g) salted roasted pepitas

Sea salt and freshly ground black pepper

1. Soak the sunflower seeds for the Velvety Sunflower Garlic Dressing.
2. Meanwhile, make the Addictive Smoky Roasted Cauli, Chickpeas, and Taters.
3. While the potatoes, chickpeas, and cauliflower are roasting, make the Velvety Sunflower Garlic Dressing.
4. Meanwhile, prepare the lettuce, tomatoes, cucumber, and green onions.
5. Assemble: Gather 5 large bowls. To each bowl, add 1½ cups of packed romaine and drizzle 2 tablespoons of dressing on top. Add ⅓ cup of halved grape tomatoes, ⅓ cup of sliced cucumber, and 2 tablespoons of green onions. When the veggies are finished roasting, add to each bowl ¾ cup of the cauliflower and chickpea mixture, a scant ⅔ cup of potatoes, and 1 tablespoon of salted roasted pepitas. Drizzle 2 to 3 more tablespoons of dressing on top of each bowl. Season to taste with salt and pepper. Serve warm.

storage

Store undressed salad in an airtight container in the fridge for up to 3 days. Reheat the cauliflower, potato, and chickpea mixture on a baking sheet lined with parchment paper in a 400°F (200°C) oven for 4 to 6 minutes, then spoon onto the salad along with more dressing.

fall and winter

Recipes

pasta and potato salads

vegan • gluten-free option • nut-free • advance prep required • kid-friendly • on the glow

Mix-and-Glow Roasted Veg Orzo Salad

makes 4 (scant 2-cup) salads • prep time: 30 minutes • total time: 55 minutes, plus pressing time

This Mix-and-Glow Roasted Veg Orzo Salad is just right for a picnic, potluck, gathering, or family meal, and it stores well to make delicious leftovers and convenient lunches. In fact, leftovers from this salad are one of my favorites to have waiting for me in the fridge, and you'll often find me eating cold (or warm) servings for breakfast! When creating a satiating, meal-worthy orzo salad to pair with my 6-Ingredient Shake-and-Glow Vinaigrette (page 235), I just had to include herbes de Provence's aromatic blend of thyme, basil, rosemary, tarragon, savory, marjoram, oregano, and bay leaf because it adds such an inviting flavor to the roasted veggies and tofu. To take it completely over the top, I highly recommend sprinkling extra herbes de Provence and drizzling spicy sriracha and runny tahini over each serving . . . it's simply luscious and extra flavorful.

Roasted Mixture

1 (12-ounce/350 g) block extra-firm tofu, pressed

2 large bell peppers (450 g total), seeded and chopped (3 cups)*

1 large jalapeño pepper (75 g), seeded and diced (6 tablespoons)

3 medium zucchini (518 g total), halved lengthwise and sliced into ½-inch (1 cm) thick half-moons (4 cups)**

3 tablespoons extra-virgin olive oil, divided***

2 teaspoons herbes de Provence, divided, plus more for garnish

½ teaspoon fine sea salt, divided

Freshly ground black pepper

Orzo Salad

1 cup (176 g) dried orzo pasta (2½ to 3 cups cooked)

1 batch 6-Ingredient Shake-and-Glow Vinaigrette (page 235)

½ cup packed (15 g) fresh basil leaves, finely chopped

1 cup (155 g) grape tomatoes, halved****

½ cup (39 g) thinly sliced green onions (3 medium)

Fine sea salt and freshly ground black pepper

For serving

Sriracha

¼ cup runny tahini

1. For the Roasted Mixture: Press the tofu for at least 30 minutes (see page 357).
2. Position the racks in the upper and lower thirds of the oven and preheat to 400°F (200°C). Line 2 large rimmed baking sheets with parchment paper.
3. Chop the pressed tofu into ½-inch (1 cm) cubes (you should have 2½ cups).
4. Prepare the bell peppers and jalapeño, adding them to one of the prepared baking sheets as you go, along with the cubed tofu. Drizzle with 2 tablespoons of the olive oil and toss with 1 teaspoon of the herbes de Provence, ¼ teaspoon of the salt, and several cranks of freshly ground black pepper. Spread into an even layer.

recipe continues

storage

Store undressed salad in an airtight container in the fridge for up to 3 days. Enjoy it chilled or reheat gently in a covered pan over medium heat for 2 to 3 minutes. Revive the flavors with a sprinkle of salt and pepper and a drizzle of the dressing, sriracha, and tahini.

tips

* You can use red, orange, or yellow bell peppers. Do not use green bell peppers.

** If your zucchini is quite wide, you can halve the half-moon slices to create smaller pieces. Both green and yellow zucchini work well (I like to use a mix of the two).

*** You can use pure avocado oil or grapeseed oil instead of the extra-virgin olive oil.

**** For an extra-colorful salad like the one shown in the photo, use red, orange, and yellow cherry tomatoes, a mix of yellow and green zucchini, and a mix of red, orange, and yellow bell peppers.

make it gluten-free

Use your favorite gluten-free orzo pasta.

5. Prepare the zucchini. Place the zucchini half-moons on the second prepared baking sheet. Drizzle the remaining 1 tablespoon olive oil over the zucchini and toss with the remaining 1 teaspoon herbes de Provence, the remaining ¼ teaspoon salt, and several cranks of freshly ground black pepper. Spread into an even layer.
6. Roast both baking sheets, uncovered, for 20 minutes. Flip the tofu mixture and the zucchini, rotate the pans from upper to lower and back to front, then continue roasting for another 13 to 20 minutes, until the tofu is lightly golden and the veggies are tender and golden brown on the bottom and around the edges. Keep an eye on the zucchini, as it may need to come out of the oven before the other pan is ready.
7. Meanwhile, cook the orzo according to the package directions (I skip salting the water), or bring 5 to 6 cups of water to a boil, add the orzo, stir, and boil uncovered, stirring occasionally, until al dente or your desired tenderness, 7 to 12 minutes. Drain the orzo and rinse under cold running water for 30 seconds, then drain very well for several minutes. Add the cooked orzo to a large serving bowl.
8. Make the 6-Ingredient Shake-and-Glow Vinaigrette.
9. Prepare the basil, tomatoes, and green onions.
10. Assemble: When ready, toss the roasted tofu and veggies with the orzo in the serving bowl until combined.
11. Shake the dressing to recombine. Drizzle 6 to 8 tablespoons of dressing over the orzo mixture and toss until coated. Add the basil, tomatoes, and green onions, tossing again to combine. Season to taste with lots of salt and pepper (I use about ¾ teaspoon salt).
12. Gather 4 large bowls. Portion the orzo salad into the bowls (scant 2 cups each). Top each bowl with a sprinkle of herbes de Provence and a generous drizzle of sriracha (about ½ teaspoon for a spicy, slightly sweet, tomatoey kick) and runny tahini (we love a full tablespoon drizzled on top). Season to taste with salt and a few cranks of freshly ground black pepper, and drizzle more dressing (about 1 tablespoon) on top, if desired. Serve warm.

vegan • gluten-free • nut-free option • soy-free • grain-free • advance prep required

Fiery 10-Spice Roasted Potato Salad

makes 6 (1½-cup) side salads • prep time: 30 minutes • total time: 55 minutes

Warm and spicy, my Fiery 10-Spice Roasted Potato Salad reimagines potato salad. I love a chilled creamy and tangy potato salad as much as the next person, but there are times when I crave savory and golden-edged roasted potatoes presented on a gorgeous platter. Crisp on the outside and soft on the inside, these spicy, smoky, and herby potatoes are coated in my Community-Fave 10-Spice Mix (page 275) and are topped with cooling juicy tomatoes, crisp green onions, refreshing parsley, and my smooth and lemony Creamy Cashew, Garlic, and Lemon Dressing (page 240) to balance the heat. I like to set out cute pinch bowls with extra spice mix and dressing so everyone can tailor their bowls to their own preference (some of us really love to load on the Community-Fave 10-Spice Mix . . . you know who you are!). To change it up, this salad is also fabulous topped with my Velvety Cashew Garlic Dressing (page 226) or Velvety Sunflower Garlic Dressing (page 227).

1 batch Creamy Cashew, Garlic, and Lemon Dressing (page 240)

1 batch Community-Fave 10-Spice Mix (page 275)

10 medium unpeeled yellow potatoes (3 pounds/1.35 kg total)

3 tablespoons grapeseed oil or pure avocado oil

Fine sea salt

1 pint (283 g) grape tomatoes, thinly sliced (1¾ cups)

½ cup (39 g) thinly sliced green onions (3 medium)

⅓ cup packed (12 g) fresh flat-leaf parsley or cilantro leaves, coarsely chopped

1. Soak the cashews for the Creamy Cashew, Garlic, and Lemon Dressing. Make the Community-Fave 10-Spice Mix.

2. Position the racks in the upper and lower thirds of the oven and preheat to 425°F (220°C). Line 2 large rimmed baking sheets with parchment paper.

3. Cut the unpeeled potatoes into 1-inch (2.5 cm) chunks (you should have 8 cups). Divide the potatoes equally between the prepared baking sheets. Toss each pan of potatoes with 1½ tablespoons of the oil until thoroughly coated. Sprinkle 1 tablespoon of Community-Fave 10-Spice Mix over each pan and toss until coated. Spread the potatoes into an even layer with some space between the chunks. Very lightly sprinkle salt over the potatoes (keeping in mind the 10-spice mix already contains some salt).

recipe continues

storage

Store leftovers in an airtight container in the fridge for up to 2 days. Reheat the potatoes in a 400°F (200°C) oven for 4 to 7 minutes, until warmed through. Recombine with the tomatoes, parsley (or cilantro), and green onions, then top with the dressing and a sprinkle of spice mix, if desired.

tip

If you don't want to serve the salad on a platter, simply gather 6 bowls or plates. To each, add 1 heaping cup of roasted potatoes, then top each with a scant ⅓ cup of tomatoes, 1½ tablespoons of green onions, and a scant 1 tablespoon of chopped parsley (or cilantro). Pipe or dollop 1½ to 2 tablespoons of dressing on top, and sprinkle with Community-Fave 10-Spice Mix.

make it nut-free

Use Velvety Sunflower Garlic Dressing (page 227) instead of the Creamy Cashew, Garlic, and Lemon Dressing.

4. Roast the potatoes, uncovered, for 20 minutes. Flip the potatoes, then rotate the pans from upper to lower and back to front. Continue roasting for another 15 to 20 minutes, until the potatoes are fork-tender and golden brown around the edges.
5. Meanwhile, make the Creamy Cashew, Garlic, and Lemon Dressing (page 240). Set aside at room temperature.
6. While the potatoes are roasting, prepare the tomatoes, green onions, and parsley (or cilantro). Pour a scant ½ cup of dressing into a small ziplock bag and seal.
7. When the potatoes come out of the oven, let them cool on the pans for just a few minutes before assembling the salad.
8. Assemble: Spread all the roasted potatoes onto a large rectangular rimmed tray or platter. Immediately scatter the sliced tomatoes and green onions over the potatoes. Snip a tiny corner off the ziplock bag and "pipe" the dressing in a diagonal pattern across the potatoes as shown in the photo. Sprinkle on about half of the chopped parsley (or cilantro). Place the leftover parsley (or cilantro), dressing, and Community-Fave 10-Spice Mix in small bowls with spoons on the table so others can add more herbs, dressing, and spice mix to their salads as desired. Serve immediately, using a spatula to lift each portion off the tray or platter (this keeps the layers mostly intact!).

vegan • gluten-free • nut-free option • soy-free • grain-free • on the glow

Herby Baked Green Bean and Potato Salad

makes 8 (1-cup) side salads • prep time: 35 minutes • total time: 1 hour

This potato salad absolutely explodes with tangy, mustardy, and herby flavor. Oven-roasting earthy green beans and yellow or baby potatoes until golden adds so much depth to their taste. The invigorating dill and parsley and crisp green onions provide a lively flavor contrast to the veggies, and the piping hot fresh-out-of-the-oven veggies are all coated in my bold and assertive Grainy Mustard and Lemon Dressing (page 234). Served warm, this potato salad has such a comforting feel. I love making this year-round, and I often change up the crunchy topping, sprinkling either garlicky and nutty Garlic Lovers' Cashew Parmesan (page 281) or chopped salted roasted pepitas over each serving. I also love to boost the protein by adding a cup of cooked and drained French green (du Puy) lentils. This salad tends to be a go-to in the early fall and winter months, because who doesn't need more warm carbs and veggies at those times of the year? For this recipe, you'll need an extra-large rimmed baking sheet to ensure all of the chopped potatoes fit on the pan, and also one large rimmed baking sheet for the green beans.

3 pounds (1.36 kg) unpeeled yellow or baby potatoes*

3 tablespoons extra-virgin olive oil, divided

¾ teaspoon fine sea salt, divided

Freshly ground black pepper

12 ounces (340 g) fresh green beans**

1 batch Grainy Mustard and Lemon Dressing (page 234)

½ cup (39 g) thinly sliced green onions (3 medium)

⅓ cup packed (13 g) fresh dill, minced

⅓ cup packed (12 g) fresh flat-leaf parsley leaves, minced

2 to 3 tablespoons chopped salted roasted pepitas or Garlic Lovers' Cashew Parmesan (page 281)

1. Position the racks in the upper and lower thirds of the oven and preheat to 425°F (220°C). Line 1 extra-large rimmed baking sheet and 1 large rimmed baking sheet with parchment paper.

2. Chop the unpeeled potatoes into ½- to ¾-inch (1 to 2 cm) pieces, adding them to the prepared extra-large baking sheet as you go (you should have 9 cups). Toss with 2 tablespoons of the olive oil. Spread into an even layer (the pan will be crowded, which is fine) and sprinkle with ½ teaspoon of the salt and several cranks of freshly ground black pepper.

3. Bake the potatoes, uncovered, on the lower rack for 20 minutes.

recipe continues

storage

This salad shines when served right away while it's still warm. Store dressed leftovers in an airtight container in the fridge for up to 2 days. Reheat in a 400°F (200°C) oven on a baking sheet lined with parchment paper, covered with foil, for about 10 minutes. Revive the flavors by drizzling with remaining dressing and sprinkling a little extra minced fresh dill on top.

tips

* If you don't have baby potatoes, feel free to use Yukon Gold or red potatoes.

** Regular green beans and French green beans both work well.

make it nut-free

Use the salted roasted pepitas option instead of the parmesan.

4. Meanwhile, prepare the green beans by trimming off the ends, then chopping them into 1- to 2-inch (2.5 to 5 cm) pieces (you should have about 3 cups). Place the green beans on the prepared large baking sheet. Toss with the remaining 1 tablespoon olive oil. Spread into an even layer and sprinkle with the remaining ¼ teaspoon salt and a few cranks of freshly ground black pepper.
5. After the potatoes have roasted for 20 minutes, flip them, then return the pan to the lower rack. Add the pan of green beans to the upper rack and roast the potatoes and green beans for another 20 to 30 minutes, until the potatoes are tender and golden brown on the bottom and the green beans are tender and starting to char around the edges. Keep an eye on the veggies: you may need to pull the green beans out of the oven a bit earlier than the potatoes (or vice versa). Slightly cool the potatoes and green beans for just a few minutes on the pans.
6. While the veggies are roasting, make the Grainy Mustard and Lemon Dressing.
7. Prepare the green onions, dill, parsley, and pepitas or parmesan.
8. Assemble: Add the roasted potatoes and green beans to a large serving bowl, along with the green onions. Set aside a large pinch each of minced dill and parsley for garnish, then add the remaining herbs to the bowl. Toss well with about ½ cup of the dressing until coated (you'll have some dressing left over). Season to taste with salt and pepper. Sprinkle on the reserved dill and parsley, along with the chopped pepitas or parmesan (you may want to use more than 2 to 3 tablespoons if using parmesan). Serve immediately, drizzled with a bit of leftover dressing, if desired.

vegan • gluten-free • nut-free option • soy-free • grain-free • kid-friendly • on the glow

Wintry Day Two-Potato, Apple, and Cranberry Kale Salad

makes 5 (2-cup) salads • prep time: 35 minutes • total time: 50 minutes

Brighten up the dull and dreary days of winter with this colorful Wintry Day Two-Potato, Apple, and Cranberry Salad. It came to be when I needed a gorgeous and nutritious winter-themed dish to complete a New Year's brunch I was hosting. Cozy caramelized sweet and yellow potatoes are so satisfying, the nutty and slightly bitter pecans and walnuts contrast perfectly with the sweet and tart green apple and dried cranberries, and it's all tossed with a base of earthy, packed-with-nutrition kale. Needless to say, everyone always has extra helpings and asks for this recipe (a special someone even said this is the best kale salad she has eaten in her whole life!). Try serving it with mimosas, as their sweet orange flavor pairs delightfully with the sweet orange juice, floral apple cider vinegar, and wine vinegar in my Cold Moon Orange Vinaigrette (page 217). Of course, this salad is flawless any time of the day, whether it be for brunch, lunch, or dinner!

2 medium sweet potatoes (1.3 pounds/605 g total), peeled

2 medium yellow potatoes (311 g total), peeled

2 tablespoons extra-virgin olive oil

½ teaspoon fine sea salt, plus more to taste

Freshly ground black pepper

½ cup (58 g) raw pecan halves

½ cup (50 g) raw walnut halves

1 batch Cold Moon Orange Vinaigrette (page 217)

½ cup (60 g) diced red onion (½ small)

1 medium bunch curly kale (257 g), stemmed and finely chopped (5 cups packed)

½ medium Granny Smith apple (90 g), diced (¾ scant cup)

⅓ cup (49 g) sweetened dried cranberries

1. Preheat the oven to 400°F (200°C) and line an extra-large rimmed baking sheet with parchment paper.
2. Chop the peeled sweet potatoes and yellow potatoes into ¾-inch (2 cm) chunks and place them on the prepared baking sheet (you should have 4 cups sweet potatoes and 2 cups yellow potatoes). Toss the potatoes with the olive oil, spread into an even layer, and sprinkle with the salt and several cranks of freshly ground black pepper.
3. Roast the potatoes, uncovered, for 30 to 42 minutes, until tender and lightly browned in some spots, flipping once halfway through roasting. During the final 4 to 6 minutes of roasting time, sprinkle the pecans and walnuts over the potatoes (no need to be fussy, just toss them onto the pan). Roast the potatoes and nuts together for 4 to 6 minutes, watching the nuts closely so they don't burn.

recipe continues

storage

This salad is best served fresh. Store leftovers in an airtight container in the fridge for up to 1 day. Add a drizzle of the vinaigrette to revive the flavors.

make it nut-free

Omit the pecans and walnuts and sprinkle 1 tablespoon of salted roasted pepitas on top of each serving.

4. Meanwhile, make the Cold Moon Orange Vinaigrette.
5. Toss the diced red onion into a small bowl. Cover with cold water and let sit for 5 minutes. Drain well.
6. Prepare the kale and add it to a large bowl. Pour ½ cup of vinaigrette over the kale and massage it into the kale with your hands, squeezing the kale between your hands for a couple of minutes to soften it.
7. Prepare the apple, then add it, along with the drained red onion and dried cranberries, to the bowl with the kale.
8. When the cooked potatoes and nuts are out of the oven, allow them to sit on the pan for 3 to 5 minutes to cool slightly. Then, using the parchment paper as a sling, lift and slide them into the bowl with the kale. Toss gently to combine, and season to taste with salt and pepper.
9. Assemble: Gather 5 large bowls. Divide the salad among the bowls (about 2 cups per bowl). Shake the vinaigrette to recombine, then drizzle another tablespoon over each salad. Serve warm.

vegan • gluten-free • nut-free • soy-free option • grain-free

Cinnamon Sweet Potato Wedge Salad with Sriracha Honey-Mustard Dressing

makes 4 (2¼-cup) salads • prep time: 20 minutes • total time: 50 minutes

Imagine cinnamon-scented sweet potato wedges, roasted until caramelized, resting atop leaves of delicate baby spinach. Now add a little bite from crisp green onions, some crunch from salty roasted pepitas, and creamy chopped avocado. Bring it all home with a drizzle of dressing that's sweet from honey, spicy from sriracha, and tangy from old-fashioned Dijon. It's uncomplicated and budget-friendly while still tasting fancy! To turn this into a heartier meal, I love to serve the salad over a bed of cooked and seasoned grains such as quinoa, millet, or my Easy Garlic-Infused Farro (page 268) or Cilantro-Jalapeño Rice (page 273).

- 3 to 4 medium sweet potatoes (1.7 pounds/785 g total)
- 2 tablespoons extra-virgin olive oil
- ½ teaspoon fine sea salt
- ½ teaspoon cinnamon
- 1 batch Sriracha Honey-Mustard Dressing (page 242)
- 1 cup (78 g) thinly sliced green onions (4 large)
- 4 cups lightly packed (120 g) baby spinach, thick stems removed*
- 1 cup (125 g) pitted, peeled, and chopped ripe avocado (1 large) or Vegan Feta Cheese (page 259)
- ¼ cup (34 g) salted roasted pepitas
- Sriracha, for garnish (optional)

1. Preheat the oven to 400°F (200°C) and line an extra-large baking sheet (or 2 medium sheets) with parchment paper.
2. Peel the sweet potatoes, then cut into wedges about ¾ inch (2 cm) wide and 3 to 4 inches (8 to 10 cm) long (you should have about 6 cups). Place the potato wedges on the prepared baking sheet and toss with the olive oil until completely coated. Spread into an even layer and sprinkle with the salt and cinnamon.
3. Roast, uncovered, for 30 to 40 minutes, until tender and lightly browned in some spots, flipping once halfway through roasting.

recipe continues

storage

Store undressed salad in an airtight container in the fridge for up to 3 days. Reheat the sweet potatoes in a 400°F (200°C) oven for 6 to 8 minutes, until warmed through, then return to the salad and add the dressing.

tip

* Mixed baby greens work well, too.

make it soy-free

If using store-bought vegan mayo in the Sriracha Honey-Mustard Dressing (page 242), be sure to select a soy-free variety. Use avocado instead of feta.

4. Meanwhile, make the Sriracha Honey-Mustard Dressing.
5. Prepare the green onions, spinach, and avocado (or feta).
6. Assemble: Gather 4 large bowls. To each bowl add a lightly packed cup of spinach, followed by a generous ¾ cup roasted sweet potato, 3 to 4 tablespoons of green onions, ¼ cup of avocado or feta cheese, and 1 tablespoon of pepitas. Drizzle with 2 to 3 tablespoons of dressing. Add a drizzle of sriracha, if desired. Serve warm.

vegan • gluten-free option • soy-free • grain-free option • advance prep required • on the glow

Warm Mushroom and Spinach Pasta Salad

makes 5 (generous 1½-cup) salads • prep time: 25 minutes • total time: 45 minutes

Though this isn't your typical pasta salad as we tend to know them (served chilled in the summertime), I just had to sneak this one into the book. Created for colder days, it's served warm, filled with fall- and winter-friendly savory flavors like thyme and parsley, and is mixed with my luxurious Creamy Cashew, Garlic, and Lemon Dressing (page 240), which feels like a cozy hug. The comforting warm noodles and herby, umami-rich cremini mushrooms are cold-weather hearty, and baby spinach adds green-powered nutrition. This pasta is fantastic served with my Garlic Lovers' Cashew Parmesan (page 281) and it's lovely with Garlic-Infused Olive Oil Crostini (page 249). The leftovers are even wonderful served chilled straight from the fridge (the next day, that's what you'll find me doing for a quick lunch!). We often add a squeeze of lemon juice over our bowls; its bright zip brings out all the flavor in this salad in the best way.

- 1 batch Creamy Cashew, Garlic, and Lemon Dressing (page 240)
- 2 heaping cups (200 g) dried short-cut pasta (such as penne or rotini)
- 2½ cups (275 g) diced sweet onion (1 large)
- 2 large garlic cloves (12 g total), minced
- 3 tablespoons extra-virgin olive oil
- ¼ teaspoon fine sea salt, plus more for seasoning
- Freshly ground black pepper
- 1½ pounds (681 g) cremini mushrooms, sliced (10 cups)
- ½ cup packed (17 g) fresh flat-leaf parsley leaves, minced
- 1 tablespoon fresh thyme leaves (or 1½ teaspoons dried thyme)
- 5 ounces (142 g) baby spinach, thick stems removed
- 5 lemon wedges

1. Make the Creamy Cashew, Garlic, and Lemon Dressing.
2. Bring a large pot of water to a boil. Cook the pasta according to the package directions, until tender (you should have 3½ to 4 cups of cooked pasta). Drain and rinse under cold running water.
3. While the pasta cooks, prepare the onion and garlic.
4. Heat the olive oil in a large 5-quart (5 L) pot over medium-low heat. Add the onion, garlic, salt, and several cranks of freshly ground black pepper. Cook, uncovered, stirring occasionally, for 10 to 14 minutes, until the onion is very soft and translucent.
5. While the onion mixture cooks, prepare the mushrooms.

recipe continues

storage

Store leftovers in an airtight container in the fridge for up to 3 days.

make it gluten- and/or grain-free

Use gluten-free pasta and/or grain-free pasta. Keep in mind that some gluten-free pastas don't store well in the fridge, so I recommend you test the shelf life of your chosen pasta before using it in this salad.

6. Stir the sliced mushrooms into the onion mixture. Increase the heat to medium and continue cooking, uncovered, stirring occasionally, for 12 to 14 minutes, until the mushrooms soften and the liquid has completely evaporated. During the last 3 to 5 minutes of cooking, increase the heat to medium-high (watching closely and stirring frequently) to help cook off the remaining liquid. (Any liquid left in the bottom of the pot will dilute the sauce.)
7. Once the mushrooms are cooking, prepare the parsley and thyme, then immediately stir them into the mushroom mixture.
8. During the last couple minutes of cooking, stir in the spinach until wilted.
9. Add the cooked pasta and 1 cup of the Creamy Cashew, Garlic, and Lemon Dressing to the pot, stirring to combine. Season to taste with salt and pepper, and cook over low heat until warmed through.
10. Assemble: Gather 5 large bowls. Portion a generous 1½ cups of pasta mixture into each bowl. Serve with another 1½ to 2 tablespoons of dressing dolloped on top of the pasta, a lemon wedge on the side (for drizzling a pop of brightness over top), and a sprinkling of salt and pepper, if desired.

protein toppers, dressings, and flavor boosters

protein toppers

Recipes

and more

vegan • nut-free • advance prep required • kid-friendly option • freezer-friendly • on the glow

Crispy Breaded Tofu Tenders

makes 16 tofu tenders • prep time: 15 minutes • total time: 37 minutes, plus pressing time

As a mom of three kids, all with varying food interests, I'm delighted that these crispy, chewy tofu tenders are approved by our whole family (not an easy feat, let me tell you). They are a tasty, protein-rich handheld dipper, are wonderful in wraps, and make an addictive and satisfying salad topper. We love to load up our Breaded Tofu Tender Salads (page 79) with these crunchy, savory tenders and liberally drizzle my Barbecue Apple Cider Vinaigrette (page 243) for the most delightful combo. These tenders freeze well, too, for the ideal thaw, heat, and serve last-minute dinners on busy weeknights. They are also tasty dipped in my Ranch Buttermilk Dressing (page 232). You'll often find us snacking on leftovers straight from the fridge. A big thank you to the lovely Richa Hingle, a cookbook author and blogger on Vegan Richa, for inspiring this recipe.

Tofu and Sauce

1 (12-ounce/350 g) block extra-firm tofu, pressed

1½ teaspoons arrowroot starch*

1½ teaspoons light tamari**

1½ teaspoons extra-virgin olive oil***

3 tablespoons tomato paste

1½ tablespoons old-fashioned Dijon mustard

1 tablespoon pure maple syrup

1½ teaspoons sriracha

¼ + ⅛ teaspoon fine sea salt

Freshly ground black pepper

Breaded Coating

¾ cup (64 g) panko breadcrumbs

1 teaspoon garlic powder

¼ teaspoon fine sea salt

Freshly ground black pepper

1. Press the tofu for at least 30 minutes (see page 357).
2. Preheat the oven to 375°F (190°C) and line a large rimmed baking sheet with parchment paper.
3. Make the Sauce and Brush the Tofu: In a medium bowl, whisk together the arrowroot starch, tamari, and olive oil until smooth. Add the tomato paste, mustard, maple syrup, sriracha, salt, and pepper and whisk until combined.
4. Halve the tofu block lengthwise so you have 2 large rectangular slabs about ¾ inch (2 cm) thick. Slice each slab crosswise into about eight ½- to ¾-inch (1 to 2 cm) wide strips (you should have about 16 strips). Using a silicone pastry brush, brush both sides of each strip generously with sauce until completely coated, placing them on a large plate as you go.

recipe continues

storage

Store cooled leftover tofu in an airtight container in the fridge for up to 4 days. Reheat in a 375°F (190°C) oven for 10 to 12 minutes, until warmed through. Freeze for up to 3 weeks. Reheat from frozen in a 375°F (190°C) oven for 13 to 15 minutes.

tips

* Cornstarch is a great swap for arrowroot starch.

** It's important to use light tamari (not regular full-sodium tamari) or the tofu mixture will be too salty.

*** Pure avocado oil can be swapped for extra-virgin olive oil.

make it kid-friendly

Omit the sriracha if your young eaters don't like spice.

5. Make the Breading and Coat the Tofu: In a large shallow bowl, stir together the breadcrumbs, garlic powder, salt, and about 10 cranks of freshly ground black pepper. Fully coat each tofu piece by dipping it into the breadcrumb mixture and tossing it around until all sides are completely coated. (I like to go at a brisk pace, and I don't fuss too much about them being "perfectly" coated.) Transfer the tofu strips to the prepared baking sheet, at least 1 inch (2.5 cm) apart.

6. Bake the tofu for 15 minutes, then flip the strips and bake for another 8 to 12 minutes, until the coating is golden and crispy. Cool on the pan for a few minutes and serve warm.

vegan • gluten-free option • nut-free • grain-free • advance prep required • kid-friendly • on the glow

Crispy and Chewy Barbecue Tofu

makes 2 scant cups • prep time: 10 minutes • total time: 30 minutes, plus pressing time

Tossing hand-torn tofu in smoky spices like chili powder and smoked paprika, then baking until lightly charred, makes this tofu super flavorful with crisp, chewy edges. It's delectably saucy after being tossed with my gently spicy Sweet and Tangy No-Chop Barbecue Sauce (page 262). One of our amazing recipe testers, Anne, says about this barbecue tofu, "It is, in my opinion, worth the price of this cookbook alone. This is a game changer, and I honestly think it could convert a lot of non-vegans!" Audrey's husband says it is the best tofu recipe he's ever tried. We'd have to humbly agree! This recipe keeps things really simple by serving the tofu topped with crisp, chopped green onion, but you can enjoy it in my Backyard Barbecue Tofu and Jalapeño-Tomato Rice Salad (page 43), and it pairs beautifully with any salad drizzled with my Velvety Cashew Garlic Dressing (page 226), as that balances out the tanginess and gentle heat of the barbecue sauce. A special thanks to Lauren Kodiak for sharing her method for tear-apart tofu, and to Kelli Foster for inspiring this scrumptious barbecue tofu!

1 (12-ounce/350 g) block extra-firm or firm tofu, pressed*

⅓ cup Sweet and Tangy No-Chop Barbecue Sauce (page 262) or store-bought*

1 teaspoon chili powder

1 teaspoon smoked paprika

¾ teaspoon garlic powder

½ teaspoon sweet paprika

½ teaspoon fine sea salt

2 tablespoons grapeseed oil**

½ cup (39 g) thinly sliced green onions, for garnish (3 medium; optional)

1 teaspoon sesame seeds, for garnish (optional)

1. Press the tofu for at least 30 minutes (see page 357). While the tofu is pressing, prepare the Sweet and Tangy No-Chop Barbecue Sauce (if using).
2. Preheat the oven to 400°F (200°C) and line a large rimmed baking sheet with parchment paper.
3. In a small bowl, stir together the chili powder, smoked paprika, garlic powder, sweet paprika, and salt until combined.
4. Using your hands, break apart the tofu block into small, bite-size pieces (1- to 2-inch/2.5 to 5 cm pieces with some tinier bits), placing the tofu in a large ziplock bag as you go. Drizzle the grapeseed oil over the tofu, secure the bag, and shake gently until all the tofu is coated. Unzip the bag and sprinkle the spices over the tofu. Secure the bag again and shake gently until the tofu pieces are coated in the spice mix.

recipe continues

storage

Store cooled leftover tofu in an airtight container in the fridge for up to 4 days. Reheat in a 400°F (200°C) oven for 4 to 7 minutes, until warmed through, then toss with a little warm barbecue sauce, if desired.

tips

* In a time crunch? Use pre-pressed tofu (such as Soyganic organic pressed tofu) to save a half hour of pressing time, and use your favorite store-bought barbecue sauce to save yourself 10 minutes of prep time.

** Extra-virgin olive oil works as a swap for grapeseed oil.

make it gluten-free

Use gluten-free vegan Worcestershire sauce in the Sweet and Tangy No-Chop Barbecue Sauce (if using) or select a gluten-free store-bought barbecue sauce.

5. Spread the tofu into an even layer on the prepared baking sheet.
6. Bake the tofu for 20 to 30 minutes, until crispy and lightly charred around the edges, flipping once halfway through baking. (I bake for about 25 minutes total.)
7. When the tofu is nearly finished baking, warm ⅓ cup of the barbecue sauce. Spoon it over the baked tofu, directly on the pan, and toss to coat. Serve immediately, topped with a sprinkle of sliced green onions and sesame seeds, if desired.

vegan • gluten-free option • nut-free • grain-free • advance prep required • kid-friendly • on the glow

Double Batch Crispy and Chewy Barbecue Tofu

makes 4 cups • prep time: 10 minutes • total time: 35 minutes, plus pressing time

2 (12 ounces/350 g each) blocks extra-firm or firm tofu, pressed*

⅔ cup Sweet and Tangy No-Chop Barbecue Sauce (page 262) or store-bought*

2 teaspoons chili powder

2 teaspoons smoked paprika

1½ teaspoons garlic powder

1 teaspoon sweet paprika

¾ teaspoon fine sea salt

¼ cup grapeseed oil**

1 cup (78 g) thinly sliced green onions, for garnish (4 large; optional)

2 teaspoons sesame seeds, for garnish (optional)

My Crispy and Chewy Barbecue Tofu (page 187) was such a hit with my family and friends that their only complaint was that it disappeared too fast. Now that's a complaint I love to hear! For easy reference, I wrote up my recipe for a double batch of sweet, tangy, lightly charred, you-won't-believe-it's-not-barbecued Crispy and Chewy Barbecue Tofu. This double batch makes just the right amount of saucy roasted tofu for serving with The Ultimate Ranch Barbecue Tofu Cobb Salad (page 85) or Dreamy Barbecue Tofu and Roasted Green Bean Salad (page 57), or alongside Sunny Day Charred Corn and Feta Salad (page 71) for the best summertime meal. It makes 4 cups, which is just right for a family of four or five when served with a salad. Coat yours in our family's favorite Sweet and Tangy No-Chop Barbecue Sauce (page 262) or use your favorite store-bought sauce to save a little time.

1. Press the tofu for at least 30 minutes (see page 357). While the tofu is pressing, prepare the Sweet and Tangy No-Chop Barbecue Sauce (if using).
2. Preheat the oven to 400°F (200°C) and line a large rimmed baking sheet with parchment paper.
3. In a small bowl, stir together the chili powder, smoked paprika, garlic powder, sweet paprika, and salt until combined.
4. Using your hands, break apart the tofu blocks into small, bite-size pieces (1- to 2-inch/2.5 to 5 cm pieces with some tinier bits), placing the tofu in a large ziplock bag as you go. Drizzle the grapeseed oil over the tofu, secure the bag, and shake gently until all the tofu is coated. Unzip the bag and sprinkle the spices over the tofu. Secure the bag again and gently shake until the tofu pieces are coated in the spice mix.

5. Spread the tofu into an even layer on the prepared baking sheet.

6. Bake the tofu for 20 to 30 minutes, until crispy and lightly charred around the edges, flipping once halfway through baking. (I bake for about 25 minutes total.)

7. When the tofu is nearly finished baking, warm ⅔ cup of the barbecue sauce. Spoon it over the baked tofu, directly on the pan, and toss to coat. Serve immediately, topped with a sprinkle of sliced green onions and sesame seeds, if desired.

storage

Store cooled leftover tofu in an airtight container in the fridge for up to 4 days. Reheat in a 400°F (200°C) oven for 4 to 7 minutes, until warmed through, then toss with a little warm barbecue sauce, if desired.

tips

* In a time crunch? Use pre-pressed tofu (such as Soyganic organic pressed tofu) to save a half hour of pressing time per tofu block, and use your favorite store-bought barbecue sauce to save yourself 10 minutes of prep time.

** Extra-virgin olive oil works as a swap for grapeseed oil.

make it gluten-free

Use gluten-free vegan Worcestershire sauce in the Sweet and Tangy No-Chop Barbecue Sauce (if using) or select a gluten-free store-bought barbecue sauce.

vegan • gluten-free option • nut-free • grain-free • advance prep required • kid-friendly
freezer-friendly • one bowl

Taco Tofu Crumble

makes 2 cups • prep time: 10 minutes • total time: 33 minutes, plus pressing time

Rich in protein, calcium, and iron, my Taco Tofu Crumble is such a hit at our house. We adore its chewy texture with just the right amount of crispy bits, the lightly sweet yet spicy flavor from the chipotle, the umami-rich vegan Worcestershire sauce, and the smoky chili powder and cumin. I could seriously snack on this crumble right off the pan, but I do my best to reserve it for serving in my Toppled Taco Salad (page 49) or over my Savory Jalapeño-Tomato Rice (page 270) and top it all with Glow Up Garden Guacamole (page 283). For a "non-recipe recipe" taco-bowl style, simply add generous scoops of Taco Tofu Crumble to serving bowls and load on your favorite toppings: chopped avocado, cilantro, cherry tomatoes, lettuce, cashew sour cream, pico de gallo, salsa—the options are nearly endless!

1 (12-ounce/350 g) block extra-firm or firm tofu, pressed
2 tablespoons extra-virgin olive oil
2 tablespoons ketchup
4 teaspoons vegan Worcestershire sauce
1½ teaspoons chili powder
1½ teaspoons ground cumin
1 teaspoon dried onion flakes
½ teaspoon fine sea salt, or to taste
½ teaspoon garlic powder
¼ teaspoon chipotle powder*

1. Press the tofu for at least 30 minutes (see page 357).
2. Preheat the oven to 400°F (200°C) and line a large baking sheet with parchment paper.
3. In a large bowl, crumble the pressed tofu into pea- and almond-size pieces. I like to squish it with my fingers as I crumble it, which results in a lot of tiny bits in addition to the bigger pieces.
4. Add the olive oil, ketchup, and Worcestershire sauce. Stir until well coated.
5. Sprinkle on the chili powder, cumin, onion flakes, salt, garlic powder, and chipotle powder. Stir well to combine.
6. Spread the seasoned tofu on the prepared baking sheet in an even layer.
7. Bake for 18 to 22 minutes, until golden, flipping once halfway through baking. The tofu will still be fairly soft when finished baking—this is so we don't dry it out. It'll firm up a bit as it cools.
8. Cool for 5 minutes on the pan, if desired, before serving.

storage

Store cooled leftover tofu in an airtight container in the fridge for up to 4 days or in the freezer for up to 3 weeks. Thaw at room temperature, then reheat in a lightly oiled covered skillet over medium heat for 3 to 4 minutes, stirring occasionally, until warm.

tip

* This dish is moderately spicy. If you are spice shy, feel free to reduce the chipotle powder to ⅛ teaspoon.

make it gluten-free

Use a gluten-free vegan Worcestershire sauce.

vegan • gluten-free • nut-free • grain-free • oil-free • advance prep required • kid-friendly • on the glow

Shake-and-Bake Sesame-Crusted Tofu

makes 6 (½-cup) salads • prep time: 10 minutes • total time: 35 minutes, plus pressing time

Say hello to your new favorite salad topper! Shake-and-Bake Sesame-Crusted Tofu is my go-to baked tofu, as it is so versatile, working with a variety of different dishes. It's a must-try for tofu skeptics and enthusiasts alike (even my three kids gobble it up when it's served in a wrap). Extra-firm or firm tofu is coated in a delightfully garlicky, "noochy" sesame seed coating and baked to chewy perfection with a lightly crisp outer shell. Try it paired with my Magnificent Miso Salad (page 149) or Edamame and Pistachio Soba Noodle Spinach Salad (page 99). You can also enjoy it on its own—it makes the perfect protein-rich snack when served with Roasted Almond Butter, Ginger, and Lime Dressing (page 222), Nut-Free Sunflower, Ginger, and Lime Dressing (page 224), my Immunity-Boosting Tahini Dressing (page 229), or Sweet and Tangy No-Chop Barbecue Sauce (page 262). I mean, what *doesn't* it go well with is the real question! No time to whip up a sauce? Rest assured this tofu is delicious served with simple ketchup or vegan mayonnaise, too, as a side or stuffed into a soft tortilla wrap.

1 (12-ounce/350 g) block extra-firm or firm tofu, pressed
¼ cup (33 g) arrowroot starch*
½ cup unsweetened non-dairy milk**
½ cup (76 g) sesame seeds
2 tablespoons nutritional yeast
1½ teaspoons garlic powder
1 teaspoon Herbamare or fine sea salt

1. Press the tofu for at least 30 minutes (see page 357).
2. Preheat the oven to 400°F (200°C) and line a large baking sheet with parchment paper.
3. Slice the block of pressed tofu in half lengthwise into two thinner rectangles. Cut each rectangle into 15 (1-inch/2.5 cm) cubes (you should have 30 cubes total). (Don't stress if the tofu cubes aren't all the same size.)
4. Gather 2 large ziplock bags and 1 large bowl. To the first bag, add the arrowroot starch. To the large bowl, add the milk. To the second bag, add the sesame seeds, nutritional yeast, garlic powder, and Herbamare or salt; secure the bag and toss to combine. Arrange the bags and bowl on the kitchen counter in the following order, from left to right: arrowroot bag, milk bowl, sesame mixture bag, and the lined baking sheet.

recipe continues

storage

Store cooled leftover tofu in an airtight container in the fridge for up to 4 days. The crusty coating will soften as it sits, but the tofu reheats beautifully. Reheat on a parchment-lined baking sheet in a 400°F (200°C) oven for 7 to 8 minutes, until warmed through. Or simply enjoy it chilled from the fridge, as we often do.

tips

* You can swap the arrowroot starch for cornstarch. The recipe will no longer be grain-free.

** Be sure to use unsweetened and unflavored milk—without vanilla or sweetener added.

If you don't have large ziplock bags, use large bowls and simply toss the tofu in the bowls using a spoon.

5. Place all the tofu cubes in the arrowroot bag, secure the bag, and gently shake several times until all the cubes are fully coated. Add all the arrowroot-coated cubes to the bowl with the milk and carefully toss with a spoon until fully coated. Using a large slotted spoon, lift the cubes out of the milk (you can do this in a few batches, if necessary), allowing the milk a few seconds to drain back into the bowl. Lower all the drained tofu cubes into the sesame bag. Immediately secure the bag and shake until the cubes are completely coated. (If some cubes clump together, simply break them apart with your fingers and dip any uncovered tofu sides directly into the sesame mixture.) Place the coated cubes on the baking sheet, about 1 inch (2.5 cm) apart.
6. Bake for 20 to 24 minutes, until lightly golden and firm, flipping once halfway through baking. Allow the tofu to cool on the pan for a few minutes before using.

vegan • gluten-free • soy-free • grain-free • advance prep required • kid-friendly • freezer-friendly • on the glow

Protein-Powered Cashew-Hemp Cheese

makes 3 to 4 cups small cubes • prep time: 15 minutes • total time: 28 minutes, plus soaking and chilling time

Tender cubes of my punchy, lightly sweet, melt-in-your-mouth Protein-Powered Cashew-Hemp Cheese are one of our fave things to top a salad. This cheese is versatile and brimming with health-promoting, satisfying protein and healthy omega fats thanks to the hemp hearts. In this herby cashew cheese, I blend savory garlic, dried oregano, and dried dill right into the mixture for a bright, garden-fresh flavor. Before baking, I press freeze-dried chives and hemp hearts into the cheese, which add protein, fiber, healthy fats, and that savory chive flavor we know and love. Keep this cheese handy to try on The Ultimate Ranch Barbecue Tofu Cobb Salad (page 85). It's also a nice alternative in my On the Glow Pasta Salad (page 107) and Sunny Day Charred Corn and Feta Salad (page 71). Really, it's delightful served on top of just about any warm or chilled pasta salad, such as my Sun-Kissed On the Glow Pasta Salad (page 111), to lend a creamy, vibrant kick.

2 cups (268 g) raw cashews, soaked

1 large garlic clove (6 g)

¼ cup refined coconut oil, melted*

5 to 6 tablespoons fresh lemon juice, to taste

2 tablespoons apple cider vinegar, or to taste

1½ to 2 teaspoons fine sea salt, to taste (I use 2 teaspoons)

1 teaspoon dried oregano

½ teaspoon dried dill

1½ tablespoons hemp hearts

1 tablespoon freeze-dried chives**

1. Place the cashews in a small bowl and add boiling water to cover. Soak for 15 minutes, then drain.
2. Preheat the oven to 325°F (160°C) and line an 8-inch (2 L) square pan with 2 pieces of parchment paper placed perpendicular to each other, cut to fit the width of the pan with a few inches of overhang on each side for easy removal.
3. Meanwhile, in a large heavy-duty food processor, process the garlic until minced.
4. Add the melted coconut oil, lemon juice, apple cider vinegar, 1½ teaspoons of salt, dried oregano, and dried dill. Add the drained cashews and process until completely smooth, 3 to 7 minutes, stopping to scrape down the sides of the bowl as necessary. There shouldn't be any gritty texture or pieces of cashew left. Taste, and add more lemon juice, apple cider vinegar, and/or salt, if desired.

recipe continues

storage

Store in an airtight container in the fridge for up to 1 week or in the freezer for up to 1 month. If frozen, thaw on the counter.

tips

* It's important to use refined coconut oil in this cheese, as virgin coconut oil will impart a light coconut flavor and aroma.

** Freeze-dried chives are usually located in the spice and seasoning aisle. I love having these handy, as they are very flavorful. You can swap an equal amount of minced fresh chives.

5. Spoon the creamy mixture into the prepared pan, spreading it out until smooth. Sprinkle the hemp hearts and chives over top, then press them gently into the cheese to adhere.
6. Bake, uncovered, for 8 minutes (this cooks off some of the moisture, resulting in a firmer cheese).
7. Cool the cheese in the pan for 10 minutes, then refrigerate, uncovered, for at least 3 hours or up to 6 hours, until firm to the touch. (If chilling for longer than 6 hours, cover the pan with plastic wrap.)
8. Lift the cheese from the pan and slice into small cubes. Transfer to an airtight container.

Dill Version

For a dill version, swap the dried chives for 2 to 2½ teaspoons dried dill sprinkled on top.

vegan • gluten-free • nut-free • soy-free • grain-free • kid-friendly • on the glow

Addictive Smoky Roasted Cauli, Chickpeas, and Taters

makes 6 generous cups • prep time: 15 minutes • total time: 41 minutes

4 medium unpeeled yellow potatoes (1.3 pounds/610 g total)

¼ cup untoasted sesame oil, divided

2¼ teaspoons garlic powder, divided

2¼ teaspoons sweet paprika, divided

2¼ teaspoons smoked paprika, divided

1½ teaspoons fine sea salt, divided

1 large head cauliflower (2.2 pounds/1 kg)

1½ cups (228 g) cooked chickpeas, drained and rinsed

Extra-virgin olive oil spray*

¼ cup (35 g) hemp hearts, divided

Cayenne pepper, to taste (optional)

The humble cauliflower and potato can be dressed up a million delicious ways; in this recipe, they're flavored robustly with smoked paprika, sweet paprika, garlic powder, and a hint of spicy cayenne pepper if you like some heat, then roasted until golden with little flavorful charred bits. You'll have to stop yourself from eating it all off the pan! After roasting, I toss the florets and potatoes with a sprinkle of hemp hearts to boost the protein by 13 grams and add those important healthy omega fats. Try these smoky florets in my Smoky Seasoned Roasted Cauliflower and Potato Salad (page 159) or to top any kind of salad you enjoy. They make a wonderful swap for the roasted chickpeas in my Roasted Chickpea and Parm Romaine Crunch Salad (page 91), as well as a savory, chewy protein topper for Busy Bee Big Salad (page 69) and my Radiant Garden Side Salad (page 89). We even love this as a side dish, with a little bowl of Sweet and Tangy No-Chop Barbecue Sauce (page 262) or Velvety Cashew Garlic Dressing (page 226) for dipping.

1. Position the racks in the upper and lower thirds of the oven and preheat to 425°F (220°C). Line 2 large rimmed baking sheets with parchment paper.
2. Chop the unpeeled potatoes into pieces ¾ to 1 inch (2 to 2.5 cm) long by ½ inch (1 cm) wide (you should have about 4½ cups). Place the potatoes on one of the prepared baking sheets and toss well with 2 tablespoons of the sesame oil until coated. Evenly sprinkle on 1 teaspoon of the garlic powder, 1 teaspoon of the smoked paprika, 1 teaspoon of the sweet paprika, and ¾ teaspoon of the salt and toss until combined. Spread the potatoes into an even layer.
3. Set a timer for 7 minutes and start roasting the potatoes, uncovered.

4. Immediately start chopping the cauliflower into small, bite-size (1-inch/2.5 cm) florets (you should have about 5 cups, including the little bits). I love how these turn out when the florets are chopped nice and small, so avoid chopping overly large florets. Transfer the cauliflower to the second prepared baking sheet, along with the drained chickpeas. Toss well with the remaining 2 tablespoons sesame oil until coated. Evenly sprinkle on the remaining 1¼ teaspoons garlic powder, remaining 1¼ teaspoons smoked paprika, remaining 1¼ teaspoons sweet paprika, and remaining ¾ teaspoon salt and toss until combined. Spread the florets into an even layer.

5. When the 7-minute timer goes off, add the cauliflower mixture to the oven, uncovered. Roast both baking sheets, uncovered, for 25 to 35 minutes, until the potatoes are tender, the bottoms are golden brown, and the florets are tender with little charred bits, flipping once and rotating the pans from upper to lower and back to front halfway through roasting. (The chickpeas won't turn crispy because of the moisture from the cauliflower cooking beside them.)

6. As soon as you remove both baking sheets from the oven, very lightly spray the cauliflower and chickpeas with olive oil spray, then quickly sprinkle on 2 tablespoons of the hemp hearts and toss to combine. Season with a small sprinkle of more salt, if desired. Repeat for the potatoes with the remaining 2 tablespoons hemp hearts and a sprinkle of salt, if desired. If you like a spicy kick, sprinkle a light dusting of cayenne pepper over the potatoes and/or cauliflower and chickpeas, to taste.

7. Using a spatula, scoop up the cauliflower, chickpeas, and potatoes (being sure to scoop all the tiny hemp bits, too!) and serve warm on top of a salad or as a delectable side.

storage

Store cooled leftovers in an airtight container in the fridge for up to 4 days. Reheat in a 400°F (200°C) oven for 4 to 6 minutes. If needed, revive the flavors with a pinch each of cayenne pepper and salt.

tips

* If you don't have extra-virgin olive oil spray, you can use a very light drizzle of extra-virgin olive oil from a bottle. I use this additional oil so the hemp hearts have a little something-something to stick to.

Don't have any cauliflower or chickpeas on hand? This recipe is just as delicious using only potatoes.

vegan • gluten-free • nut-free • soy-free • grain-free • kid-friendly • on the glow • one pan

Garlic-Cayenne Roasted Chickpeas

makes 1 heaping cup • prep time: 5 minutes • total time: 35 minutes plus cooling time

1½ cups (228 g) cooked chickpeas, drained and rinsed

2 teaspoons pure avocado oil, grapeseed oil, or extra-virgin olive oil

1 teaspoon garlic powder, plus more to taste

½ teaspoon Herbamare or fine sea salt, plus more to taste

⅛ to ¼ teaspoon cayenne pepper, to taste*

storage

While leftovers can be stored in an airtight container at room temperature for up to 3 days, I always prefer roasted chickpeas fresh out of the oven. The chickpeas will soften when stored, but can be re-crisped in a 375°F (190°C) oven for 5 to 6 minutes.

tip

* Use ⅛ teaspoon cayenne pepper for a mild spice level; use ¼ teaspoon for a moderate to strong spice level. I like to use ⅛ teaspoon and then sprinkle on a bit more after cooking.

I've been making roasted chickpeas to add flavor, crunch, protein, and fiber to my salads for years, as they are such a fun protein-packed topper. I love how these chickpeas sprinkled liberally with zippy garlic powder and spicy cayenne bring a kick of heat to my Roasted Chickpea and Parm Romaine Crunch Salad (page 91) and Sweater Weather Toasted Sesame, Tamari, and Garlic Kale Salad (page 123). Making these couldn't be simpler: just drain and dry the cooked chickpeas (either homemade or from a can), toss them with a little oil, spices, and some sea salt, and throw the pan in the oven. Roasted chickpeas aren't just for salads; they make a nice snack eaten straight from the pan, too.

1. Preheat the oven to 375°F (190°C) and line a large baking sheet with parchment paper.
2. With a clean kitchen towel, pat the chickpeas mostly dry, then spread them onto the prepared baking sheet. Toss with the avocado oil until coated. Sprinkle on the garlic powder, Herbamare (or salt), and cayenne pepper, and toss the chickpeas until evenly coated. Spread into an even layer.
3. Roast the chickpeas, uncovered, for 25 to 35 minutes, until golden and slightly firm, giving the pan a gentle shake halfway through roasting. Cool the chickpeas on the pan for 3 to 5 minutes before serving. Taste, and sprinkle on more garlic powder, Herbamare (or salt), and cayenne, if desired.

vegan • gluten-free option • soy-free option • grain-free • oil-free • on the glow • one bowl

Sticky Roasted Tamari-Maple Almonds

makes ¾ cup • prep time: 5 minutes • total time: 15 minutes, plus cooling time

Sticky Roasted Tamari-Maple Almonds, mmmm . . . what have we here? How about crisp, crunchy, caramelized, sweet and sticky roasted almond delights! This nutty topper is so quick to whip up; in only 5 minutes they are in the oven, allowing you to start prepping your salad. With a salty umami tone from the light tamari and that sweet maple goodness, these nuts are so tasty to snack on all on their own. They are even more delightful with sesame seeds stirred into the mixture. We love the crunch they add to Glow Girl Kale Slaw (page 39). My delicate-textured sliced version (see page 204) cooks up into sweet and savory little candied bundles that are simply irresistible on my Sweet Potato and Edamame Salad with Roasted Almond Butter, Ginger, and Lime Dressing (page 143). Be sure to use light tamari, as full-sodium tamari will result in a mixture that's too salty.

½ cup (78 g) raw almonds, chopped into pea-size and smaller pieces

1 tablespoon + 1 teaspoon light tamari*

1 tablespoon pure maple syrup

2 teaspoons sesame seeds

Sprinkle of fine sea salt (optional)

1. Preheat the oven to 325°F (160°C). Line a large rimmed baking sheet with parchment paper.
2. In a small bowl, stir together the chopped almonds, tamari, and maple syrup until the nuts are completely coated. Add the sesame seeds and stir to combine. Using a spatula, scrape the coated almond and sesame seed mixture, along with every last bit of the tamari-maple liquid, onto the prepared baking sheet and spread in an even layer.
3. Roast for 10 to 15 minutes, until lightly golden. The tamari-maple liquid should be somewhat dried up, but the mixture will be very sticky when it first comes out of the oven.
4. Allow the mixture to cool completely on the pan, about 30 minutes. The almonds will firm up and the mixture will become slightly less sticky. Taste, and add a sprinkle of salt, if desired (I usually don't need to add any). Using a spatula, scrape the almonds off the parchment.

recipe continues

storage

Store in an airtight container in the fridge for up to 3 weeks. The almonds will firm up slightly when chilled but will remain sticky. At room temperature, they'll have a slightly softer consistency.

tips

* It's important to use light tamari (not regular full-sodium tamari) or the mixture will be too salty.

This recipe doubles and triples beautifully.

make it gluten-free

Use gluten-free light tamari.

make it soy-free

Swap the light tamari for an equal amount of coconut aminos (also called soy-sauce substitute or soy-free seasoning) and add ¼ to ½ teaspoon fine sea salt to the mixture (coconut aminos are less salty than light tamari).

Sliced Version

For a sliced version, use ½ cup (56 g) thinly sliced almonds and reduce the roasting time to 10 to 13 minutes, until the edges are golden and the almonds are fragrant. When they come out of the oven, the almonds will be very sticky. This is normal, and it leads to delicious clusters! Immediately scrape the almonds to release them from the parchment paper, using a spatula while holding the parchment in place with one hand. Leave the almonds on the parchment paper to cool. At the 5-minute cooling mark, I recommend giving the almonds another scrape with the spatula to release them from the parchment paper, as they tend to stick to it again. After fully cooling (about 15 minutes), scoop the sliced almond clusters into a small bowl or container. Makes ⅔ cup.

HOME

vegan • gluten-free • nut-free • soy-free • kid-friendly • freezer-friendly • on the glow • one pot

Savory Brown Rice and Lentils

makes 6 cups • prep time: 10 minutes • total time: 55 minutes

I love having this whole-grain Savory Brown Rice and Lentils dish in the fridge during the week, as it is the ideal high-protein addition to almost any salad or other dish. Its gentle taste of roasty brown rice, earthy lentils, sautéed sweet onion and garlic, and savory bay leaf guarantees that its flavor will meld nicely with most salads and dressings. Fiber-filled brown lentils and rice add staying power, which I especially love when using this as a base for simple green salads. You'll find me serving it with my Busy Bee Big Salad (page 69) and even as its own salad, piled high atop a bed of baby spinach or other greens, dressed with my Perfect Balsamic-Maple Vinaigrette (page 218). A big thank you to Chef Michael Smith for inspiring a vegan version of his delectable grain and legume recipe.

2 cups (220 g) diced sweet onion (1 medium)

3 large garlic cloves (18 g total), minced

1 tablespoon extra-virgin olive oil

¼ teaspoon fine sea salt, more as needed

¼ teaspoon freshly ground black pepper, more as needed

4 cups vegetable broth

1 cup (178 g) uncooked long-grain brown rice

1 cup (187 g) uncooked brown lentils*

2 bay leaves

1. Prepare the onion and garlic.
2. Heat the olive oil in a medium pot over medium heat. Stir in the diced onion, minced garlic, salt, and pepper. Cook, uncovered, stirring frequently, for 8 to 10 minutes, until the onion is soft and translucent.
3. Stir in the broth, rice, lentils, and bay leaves. Increase the heat to high and bring to a boil. Immediately reduce the heat to low, cover with a tight-fitting lid, and gently simmer for 33 to 43 minutes (I cook mine for about 35 minutes), until most of the liquid has been absorbed and the lentils and rice are tender and fluffy. Uncover and cool for 10 minutes, stirring occasionally. Remove and discard the bay leaves, and drain any excess liquid, if needed. Season to taste with salt and pepper, if desired.

storage

Store in an airtight container in the fridge for up to 5 days or in the freezer for up to 3 weeks.

tip

* Green lentils (not French lentils) work well as a swap for brown lentils. This recipe hasn't been tested using smaller green French (du Puy) lentils.

fl oz 16
8

vegan • gluten-free • soy-free • grain-free • oil-free • kid-friendly • on the glow • one bowl

Rosemary, Maple, and Cayenne Roasted Pecans and Walnuts

makes 2⅓ cups • prep time: 8 minutes • total time: 25 minutes, plus cooling time

Get ready for a crowd-pleasing and addictive candied nut recipe that you're going to be gifting in mason jars to all of your family and friends! Candied nuts have to be the quickest, simplest way to elevate a salad to "impress your guests" level, but you don't have to wait for a special occasion to enjoy them. With less than 10 minutes of simple prep, you can have a bowl of sweet, savory, nutty, aromatic candied nuts at the ready for salads or snacks. I love them in my Strawberry Arugula Salad with Feta and Rosemary-Maple Nuts (page 86), Butternut, Cranberry, and Rosemary-Maple Pecan and Walnut Arugula Salad (page 153), and Nourishing Warm Brunch Salad Bowls (page 113). I often set them out on a veggie platter alongside my Garlic-Infused Olive Oil Crostini (page 249), too.

1 cup (116 g) raw pecan halves

1 cup (100 g) raw walnut halves

3½ tablespoons pure maple syrup

3 tablespoons unpacked (31 g) brown sugar

1½ tablespoons minced fresh rosemary leaves

½ teaspoon fine sea salt

⅛ to ¼ teaspoon cayenne pepper, to taste*

1. Preheat the oven to 325°F (160°C) and line a large rimmed baking sheet with parchment paper.
2. In a medium bowl, stir together the pecans, walnuts, maple syrup, brown sugar, minced rosemary, salt, and cayenne. Stir very well until all the nuts are coated.
3. Using a silicone spoon, scrape the nut mixture onto the prepared baking sheet, being sure to scoop all the juicy bits of rosemary and syrup onto the pecans and walnuts. Spread the nuts into an even layer.
4. Roast, uncovered, for 10 minutes. Remove from the oven and toss the nuts with a spatula. Spread them back into an even layer. The nuts will look bubbly from the syrupy mixture. Rotate the pan, then return to the oven and roast, uncovered, for another 5 to 8 minutes, until fragrant and lightly golden.

recipe continues

storage

Store completely cooled nuts in an airtight container at room temperature for up to 1 month.

tips

* Use ⅛ teaspoon cayenne pepper for a very mild heat or use ¼ teaspoon for a mild to moderate heat level.

For a slightly sticky end result, roast for the shorter time, and for nuts with a drier consistency, roast for the longer time.

5. Cool the nuts on the pan for 10 minutes. Using one hand to hold the parchment paper in place, scoop the nuts up with a spatula or metal spoon to unstick and flip them. Leave the nuts on the pan for another 20 minutes, until fully cooled, before transferring to an airtight container. The nuts will firm up as they cool on the pan and a bit more once stored. Feel free to chop the nuts before using on salads, if desired, or leave whole.

Rosemary-Free Version

For a rosemary-free version, simply omit the rosemary. This recipe still works beautifully without rosemary; however, the flavor will be less savory and complex without it, and the maple and brown sugar will be more pronounced.

vegan • gluten-free • soy-free • grain-free • oil-free • raw/no bake • freezer-friendly • on the glow • one bowl

The Crunch Nutty Protein Topper

makes 3 cups • prep time: 8 minutes • total time: 8 minutes

Garlicky, herby, *crunchtastic*, packed with protein and healthy fats . . . what's not to love about this easy-to-throw-together protein topper? Rich and buttery hazelnuts, lightly sweet cashews, bitter walnuts, fragrant parsley, and assertive garlic are pulsed into small pieces to create the perfect texture for scattering. This is one of my go-tos for topping all kinds of salads, from raw green leafy salads to pasta salads to roasted salads. You could honestly use this on just about any salad! For a flavor and protein knockout, try it on my Fall Crunch Farro Kale Salad (page 121), Warm Mushroom and Spinach Pasta Salad (page 177), and Roasted Chickpea and Parm Romaine Crunch Salad (page 91), just to name a few. Have fun experimenting with different kinds of fresh herbs in season to create different flavor profiles, too.

2 large garlic cloves (12 g total)

⅓ cup packed (12 g) fresh flat-leaf parsley leaves

⅓ heaping cup (55 g) raw hazelnuts, coarsely chopped* (see Variation)

¾ cup (101 g) raw cashews (see Variation)

¾ cup (75 g) raw walnut halves (see Variation)

6 tablespoons (53 g) hemp hearts

3 tablespoons nutritional yeast

¾ teaspoon fine sea salt, or to taste**

1. In a large food processor, process the garlic and parsley until minced, 5 to 10 seconds, scraping down the bowl if needed.
2. Add the chopped hazelnuts, cashews, walnut halves, hemp hearts, nutritional yeast, and salt and pulse the mixture only 18 to 25 times, until coarsely chopped with some larger chunks of nuts (the nut mixture should include pea-size pieces and smaller pieces). Be careful not to overprocess the nuts, as you want the topping to be very textural and crunchy.

recipe continues

Storage

Store leftovers (cooled, if you toasted the nuts) in an airtight container in the fridge for up to 1 week or in the freezer for up to 3 weeks. Set on the counter until room temperature before using.

Tips

* Don't chop the hazelnuts too small. I only chop them into halves or at the most into thirds. You just want to break them down slightly before they go in the processor. During testing, I found if I didn't give the hazelnuts a bit of a chop before processing, they wouldn't break down into small enough pieces before the other nuts had.

** Using ¾ teaspoon salt results in a fairly salty mixture (just slightly more salty than I would normally season a dish), but I find the extra bit of salt helps this topper "pop" when scattered over recipes. If too little salt is used, it may fall flat once over a salad or other dish. As always, feel free to add it slowly and keep tasting.

Toasted Nut Variation

This recipe uses untoasted nuts, but I slightly prefer its deep, toasty flavor when using toasted nuts. To toast the nuts, simply preheat the oven to 325°F (160°C). Spread the cashews, walnuts, and coarsely chopped hazelnuts on a parchment-lined large rimmed baking sheet and roast, uncovered, for 10 to 15 minutes, until lightly golden, watching closely during the last few minutes to avoid burning. Cool on the pan for a few minutes. There's no need to remove any skins from the hazelnuts before adding them to the processor. (How's that for easy!)

dressings

Recipes

and vinaigrettes

Back row, left to right: Barbecue Apple Cider Vinaigrette; Cold Moon Orange Vinaigrette; Perfect Balsamic-Maple Vinaigrette

Front row, left to right: Sriracha Honey-Mustard Dressing; Cilantro, Lime, Cumin, and Jalapeño Dressing; Toasted Sesame, Tamari, and Garlic Dressing

vegan • gluten-free • nut-free • soy-free • grain-free • raw/no bake • kid-friendly • on the glow • one bowl

Cold Moon Orange Vinaigrette

makes 1 cup plus 3 tablespoons • prep time: 11 minutes • total time: 11 minutes

The first full moon in December is called the Cold Moon, and it just happened to be when I whipped up this delightful vinaigrette. This warming, golden-hued dressing, with its sweet orange juice, tangy apple cider and wine vinegars, bitey shallots, robust old-fashioned Dijon, and lightly sweet pure maple syrup is a delight over leafy salads in the wintertime (or any time). I love pairing it with kale, as its tangy sweetness softens and sweetens the greens. Try it with my Wintry Day Two-Potato, Apple, and Cranberry Kale Salad (page 171) and Stuffed Butternut Squash Wild Rice Salad (page 129). We'll sometimes throw it together to drizzle over cooked grains or roasted veggies like sweet or yellow potatoes and green beans, for a quick and simple glow up.

2 medium shallots (58 g total), minced (¼ cup)

6 tablespoons freshly squeezed orange juice (1 large navel orange)

¼ cup extra-virgin olive oil

3 tablespoons apple cider vinegar

1 tablespoon + 2 teaspoons red or white wine vinegar* (I use a mix of both)

1 tablespoon pure maple syrup

1 tablespoon old-fashioned Dijon mustard

¼ to ½ teaspoon fine sea salt, to taste

Freshly ground black pepper

1. To a medium mason jar, add the minced shallots, orange juice, olive oil, apple cider vinegar, red or white wine vinegar (or use a mix of both vinegars), maple syrup, mustard, salt, and pepper to taste. Secure the lid and shake vigorously to combine. Taste and adjust any flavors, if desired.

Double Batch Variation

For a double batch of vinaigrette, use 4 medium shallots (116 g total), minced (½ cup); ¾ cup freshly squeezed orange juice (2 large navel oranges); ½ cup extra-virgin olive oil; 6 tablespoons apple cider vinegar; 3 tablespoons + 1 teaspoon red and/or white wine vinegar; 2 tablespoons pure maple syrup; 2 tablespoons old-fashioned Dijon mustard, or to taste; and fine sea salt and freshly ground black pepper to taste (I use ½ teaspoon of salt or a bit more). Makes 2⅓ cups.

storage

Store in the jar or an airtight container in the fridge for up to 5 days. Shake before each use, if needed.

tip

* This vinaigrette has a slightly sharper flavor when made with red wine vinegar, while white wine vinegar yields a slightly sweeter flavor. I like using a mix of both for the most complexity of flavor.

vegan • gluten-free • nut-free • soy-free • grain-free • raw/no bake • kid-friendly • on the glow • one bowl

Perfect Balsamic-Maple Vinaigrette

makes ¾ cup plus 1 tablespoon • prep time: 5 minutes • total time: 5 minutes

1 large garlic clove (6 g), minced

1 medium shallot (30 g), minced (3 tablespoons)

½ cup extra-virgin olive oil

4 to 5 tablespoons balsamic vinegar, to taste (I use 5 tablespoons)

2 to 3 teaspoons pure maple syrup, to taste (I use 3 teaspoons)

½ teaspoon fine sea salt, or to taste

Freshly ground black pepper

storage

Store in the jar or an airtight container in the fridge for up to 9 days. Let sit at room temperature until softened, then shake before each use, if needed.

Sweet, lightly garlicky, a hint of shallot, tangy and rich balsamic, sweet pure maple syrup . . . this is sure to be your new favorite balsamic vinaigrette. It's so simple: all the ingredients get added directly to a jar so you can just shake it up. Serve it with my Strawberry Arugula Salad with Feta and Rosemary-Maple Nuts (page 86), Stuffed Butternut Squash Wild Rice Salad (page 129), Roasted Vegetable Medley with Sun-Dried Tomato, Walnut, and Basil Whipped Feta (page 155), and Radiant Garden Side Salad (page 89).

1. To a medium mason jar, add the minced garlic, minced shallot, olive oil, balsamic vinegar, maple syrup, salt, and pepper to taste. Secure the lid and shake vigorously until combined, 10 to 15 seconds. Adjust the flavors to taste, if desired. For example, if you find the dressing to be a bit too tangy, add a bit more olive oil, shake it again to recombine, and adjust until it suits your tastes.

Double Batch Variation

For a double batch of vinaigrette, use 2 large garlic cloves (12 g total), minced, 2 medium shallots (60 g total), minced (6 tablespoons), 1 cup extra-virgin olive oil, 8 to 10 tablespoons balsamic vinegar (to taste), 4 to 6 teaspoons pure maple syrup (to taste), ¾ to 1 teaspoon fine sea salt (to taste), and freshly ground black pepper (to taste). Adjust the flavors to taste, if desired. Makes a generous 1½ cups.

vegan • gluten-free option • nut-free • raw/no bake • kid-friendly • freezer-friendly • on the glow • one bowl

Toasted Sesame, Tamari, and Garlic Dressing

makes ⅔ cup • prep time: 5 minutes • total time: 5 minutes

This Toasted Sesame, Tamari, and Garlic Dressing has it all, and I bet you'll be enjoying it right off the spoon! It's umami-rich from the tamari, sweet from the pure maple syrup, tangy from the rice vinegar, creamy from the tahini, and deeply rich from the sesame oil. It goes beautifully with my Sweater Weather Toasted Sesame, Tamari, and Garlic Kale Salad (page 123), Sunflower, Ginger, and Lime Crunch Salad (page 45), and Edamame and Pistachio Soba Noodle Spinach Salad (page 99). Drizzle it over sautéed greens, roasted sweet potatoes, or steamed rice to add a lovely umami, sweet, and creamy flavor . . . mmm, yes!

1 medium garlic clove (5 g)
3 tablespoons light tamari*
3 tablespoons seasoned rice vinegar
2 tablespoons grapeseed oil or pure/refined olive oil
2 tablespoons runny tahini
1 tablespoon + 1 teaspoon toasted sesame oil
3 to 4 teaspoons pure maple syrup, to taste**

1. In a small food processor, process the garlic until minced.
2. Add the tamari, rice vinegar, grapeseed oil or olive oil, tahini, toasted sesame oil, and maple syrup to taste. Process until smooth, 10 to 15 seconds. Taste and adjust the flavors, if desired.

One and a Half Batch Variation

For 1½ batches of dressing, use 1 large garlic clove (6 g), 4½ tablespoons light tamari, 4½ tablespoons seasoned rice vinegar, 3 tablespoons grapeseed oil or olive oil, 3 tablespoons runny tahini, 2 tablespoons toasted sesame oil, and 1½ to 2 tablespoons pure maple syrup (to taste). Makes 1 cup plus 2 tablespoons.

storage

Store in an airtight container in the fridge for up to 5 days or in the freezer for up to 6 weeks. Stir before each use, if needed.

tips

* It's important to use light tamari (not regular full-sodium tamari) or the dressing will be too salty.

** If you prefer a tangier dressing, use 3 teaspoons of pure maple syrup; if you prefer a sweeter dressing, use 4 teaspoons. I prefer using 4 teaspoons when serving this in my Sweater Weather Toasted Sesame, Tamari, and Garlic Kale Salad, as the sweetness counters the slightly bitter taste of the kale.

make it gluten-free:

Use gluten-free light tamari.

vegan • gluten-free • nut-free • soy-free • grain-free • raw/no bake • kid-friendly freezer-friendly • on the glow • one bowl

Apple Cider, Shallot, Maple, and Dijon Vinaigrette

makes ⅔ cup plus 1 tablespoon • prep time: 6 minutes • total time: 6 minutes

1 medium garlic clove (5 g), minced

1 small shallot (27 g), minced (2½ tablespoons)

2 tablespoons + 1 teaspoon apple cider vinegar

¼ cup extra-virgin olive oil

1 tablespoon + 1 teaspoon to 1½ tablespoons pure maple syrup, to taste

1½ tablespoons white wine vinegar*

2 teaspoons old-fashioned Dijon mustard

¼ teaspoon + ⅛ teaspoon fine sea salt, or to taste

storage

Store in the jar or an airtight container in the fridge for up to 7 days or in the freezer for up to 2 months. Shake before each use, if needed.

tip

* If you have pear vinegar on hand, it's a lovely seasonal swap for white wine vinegar.

This lightly sweet, savory, and tangy autumnal vinaigrette complements cooler-weather salads with their heavier greens and roasted pumpkin, squash, and other seasonal veggies. It gets that cozy fall feel from the sweet and tart apple cider vinegar, mild minced shallots, and sweet hint of maple syrup. For salads you won't be able to stop eating, pair it with my Butternut, Cranberry, and Rosemary-Maple Pecan and Walnut Arugula Salad (page 153), Glow Girl Kale Slaw (page 39), and Nourishing Warm Brunch Salad Bowls (page 113)! If you love this dressing, then you need to try the creamier version—my Creamy ACV, Shallot, Maple, and Dijon Vinaigrette (page 233), which is especially delicious on my On the Glow Pasta Salad (page 107).

1. To a small mason jar, add the minced garlic, minced shallot, apple cider vinegar, olive oil, maple syrup, white wine vinegar, mustard, and salt to taste. Secure the lid and shake vigorously until combined, 10 to 15 seconds. Taste and adjust the flavors, if desired.

vegan • gluten-free • nut-free • soy-free option • grain-free • raw/no bake • kid-friendly • on the glow • one bowl

Luxurious ACV and Dijon Dressing

makes ¾ cup plus 1 tablespoon • prep time: 5 minutes • total time: 5 minutes

This dressing is decadent, velvety, tangy, and lightly garlicky and is the ideal pairing to warm roasted salads, which need a flavorful, rich dressing, and chilled salads made with sturdy greens like romaine lettuce that can handle a thick, creamy coating. Both the mayo and the apple cider vinegar add tanginess, while a hint of maple syrup lends a light sweetness, and the Dijon adds its distinctive zesty flavor that suits greens, potatoes, tomatoes, and more. Use my Soy-Free Vegan Mayonnaise (page 265) or your favorite store-bought vegan mayonnaise. This dressing is fab drizzled over my Cozy Potato, Zucchini, and Cannellini Bean Salad (page 147), and we also love serving it with my Stuffed Butternut Squash Wild Rice Salad (page 129), upping the maple syrup in the dressing to 2 teaspoons to enhance the sweetness of the squash.

1 small garlic clove (4 g)

½ cup + 2 tablespoons Soy-Free Vegan Mayonnaise (page 265) or store-bought

1 tablespoon + 1 teaspoon apple cider vinegar

1 tablespoon + 1 teaspoon old-fashioned Dijon mustard

½ teaspoon pure maple syrup, or to taste

Fine sea salt and freshly ground black pepper

1. Grate the garlic on a Microplane.
2. In a small bowl, whisk together the grated garlic, vegan mayonnaise, apple cider vinegar, mustard, and maple syrup to taste. Season to taste with salt and pepper, stirring to combine.

storage

Store in an airtight container in the fridge for up to 5 days. Stir before each use, if needed.

make it soy-free

If using store-bought vegan mayo, be sure to select a soy-free variety.

vegan • gluten-free option • nut-free option • grain-free • raw/no bake • kid-friendly • on the glow • one bowl

Roasted Almond Butter, Ginger, and Lime Dressing

makes a generous ¾ cup • prep time: 8 minutes • total time: 8 minutes

1 to 2 medium garlic cloves (5 to 10 g total), to taste*

2 teaspoons grated peeled fresh ginger (use a Microplane)

6 tablespoons natural smooth roasted almond butter**

2 tablespoons seasoned rice vinegar

2 tablespoons light tamari***

2 tablespoons fresh lime juice, or to taste

2 tablespoons pure maple syrup, or to taste

1 tablespoon toasted sesame oil

1 to 2 tablespoons water

Fine sea salt

Every time I whip up a new winning salad dressing, I think, "This is the best salad dressing I have ever created!" Of course, once I go back and serve my other dressings, I think the same thing about *them*. How's a girl to choose? (Spoiler alert: not very easily!) My Roasted Almond Butter, Ginger, and Lime Dressing is quite special; using roasted almond butter really adds depth of flavor. It has everything: a little heat from fresh ginger, sweet tanginess from the lime, savory garlic, umami tamari and toasted sesame oil, rich roasted almond butter, and more. It's an ideal pairing for my Sweet Potato and Edamame Salad with Roasted Almond Butter, Ginger, and Lime Dressing (page 143) and Summer Roll Salad with Pickled Carrots (page 101). If nuts aren't a concern for you, you can enjoy this dressing on my Sunflower, Ginger, and Lime Crunch Salad (page 45) in place of the Nut-Free Sunflower, Ginger, and Lime Dressing as a fun way to change up that salad.

1. In a small food processor, process the garlic until minced.
2. Add the grated ginger, almond butter, rice vinegar, tamari, lime juice, maple syrup, toasted sesame oil, and 1 tablespoon water, and process until smooth, about 10 seconds. Add the remaining 1 tablespoon of water, if needed, to thin the dressing. Taste and adjust any flavors, if you'd like, and season to taste with salt. The dressing will thicken as it sits; stir well before use.

One and a Half Batch Variation

For 1½ batches of dressing, use 3 medium garlic cloves (15 g total), 1 tablespoon grated peeled fresh ginger, ½ cup plus 1 tablespoon natural smooth roasted almond butter, 3 tablespoons seasoned rice vinegar, 3 tablespoons light tamari, 3 tablespoons fresh lime juice (or to taste), 3 tablespoons pure maple syrup (or to taste), 1½ tablespoons toasted sesame oil, 1½ to 3 tablespoons water (as needed), and fine sea salt to taste. Makes a generous 1½ cups.

storage

Store in an airtight container in the fridge for up to 1 week. This dressing may thicken a bit after being refrigerated; simply let it come to room temperature and stir well before each use.

tips

* For a mild garlic flavor, use 1 clove, and for a moderate garlic flavor, use 2 cloves.

** Avoid using thick and dry almond butter. Runny and smooth is the best consistency.

*** It's important to use light tamari (not regular full-sodium tamari) or the dressing will be too salty.

make it gluten-free

Use gluten-free light tamari.

make it nut-free

Make my Nut-Free Sunflower, Ginger, and Lime Dressing (page 224) instead.

vegan • gluten-free option • nut-free • grain-free • raw/no bake • kid-friendly • freezer-friendly
on the glow • one bowl

Nut-Free Sunflower, Ginger, and Lime Dressing

makes 1 scant cup • prep time: 10 minutes • total time: 10 minutes

1 medium garlic clove (5 g)
2 teaspoons freshly grated peeled ginger
6 tablespoons natural smooth roasted sunflower seed butter*
2 tablespoons seasoned rice vinegar
2 tablespoons light tamari**
2 tablespoons fresh lime juice, or to taste
2 tablespoons pure maple syrup, or to taste
1 tablespoon toasted sesame oil
1 tablespoon water, or as needed
Fine sea salt (optional)

This light-as-air dressing started out as a nut-free version of my Roasted Almond Butter, Ginger, and Lime Dressing (and it makes a fantastic swap!), but it quickly evolved into one of my favorite dressings all on its own. No nuts required. The mild, roasty taste of sunflower seed butter is the perfect canvas for spicy ginger, zesty lime, umami tamari and toasted sesame oil, and zippy seasoned rice vinegar. The flavors all blend smoothly together and are fantastic on my Sweet Potato and Edamame Salad (page 143), Sunflower, Ginger, and Lime Crunch Salad (page 45), and Summer Roll Salad with Pickled Carrots (page 101).

1. In a small food processor, process the garlic until minced.
2. Add the grated ginger, sunflower seed butter, rice vinegar, tamari, lime juice, maple syrup, toasted sesame oil, and water (starting with 1 tablespoon). Process until smooth, 10 to 15 seconds. Add more water, if needed, to thin the dressing. Taste and adjust any flavors, if you'd like, and season with a bit of salt, if desired (I add about ⅛ teaspoon salt and 1 teaspoon additional lime juice). The dressing will thicken as it sits; stir well before use.

One and a Half Batch Variation

For 1½ batches of dressing, use 2 small garlic cloves (8 g total), 1 tablespoon freshly grated peeled ginger, ½ cup + 1 tablespoon natural smooth roasted sunflower seed butter, 3 tablespoons seasoned rice vinegar, 3 tablespoons light tamari, 3 tablespoons fresh lime juice (or to taste), 3 tablespoons pure maple syrup (or to taste), 1½ tablespoons toasted sesame oil, 1½ tablespoons water (or as needed), and fine sea salt to taste. Makes 1½ cups.

storage

Store in an airtight container in the fridge for up to 6 days or in the freezer for up to 1 month. This dressing may thicken a bit after being refrigerated; simply let it come to room temperature, thin with a touch of water (if needed), and stir well before each use.

tips

* Use a roasted sunflower seed butter with a runny consistency, and avoid using sunflower seed butters with added sugar or emulsifiers.

** It's important to use light tamari (not regular full-sodium tamari) or the dressing will be too salty.

make it gluten-free

Use gluten-free light tamari.

vegan • gluten-free • nut-free option • soy-free • grain-free • raw/no bake • advance prep required
kid-friendly • freezer-friendly • on the glow • one bowl

Velvety Cashew Garlic Dressing

makes 1½ generous cups • prep time: 10 minutes • total time: 10 minutes, plus soaking time

½ cup (67 g) raw cashews, soaked
½ cup water
6 tablespoons grapeseed oil
3 to 4 large garlic cloves (18 to 24 g total), to taste
¼ cup (22 g) nutritional yeast
2 tablespoons + 2 teaspoons white wine vinegar
2 tablespoons fresh lemon juice
1 to 1½ tablespoons old-fashioned Dijon mustard, to taste
1 to 1¼ teaspoons fine sea salt, to taste
Freshly ground black pepper

One of my all-time favorite luxurious dressings, my Velvety Cashew Garlic Dressing is delectable over hearty salads like my Roasted Chickpea and Parm Romaine Crunch Salad (page 91) and Smoky Seasoned Roasted Cauliflower and Potato Salad (page 159). This dressing's sweet cashews, cheesy nutritional yeast, tart white wine vinegar, mildly spicy old-fashioned Dijon mustard, and bright lemon juice add an explosion of vibrant, citrusy, garlicky flavor that kicks everyday veggies and legumes into major overdrive! I find that salads featuring lots of roasted veggies take to a thick and creamy (yet somehow light as air at the same time) dressing like this one to really coat those ingredients.

1. Place the cashews in a small bowl and add boiling water to cover. Soak for 1 hour, then drain. (If you have a high-speed blender, you can get away with a 10-minute soak.)
2. To a blender, add the drained cashews, ½ cup water, grapeseed oil, garlic cloves, nutritional yeast, white wine vinegar, lemon juice, mustard, salt, and pepper to taste. Blend on high speed until super smooth, 30 to 90 seconds. Taste and adjust the flavors, if desired.
3. Immediately pour the dressing into an airtight container. (The dressing thickens as it sits, so if you leave it in the blender jar, it'll be hard to scoop out.)

storage

Store in an airtight container in the fridge for up to 5 days or in the freezer for up to 3 weeks. Let sit at room temperature until softened, or microwave for 15 to 20 seconds, stirring every 5 seconds. Once softened, stir in a small amount of water, ½ teaspoon at a time, to thin to your desired consistency, if necessary.

make it nut-free

Make my Velvety Sunflower Garlic Dressing (page 227) instead.

vegan • gluten-free • nut-free • soy-free • grain-free • raw/no bake • advance prep required
kid-friendly • freezer-friendly • on the glow • one bowl

Velvety Sunflower Garlic Dressing

makes 1¾ cups • prep time: 9 minutes • total time: 9 minutes, plus soaking time

When I created my Velvety Cashew Garlic Dressing (page 226), it was an instant hit with friends, family, and recipe testers alike. There were several requests for a nut-free version so that friends with allergy concerns could enjoy salads like my Roasted Chickpea and Parm Romaine Crunch Salad (page 91) and Smoky Seasoned Roasted Cauliflower and Potato Salad (page 159). It took me a while, as I wanted this version to taste as cheesy from the nutritional yeast, bright from the lemon and white wine vinegar, oh-so-garlicky and as close to the superstar-status cashew version as possible. This turned out to be a winner! I often find myself whipping it up in place of the cashew version despite not needing my dressing to be nut-free.

6 tablespoons (65 g total) raw sunflower seeds, soaked

½ cup water

6 tablespoons grapeseed oil or pure avocado oil

3 large garlic cloves (18 g total), or to taste

¼ cup + 1 tablespoon (27 g) nutritional yeast

2 tablespoons + 1 teaspoon white wine vinegar

2 tablespoons + 1 teaspoon fresh lemon juice

1½ teaspoons pure maple syrup

1¼ teaspoons fine sea salt, or to taste

Freshly ground black pepper

1. Place the sunflower seeds in a small bowl and add boiling water to cover. Soak for 1 hour, then drain. (If you have a high-speed blender, you can get away with a ten-minute soak.)
2. To a blender, add the drained sunflower seeds, ½ cup water, grapeseed oil or avocado oil, garlic cloves, nutritional yeast, white wine vinegar, lemon juice, maple syrup, salt, and pepper to taste. Blend on high speed until super smooth, 30 to 60 seconds. Taste and adjust the flavors, if desired.
3. Immediately pour the dressing into an airtight container. (The dressing thickens as it sits, so if you leave it in the blender jar, it'll be hard to scoop out.)

storage

Store in an airtight container in the fridge for up to 5 days or in the freezer for up to 3 weeks. Let sit at room temperature until softened, or microwave for 15 to 20 seconds, stirring every 5 seconds. Once softened, stir in a small amount of water, ½ teaspoon at a time, to thin to your desired consistency, if needed.

vegan • gluten-free • nut-free • soy-free • grain-free • raw/no bake • on the glow • one bowl

Sesame, Lime, and Ginger Dressing

makes ½ cup plus 1 tablespoon • prep time: 5 minutes • total time: 5 minutes

1 to 2 teaspoons grated peeled fresh ginger, to taste (use a Microplane; I use 2 teaspoons)

3 tablespoons seasoned rice vinegar

2 tablespoons grapeseed oil or pure avocado oil

2 tablespoons pure maple syrup

3 to 4 teaspoons fresh lime juice, to taste (I like 4 teaspoons)

1 tablespoon toasted sesame oil

¼ teaspoon fine sea salt, or to taste

storage

Store in the jar or an airtight container in the fridge for up to 5 days. Shake before each use, if needed.

My Sesame, Lime, and Ginger Dressing comes together in just 5 minutes and is the go-to zesty companion to my Minty Sesame, Lime, and Ginger Noodle Salad (page 105) and Super Green Bean, Rice, and Avocado Salad (page 127). Lightly roasty from the toasted sesame oil, zippy from the fresh citrusy lime juice, and with just a whisper of heat from the spicy ginger root, it adds a pop of sweetness and depth to salads and can also be stirred into warm cooked rice or your other favorite grains for a quick and simple side dish.

1. To a small mason jar, add the grated ginger, rice vinegar, grapeseed oil or avocado oil, maple syrup, lime juice, toasted sesame oil, and salt. Secure the lid and shake vigorously until combined, 10 to 15 seconds. Taste and adjust the flavors, if desired, such as adding more lime juice and/or rice vinegar for more tanginess, more syrup to sweeten or reduce tanginess, or more salt to balance the flavors.

vegan • gluten-free option • nut-free • soy-free option • grain-free • raw/no bake • on the glow • one bowl

Immunity-Boosting Tahini Dressing

makes 1 cup • prep time: 10 minutes • total time: 10 minutes

This dressing is immune-boosting thanks to the vitamin C–packed citrusy lemon, assertive garlic, and zinc-rich tahini, and it has a touch of umami flavor from light tamari. This versatile dressing will be your new fall and winter BFF (though I love it all year round!). We always try to have it on hand for drizzling over my Warm and Cozy Roasted Mediterranean Lentil Salad (page 141) and as a creamy option for my Glow Girl Kale Slaw (page 39). It adds creaminess and satiety (not to mention mega flavor) to just about any grain-based salad.

1 large garlic clove (6 g)
7 tablespoons fresh lemon juice
6 tablespoons extra-virgin olive oil or untoasted sesame oil*
¼ cup (22 g) nutritional yeast
¼ cup runny tahini
1 teaspoon light tamari**
½ teaspoon pure maple syrup
¼ teaspoon + ⅛ teaspoon fine sea salt
Freshly ground black pepper, to taste
1 to 2 tablespoons water, as needed

1. In a small food processor, process the garlic until minced.
2. Add the lemon juice, olive oil or untoasted sesame oil, nutritional yeast, tahini, tamari, maple syrup, salt, pepper, and water (starting with 1 tablespoon). Process until smooth, about 15 seconds. Add more water, if needed, to thin the dressing. Adjust the flavors to taste, if desired.

tips

* Be careful not to use *toasted* sesame oil, as its flavor is much too strong for this dressing.

** It's important to use light tamari (not regular full-sodium tamari) or the dressing will be too salty.

make it gluten-free

Use gluten-free light tamari.

make it soy-free

Use coconut aminos (also called soy-sauce substitute or soy-free seasoning) instead of light tamari.

storage

Store in an airtight container in the fridge for up to 1 week. The dressing will firm up when chilled. To soften, gently heat it for 10 to 15 seconds in the microwave, stirring every 5 seconds, or simply let it sit at room temperature until softened, then stir before using.

vegan • gluten-free • nut-free • soy-free • grain-free • raw/no bake • kid-friendly • on the glow • one bowl

Glowing House Vinaigrette

makes 1 cup • prep time: 5 minutes • total time: 5 minutes

1 large garlic clove (6 g)
½ cup extra-virgin olive oil
¼ cup + 1 tablespoon apple cider vinegar
2 tablespoons pure maple syrup
2 teaspoons smooth Dijon mustard
½ teaspoon fine sea salt, or to taste
Freshly ground black pepper

storage

Store in the jar or an airtight container in the fridge for up to 1 week. Shake before each use, if needed.

This easy five-minute vinaigrette is so quick to whip up and so wildly flavorful that I often call it my house dressing because it can be used on so many different kinds of salads. I created it specifically for one of my favorite kale salads (Fall Crunch Farro Kale Salad, page 121) because the maple and apple cider vinegar play so nicely with the kale and sweetly counteract its slightly bitter quality. Extra-virgin olive oil adds healthy, good-for-you fats and richness, and the smooth Dijon mustard adds a mild sharpness and wakes it all up. Try pouring it over my Butternut, Cranberry, and Rosemary-Maple Pecan and Walnut Arugula Salad (page 153), Mix-and-Glow Roasted Veg Orzo Salad (page 163), Busy Bee Big Salad (page 69), Nourishing Warm Brunch Salad Bowls (page 113), or any other salad where you're looking for a well-rounded all-purpose vinaigrette.

1. Grate the garlic on a Microplane.
2. To a medium mason jar, add the grated garlic, olive oil, apple cider vinegar, maple syrup, mustard, salt, and several cranks of freshly ground black pepper. Secure the lid and shake well to combine, 10 to 15 seconds. Taste and adjust the flavors, if desired.

vegan • gluten-free • nut-free • soy-free • grain-free • raw/no bake • on the glow • one bowl

Herby Lemon and White Wine Vinaigrette

makes ¾ cup plus 2 tablespoons • prep time: 6 minutes • total time: 6 minutes

My Herby Lemon and White Wine Vinaigrette can be whipped up in 6 minutes flat but tastes like you spent hours choosing the best ingredients and making tiny measurement changes until you came to the ideal combination of flavors (which is exactly what I did). A punch of vibrant lemon and garlic are the top notes, which are quickly rounded out and gently sweetened by the pure maple syrup and old-fashioned Dijon (which has less heat than regular Dijon). Made herby and a bit spicy from the oregano, basil, and optional cayenne, it's our favorite Mediterranean-inspired dressing to drizzle over my Radiant Garden Side Salad (page 89) and Herby Couscous, Sun-Dried Tomato, and Chickpea Salad (page 75). We also love it as a dip for crusty bread.

1 large garlic clove (6 g), minced

½ cup extra-virgin olive oil

¼ cup fresh lemon juice

1 tablespoon white wine vinegar

1 tablespoon pure maple syrup, or to taste

1 teaspoon old-fashioned Dijon mustard

1 teaspoon dried oregano

½ teaspoon dried basil

¼ teaspoon fine sea salt, or to taste

Freshly ground black pepper, to taste

1⁄16 to ⅛ teaspoon cayenne pepper, to taste (optional)*

1. To a medium mason jar, add the minced garlic, olive oil, lemon juice, white wine vinegar, maple syrup, mustard, dried oregano, dried basil, salt, black pepper, and cayenne (if using), to taste. Secure the lid and shake vigorously until combined, 10 to 15 seconds. Adjust the flavors to taste, if desired.

storage

Store in the jar or an airtight container in the fridge for up to 1 week. Shake before each use, if needed.

tip

* Using 1⁄16 teaspoon of cayenne pepper gives this recipe a very mild, zingy heat, while ⅛ teaspoon creates a moderate heat.

vegan • gluten-free • nut-free option • soy-free option • grain-free • raw/no bake • kid-friendly
on the glow • one bowl

Ranch Buttermilk Dressing

makes 1 cup plus 3 tablespoons • prep time: 6 minutes • total time: 6 minutes

- 1 tablespoon unsweetened and unflavored non-dairy milk
- 2 tablespoons apple cider vinegar
- 1 small garlic clove (4 g), minced
- 1 cup Soy-Free Vegan Mayonnaise (page 265) or store-bought
- 1½ teaspoons dried dill
- 1 teaspoon dried parsley
- ¾ teaspoon onion powder
- ½ teaspoon garlic powder
- Fine sea salt
- 1 teaspoon water (optional)

storage

Store in an airtight container in the fridge for up to 6 days. Stir before each use, if needed.

make it nut-free

Use a nut-free non-dairy milk.

make it soy-free

Use a soy-free non-dairy milk. If using store-bought vegan mayo, be sure to select a soy-free variety.

I've created oodles of plant-based creamy salad dressings over the years, but for some reason, I'd never made a ranch! How could this be? I envisioned a thick, lush, zippy buttermilk ranch to drizzle over The Ultimate Ranch Barbecue Tofu Cobb Salad (page 85) that would accent the smoky Crispy and Chewy Barbecue Tofu (page 187), briny Vegan Feta Cheese (page 259), and crisp veggies. The apple cider vinegar adds a hint of sweet brightness to the mayo and herby dill and parsley, and a dash of garlic and onion powders add savory depth. Make this dressing a day in advance and the flavor gets even better overnight. If you have some on hand, sprinkle a pinch of freeze-dried chives over this dressing just before serving to accent the flavors. (I don't recommend mixing the chives into the dressing, as they turn mushy over time.)

1. In a medium bowl, stir together the milk and apple cider vinegar to combine, and let sit for a minute. This makes a modified version of vegan buttermilk.
2. Add the minced garlic, vegan mayonnaise, dill, parsley, onion powder, and garlic powder. Whisk until well combined and smooth. Add salt to taste (I add about ⅛ teaspoon) and adjust any other flavors, if desired. If the dressing is a touch too thick, you can thin it by stirring in a teaspoon of water, as needed, being careful not to dilute the dressing too much.
3. Transfer to an airtight container and refrigerate for at least 1 hour to allow the flavors to develop.

vegan • gluten-free • nut-free • soy-free option • grain-free • raw/no bake • kid-friendly
on the glow • one bowl

Creamy ACV, Shallot, Maple, and Dijon Vinaigrette

makes 1¼ cups • prep time: 9 minutes • total time: 9 minutes

This is a creamier and richer version of my favorite Apple Cider, Shallot, Maple, and Dijon Vinaigrette (page 220), with the addition of vegan mayonnaise lending such a luxurious feel to the dressing. I created it specifically for my On the Glow Pasta Salad (page 107), as I wanted a dressing with a bit more heft for the pasta while remaining super light. With a gentle bite of garlic, sweet and tart apple cider vinegar, tangy mayo, sweet pure maple syrup, and a subtle kick from the old-fashioned Dijon mustard, this dressing is heavenly and is just fab on a pasta salad or any leafy salad for which you crave a rich and creamy dressing. Try it on my Cozy Potato, Zucchini, and Cannellini Bean Salad (page 147), Nourishing Warm Brunch Salad Bowls (page 113), and Busy Bee Big Salad (page 69).

- 1 large garlic clove (6 g), minced
- 1 large shallot (40 g), minced (3 tablespoons)
- 6 tablespoons extra-virgin olive oil
- 3½ tablespoons apple cider vinegar
- 3 tablespoons Soy-Free Vegan Mayonnaise (page 265) or store-bought
- 2 tablespoons + 1 teaspoon pure maple syrup, or to taste
- 2 tablespoons + 1 teaspoon white wine vinegar*
- 1 tablespoon old-fashioned Dijon mustard
- ¼ teaspoon + ⅛ teaspoon fine sea salt, or to taste

1. To a medium mason jar, add the minced garlic, minced shallot, olive oil, apple cider vinegar, vegan mayonnaise, maple syrup, white wine vinegar, mustard, and salt. Secure the lid and shake vigorously until combined, 10 to 15 seconds. Taste and adjust the flavors, if desired.

storage

Store in the jar or an airtight container in the fridge for up to 6 days. Shake before each use, if needed.

tip

* If you have pear vinegar on hand, it's a lovely seasonal swap for white wine vinegar.

make it soy-free

If using store-bought vegan mayo, be sure to select a soy-free variety.

vegan • gluten-free • nut-free • soy-free • grain-free • raw/no bake
on the glow • one bowl

Grainy Mustard and Lemon Dressing

makes 1 cup • prep time: 6 minutes • total time: 6 minutes

3 tablespoons old-fashioned Dijon mustard

1½ tablespoons smooth Dijon mustard

6 tablespoons extra-virgin olive oil

4½ tablespoons fresh lemon juice

4 teaspoons pure maple syrup, or to taste

¼ teaspoon + ⅛ teaspoon fine sea salt, or to taste

Freshly ground black pepper

storage

Store in the jar or an airtight container in the fridge for up to 6 days. Let sit at room temperature until softened (if needed), then shake before each use.

This assertive and zippy Grainy Mustard and Lemon Dressing has a nice balance of tart and tangy smooth and old-fashioned Dijon mustards, buttery olive oil, bright lemon juice, a hint of maple syrup for sweetness, and sea salt and freshly ground black pepper to bring out all the flavors. It's a lemony, punchy dressing that will add the wow flavor needed on a roasted potato salad such as my Herby Baked Green Bean and Potato Salad (page 169). Try it drizzled over smashed potatoes, too, or even over cooked lentils or grains, such as my Easy Garlic-Infused Farro (page 268).

1. To a medium mason jar, add the old-fashioned Dijon mustard, smooth Dijon mustard, olive oil, lemon juice, maple syrup, salt, and black pepper to taste. Secure the lid and shake vigorously until combined and smooth, 10 to 15 seconds. Taste and adjust the flavors, if desired.

vegan • gluten-free • nut-free • soy-free • grain-free • raw/no bake • kid-friendly • freezer-friendly • on the glow • one bowl

6-Ingredient Shake-and-Glow Vinaigrette

makes 1 scant cup • prep time: 7 minutes • total time: 7 minutes

One of my dear testers, Adrienne, says about this vinaigrette, "It's super easy, probably the perfect easy dressing for anything!" While it is so versatile, we think it's the perfect pairing for my Mix-and-Glow Roasted Veg Orzo Salad (page 163), Busy Bee Big Salad (page 69), and Nourishing Warm Brunch Salad Bowls (page 113). This little black dress of vinaigrettes features a hint of pungent garlic and buttery extra-virgin olive oil or pure avocado oil, and is made tangy and bright with the addition of apple cider vinegar, lemon juice, and smooth Dijon mustard. I created an intriguing lime flavor variation, too, which tastes just right on my Easy Breezy Deconstructed Guacamole Salad (page 95), perfectly accenting its avocado and cilantro tones.

1 large garlic clove (6 g), minced
½ cup extra-virgin olive oil or pure avocado oil*
¼ cup apple cider vinegar
2 tablespoons fresh lemon juice
1 tablespoon pure maple syrup
2 teaspoons smooth Dijon mustard
¼ to ½ teaspoon fine sea salt, to taste
Freshly ground black pepper

1. To a medium mason jar, add the minced garlic, olive oil (or avocado oil), apple cider vinegar, lemon juice, maple syrup, mustard, salt, and pepper to taste. Secure the lid and shake vigorously until smooth, 10 to 15 seconds. Taste and adjust the flavors, if desired.

Lime Variation

For a lime variation, swap the lemon juice for an equal amount of fresh lime juice. Everything else stays the same.

storage

Store in the jar or an airtight container in the fridge for up to 6 days or in the freezer for up to 1 month. Let sit at room temperature until softened, then shake before each use.

tip

* If using avocado oil, be sure to use 100% pure avocado oil and *not* extra-virgin avocado oil, which has a much stronger taste that is often overwhelming in dressings.

vegan • gluten-free • nut-free • soy-free • grain-free • raw/no bake • kid-friendly • on the glow • one bowl

Cilantro, Lime, Cumin, and Jalapeño Dressing

makes ½ cup plus 1 tablespoon • prep time: 9 minutes • total time: 9 minutes

1 medium garlic clove (5 g)

½ cup lightly packed (11 g) fresh cilantro leaves*

4½ tablespoons extra-virgin olive oil

2 tablespoons fresh lime juice

1½ tablespoons white wine vinegar

1½ teaspoons pure maple syrup, or to taste

1 teaspoon ground cumin

1 teaspoon chopped pickled jalapeño, drained and seeded (optional)

¼ + ⅛ teaspoon fine sea salt

storage

Store in an airtight container in the fridge for up to 5 days. Let sit at room temperature until softened (if needed), then stir before each use.

tip

* This dressing works beautifully if you swap the cilantro for fresh flat-leaf parsley!

My Cilantro, Lime, Cumin, and Jalapeño Dressing features refreshing and detoxifying cilantro, bright and zesty lime, smoky and earthy cumin, and lightly spicy jalapeño, with just a hint of sweetness to balance it all out. Try it in my Easy Breezy Deconstructed Guacamole Salad (page 95) as a tangier swap for the lightly sweet 6-Ingredient Shake-and-Glow Vinaigrette, Lime Variation, or in my Sunny Day Charred Corn and Feta Salad (page 71) as a swap for the Lime and Sriracha Aioli.

1. In a small food processor, process the garlic and cilantro until minced, 5 to 10 seconds.
2. Add the olive oil, lime juice, white wine vinegar, maple syrup, cumin, pickled jalapeño (if using), and salt. Process until mostly smooth, 10 to 15 seconds (you'll still have pretty green flecks from the cilantro!). Adjust the salt and other flavors to taste, if desired.

One and a Half Batch Variation

For 1½ batches of dressing, use 1 large garlic clove (6 g), ¾ cup lightly packed (16 g) fresh cilantro leaves, 6 tablespoons plus 2¼ teaspoons extra-virgin olive oil, 3 tablespoons fresh lime juice, 2 tablespoons + ¾ teaspoon white wine vinegar, 2¼ teaspoons pure maple syrup, 1½ teaspoons ground cumin, 1½ teaspoons chopped pickled jalapeño, drained and seeded (optional), and ½ teaspoon fine sea salt (or to taste). Makes a generous ¾ cup.

vegan • gluten-free • soy-free option • grain-free • raw/no bake • advance prep required • on the glow • one bowl

Creamy Chipotle Dressing

makes 1¼ cups • prep time: 8 minutes • total time: 8 minutes, plus soaking time

Tangy mayo, zesty lime juice, smoky cumin, and spicy sriracha and chipotle are a salad dressing dream team! We love this spicy, velvety Creamy Chipotle Dressing on my Spicy Chipotle Corn Salad (page 53), but you can use it on any salad that you'd like coated in a dreamy smoky, nutty dressing. I use mild sweet cashews as the base for this dressing, as they add such a smooth, thick texture and just a hint of sweetness that works so well with the chipotle. A little pure maple syrup mellows the flavors just right, adding a touch of sweet to contrast the spicy. This is also tasty served over top smashed potatoes or roasted veggies.

¼ cup + 2 tablespoons (51 g) raw cashews, soaked

¼ cup + 2 tablespoons water, plus more if needed

¼ cup + 2 tablespoons Soy-Free Vegan Mayonnaise (page 265) or store-bought

3 to 3½ tablespoons fresh lime juice, to taste

1 teaspoon ground cumin

1 teaspoon sriracha

1 teaspoon pure maple syrup

⅛ to ¼ teaspoon chipotle powder, to taste

¼ to ½ teaspoon fine sea salt, or to taste

1. Place the cashews in a small bowl and add boiling water to cover. Soak for 1 hour, then drain. (If using a high-speed blender, you can reduce the soaking time to 10 minutes.)
2. To a blender, add the drained cashews, ¼ cup + 2 tablespoons water, vegan mayonnaise, lime juice (to taste), cumin, sriracha, maple syrup, chipotle powder (starting with ⅛ teaspoon), and salt to taste. Blend on high speed until very smooth, about 1 minute. Taste; if you'd like more heat, add another 1/16 to ⅛ teaspoon chipotle powder (start small, as it's intense) and blend again.

storage

Store in an airtight container in the fridge for up to 6 days. Stir before each use, if needed.

make it soy-free

If using store-bought vegan mayo, be sure to select a soy-free variety.

vegan • gluten-free • nut-free • soy-free • grain-free • raw/no bake • kid-friendly • on the glow • one bowl

Light and Floral Lemony Garlic Vinaigrette

makes ¾ cup • prep time: 6 minutes • total time: 6 minutes

- 1 large garlic clove (6 g), minced
- 6 tablespoons extra-virgin olive oil
- 5 tablespoons fresh lemon juice, or to taste
- 1½ tablespoons white wine vinegar, or to taste
- 1½ teaspoons smooth Dijon mustard
- 1½ teaspoons pure maple syrup, or to taste
- ¼ teaspoon + ⅛ teaspoon fine sea salt, or to taste
- Freshly ground black pepper

storage

Store in the jar or an airtight container in the fridge for up to 8 days. Let sit at room temperature until softened, then shake before each use.

Light and Floral Lemony Garlic Vinaigrette tastes just as it sounds—light, breezy, lemon-scented, and floral, like spring in a jar. Bright lemon juice, sweet and tangy white wine vinegar, pungent garlic, and earthy olive oil make up this dressing, which gets a whisper of heat from smooth Dijon mustard and a hint of sweetness from pure maple syrup. It's the perfect mate for my Parsley, Sun-Dried Tomato, and Feta Quinoa Salad (page 63), and it tastes wonderful on my Mix-and-Glow Roasted Veg Orzo Salad (page 163) and Busy Bee Big Salad (page 69), too.

1. To a medium mason jar, add the minced garlic, olive oil, lemon juice, white wine vinegar, mustard, maple syrup, salt, and pepper to taste. Secure the lid and shake vigorously until combined, 10 to 15 seconds. Taste and adjust the flavors, if desired.

vegan • gluten-free • nut-free • soy-free • grain-free • raw/no bake • kid-friendly • freezer-friendly • on the glow • one bowl

Zesty Lemon, Dill, and Oregano Dressing

makes a scant 1 cup • prep time: 10 minutes • total time: 10 minutes

Brighten your salad and your day by drizzling my Zesty Lemon, Dill, and Oregano Dressing over your favorite bowls. Herby dill and oregano are brightened further with fresh lemon, and the garlic and red wine vinegar give it a zingy kick. It's so creamy from the tahini and has just a little sweetness from the maple syrup for balance. This dressing is so tasty on my Warm and Cozy Roasted Mediterranean Lentil Salad (page 141). It adds a Mediterranean flair to non-salad side dishes, too: try it over roasted potatoes, sweet potatoes, cauliflower, or cooked lentils for an instant transformation!

2 medium garlic cloves (10 g total)
½ cup + 1 tablespoon extra-virgin olive oil
3 to 4 tablespoons fresh lemon juice, to taste
2 tablespoons packed fresh dill
1 tablespoon red wine vinegar
1 tablespoon runny tahini
2½ teaspoons dried oregano
1 teaspoon pure maple syrup, or to taste
¼ + ⅛ teaspoon to ½ teaspoon fine sea salt, to taste
Freshly ground black pepper
1 teaspoon water, if needed

1. In a small food processor, process the garlic until minced.
2. Add the olive oil, lemon juice, dill, red wine vinegar, tahini, dried oregano, maple syrup, salt, and pepper to taste. Process until combined, about 15 seconds. Add the water to thin, if needed, and process again. Taste and adjust the flavors, if desired.

storage

Store in an airtight container in the fridge for up to 5 days or in the freezer for up to 1 month. Stir before each use, if needed.

tip

Add ½ teaspoon dried basil for an extra herby kick.

vegan • gluten-free • soy-free • grain-free • raw/no bake • advance prep required • kid-friendly freezer-friendly • on the glow • one bowl

Creamy Cashew, Garlic, and Lemon Dressing

makes 1⅔ cups • prep time: 7 minutes • total time: 7 minutes, plus soaking time

¾ cup raw cashews (101 g), soaked
¾ cup vegetable broth*
2 large garlic cloves (12 g total)
2 tablespoons fresh lemon juice
2 tablespoons white wine vinegar
1 tablespoon extra-virgin olive oil
1 teaspoon nutritional yeast
½ to ¾ teaspoon fine sea salt (I use ¾ teaspoon)
Freshly ground black pepper
¼ teaspoon red pepper flakes, or to taste

storage

Store in an airtight container in the fridge for up to 3 days or in the freezer for up to 2 months. Stir before each use, if needed.

tip

* I don't use low-sodium vegetable broth in this recipe. If using low-sodium, you will likely need to add more salt to taste.

I am a big fan of pestos, sauces, dressings, and cremas, as they add an appetizing kick to nearly any dish and are an integral part of a recipe's flavor profile. Give me one that's exploding with bold flavors such as tangy lemon, cheesy nutritional yeast, pungent garlic, and spicy red pepper flakes, like in my Creamy Cashew, Garlic, and Lemon Dressing, and I am a happy camper. This dressing is nutty, with a velvety texture and bright flavor! The lemon comes through just right, and the dressing has the ideal balance of tangy from the lemon and white wine vinegar and lightly sweet from the cashews. It's my chosen pairing for Dreamy Barbecue Tofu and Roasted Green Bean Salad (page 57) and Fiery 10-Spice Roasted Potato Salad (page 165). You'll also always find me stirring this bright sauce into my Warm Mushroom and Spinach Pasta Salad (page 177). I often use this dressing to jazz up roasted potatoes and steamed veggies, too.

1. Place the cashews in a small bowl and add boiling water to cover. Soak for 1 hour, then drain. (If using a high-speed blender, you can reduce the soaking time to 10 minutes.)
2. To a blender, add the drained cashews, broth, garlic, lemon juice, white wine vinegar, olive oil, nutritional yeast, salt, several cranks of freshly ground black pepper, and red pepper flakes to taste. Blend on high speed until very smooth, 30 to 60 seconds. Taste and adjust the flavors, if desired, and blend again until smooth.

vegan • gluten-free option • nut-free • grain-free • raw/no bake • kid-friendly
on the glow • one bowl

Miso, Maple, and Ginger Dressing

makes 1 scant cup • prep time: 10 minutes • total time: 10 minutes

Tangy, salty, and umami-rich white (shiro) miso provides the base for this super-flavored dressing. I added lots and lots of freshly grated ginger for zing, a touch of pure maple syrup for a light sweetness, and untoasted sesame oil for just a hint of sesame flavoring. Zesty lime and seasoned rice vinegar bring a bright tone to this dressing, and I love the addition of tahini to thicken and up the sesame a touch. I drizzle this dressing generously over my Magnificent Miso Salad (page 149); they make the perfect pair! The sodium content of miso paste varies greatly from brand to brand, which affects the saltiness (and outcome) of the dressing. Check my Tips before starting to see how much of your white miso I recommend as a starting amount.

1 tablespoon + 1 teaspoon grated peeled fresh ginger (use a Microplane)

2 teaspoons to 3 tablespoons white miso paste*

3 tablespoons + 1 teaspoon untoasted sesame oil

3 tablespoons pure maple syrup

2½ tablespoons fresh lime juice

2 tablespoons light tamari**

1½ tablespoons seasoned rice vinegar

1 tablespoon runny tahini

Fine sea salt (optional)

1. To a small food processor, add the grated ginger, miso paste, untoasted sesame oil, maple syrup, lime juice, tamari, seasoned rice vinegar, and tahini. Process until smooth, 8 to 10 seconds. Taste, add bit more salt if needed, and process again.

storage

Store in an airtight container in the fridge for up to 5 days. Stir before each use, if needed.

tips

* Brands of white (shiro) miso pastes vary in sodium content. If your miso contains around 440 mg of sodium per tablespoon, I recommend using 2 to 3 tablespoons of miso in this dressing (to taste). If your miso contains around 720 mg of sodium or more per tablespoon, I suggest starting with just 2 teaspoons and adding more slowly, to taste, if needed.

** It's important to use light tamari (not regular full-sodium tamari) or the dressing will be too salty.

make it gluten-free

Use gluten-free light tamari.

vegan • gluten-free • nut-free • soy-free option • grain-free • raw/no bake • kid-friendly • on the glow • one bowl

Sriracha Honey-Mustard Dressing

makes ¾ cup • prep time: 5 minutes • total time: 5 minutes

- 6 tablespoons Soy-Free Vegan Mayonnaise (page 265) or store-bought
- 3 tablespoons vegan liquid honey*
- 2 tablespoons + 1 teaspoon old-fashioned Dijon mustard
- 1 tablespoon apple cider vinegar
- ⅛ teaspoon fine sea salt, or to taste
- 1 to 3 teaspoons sriracha, to taste

storage

Store in an airtight container in the fridge for up to 5 days. Stir before each use, if needed.

tip

* Feel free to use traditional liquid honey if you consume it. See "Pantry Staples" (page 342) for information on vegan honey.

make it soy-free

If using store-bought vegan mayo, be sure to select a soy-free variety.

Sweet? Spicy? Tangy? Creamy? You don't have to choose with my Sriracha Honey-Mustard Dressing—it features all of those and more! Vegan honey and apple cider vinegar add a delicate sweetness to this dressing, while sriracha adds heat (just how much is up to you). The distinctive sharp taste of old-fashioned Dijon and the tang of mayo round out the full flavor. Try this delectable dressing on my Cinnamon Sweet Potato Wedge Salad (page 175) and Spring Fever Lentil and Quinoa Salad (page 51), or drizzled over your favorite roasted root veggies for a fancy, flavorful side dish.

1. In a medium bowl, whisk together the vegan mayonnaise, liquid honey, mustard, apple cider vinegar, salt (to taste), and sriracha (to taste, starting with 1 teaspoon) until smooth. Taste and adjust the flavors as desired, such as adding more sriracha for a spicy kick, more honey for sweetness, or more vinegar for brightness, or simply leave as is.

Double Batch Variation

For a double batch of dressing, use ¾ cup Soy-Free Vegan Mayonnaise (page 265) or store-bought, 6 tablespoons vegan liquid honey, ¼ cup + 2 teaspoons old-fashioned Dijon mustard, 2 tablespoons apple cider vinegar, ¼ teaspoon fine sea salt (or to taste), and 2 to 6 teaspoons sriracha (to taste). Makes 1½ cups.

vegan • gluten-free option • nut-free • soy-free option • grain-free • on the glow

Barbecue Apple Cider Vinaigrette

makes 1 cup • prep time: 10 minutes • total time: 10 minutes

Barbecue-inspired vinaigrette? It may sound unusual, but trust me on this one. This dressing evokes summer days lounging outside with all the delicious, bold flavors you could hope for. It starts with my flavor-bursting Sweet and Tangy No-Chop Barbecue Sauce (page 262), ready in just 12 minutes—or use your favorite store-bought version. While the sauce simmers, I whisk together the creamy vegan mayo, apple cider vinegar, floral vegan honey, and a spoonful of Dijon mustard. Stir in the barbecue sauce and you've got my go-to summer vinaigrette. Drizzle it over our Breaded Tofu Tender Salad (page 79), use it as a dip, or serve over grains like brown rice or quinoa. Leftover barbecue sauce? Use it for my Crispy and Chewy Barbecue Tofu (page 187). Spice lovers can even add sriracha to this vinaigrette for a subtle kick!

- ⅓ cup + 1 tablespoon Sweet and Tangy No-Chop Barbecue Sauce (page 262) or store-bought*
- 1 small garlic clove (4 g), grated on a Microplane
- 6 tablespoons Soy-Free Vegan Mayonnaise (page 265) or store-bought
- 2½ to 3 tablespoons apple cider vinegar, to taste
- 1 tablespoon vegan liquid honey, or to taste**
- 1 teaspoon old-fashioned Dijon mustard
- ¼ + ⅛ teaspoon fine sea salt, or to taste

1. Make the Sweet and Tangy No-Chop Barbecue Sauce (if using). While the sauce simmers, get the ingredients for the vinaigrette ready to go.
2. In a medium bowl, whisk together the grated garlic, vegan mayonnaise, apple cider vinegar, honey (to taste), mustard, salt (to taste), and barbecue sauce until smooth. Taste and adjust the flavors as desired, such as adding more honey for sweetness or more vinegar for brightness, or simply leave as is.

tips

* If using store-bought barbecue sauce, the flavor profile will likely change quite a bit, so you may need to adjust the ingredient amounts provided.

** Feel free to use traditional liquid honey if you consume it. See "Pantry Staples" (page 342) for information on vegan honey.

storage

Store in an airtight container in the fridge for up to 1 week. Stir before each use, if needed.

make it gluten-free

Use gluten-free vegan Worcestershire sauce in the Sweet and Tangy No-Chop Barbecue Sauce, or use gluten-free store-bought barbecue sauce.

make it soy-free

If using a store-bought vegan mayo, be sure to select a soy-free variety. Use a soy-free vegan Worcestershire sauce in the Sweet and Tangy No-Chop Barbecue Sauce.

flavor boosters

sauces, cheeses, nuts, and more

vegan • gluten-free • grain-free • advance prep required • kid-friendly

Sun-Dried Tomato, Walnut, and Basil Whipped Feta Spread

makes 2½ cups • prep time: 16 minutes • total time: 20 minutes, plus pressing time

My Sun-Dried Tomato, Walnut, and Basil Whipped Feta Spread is packed with protein, healthy fats, and antioxidants, not to mention it's hard to stop eating! We enjoy having a batch on hand in the fridge to serve with crackers for a delicious snack whenever hunger strikes. Sweet fresh basil and umami-rich, chewy sun-dried tomatoes, along with bright lemon juice and apple cider vinegar add vibrance, while walnuts impart a rich and nutty flavor. Try it with my Roasted Vegetable Medley (page 155), as it's so dreamy when served with caramelized roasted vegetables. We also love scooping it up with my Garlic-Infused Olive Oil Crostini (page 249), raw veggies, and favorite crackers.

Whipped Feta

1 (12-ounce/350 g) block extra-firm or firm tofu, pressed

1 cup (100 g) raw walnut halves, coarsely chopped

⅓ cup (53 g) oil-packed sun-dried tomatoes, drained and coarsely chopped

½ cup lightly packed (10 g) fresh basil leaves, finely chopped

¼ cup extra-virgin olive oil

4½ tablespoons fresh lemon juice, or more to taste

1½ tablespoons apple cider vinegar, or to taste

1½ to 2 teaspoons fine sea salt, to taste

Toppings

2 teaspoons extra-virgin olive oil*

¼ teaspoon dried oregano

1. Press the tofu for at least 30 minutes (see page 357).
2. Preheat the oven to 350°F (180°C). Spread the chopped walnuts on a small baking sheet. Toast for 5 to 9 minutes, until fragrant and lightly golden.
3. Prepare the sun-dried tomatoes and fresh basil. Set aside 1 tablespoon each of the chopped tomatoes and basil to use for the topping.
4. Using your hands, break apart the pressed tofu into about 8 chunks, adding them to a large heavy-duty food processor as you go. Add the ¼ cup olive oil, lemon juice, apple cider vinegar, and salt (starting with 1½ teaspoons). Process until very smooth, about 1 minute. The mixture will be thick and creamy.
5. Add ¾ cup of the toasted walnuts (reserving ¼ cup for the topping), along with the larger portion of the sun-dried tomatoes and basil. Pulse 7 to 9 times, just until the additions are incorporated into the feta mixture. Avoid overprocessing, as you want lots of crunchy texture!

recipe continues

storage

Store in an airtight container in the fridge for up to 1 week.

tip

* I like to use the oil from the jar of oil-packed sun-dried tomatoes instead of the 2 teaspoons olive oil for topping the feta spread.

6. Taste and add more salt, if needed (I like to use 2 teaspoons in total). Add a touch more lemon juice, if desired (I add another ½ tablespoon). With a spoon, stir to combine. It should taste tangy and salty.
7. Assemble: Remove the processor blade. Using a spatula, spoon the mixture into a shallow 3- to 4-cup (750 mL to 1 L) serving bowl. Gently spread out the mixture evenly. Create a small divot in the center of the mixture.
8. For the Topping: Sprinkle the reserved walnuts, tomatoes, and basil in and around the divot. Drizzle the 2 teaspoons of olive oil in a swirl over the surface. Sprinkle on the oregano. Serve immediately or cover and refrigerate until ready to use.

vegan • nut-free • soy-free • kid-friendly • freezer-friendly • on the glow • one bowl

Garlic-Infused Olive Oil Crostini

makes 24 to 30 crostini • prep time: 16 minutes • total time: 24 minutes

Buttery and crisp on the outside and chewy on the inside, with a mellow, gentle tang from the garlic and an aromatic herbal tone from the oregano, my Garlic-Infused Olive Oil Crostini taste as delectable as they sound! They're divine served with my Roasted Vegetable Medley with Sun-Dried Tomato, Walnut, and Basil Whipped Feta (page 155), and we also adore them alongside my Herby Couscous, Sun-Dried Tomato, and Chickpea Salad (page 75). Spread these crostini with my Vegan Feta Cheese (page 259), Sun-Dried Tomato, Walnut, and Basil Whipped Feta Spread (page 247), or Protein-Powered Cashew-Hemp Cheese (page 197) for an appetizer that's sure to impress!

¼ cup extra-virgin olive oil, plus more if needed

3 medium garlic cloves (15 g total), grated on a Microplane

1 medium or large baguette (250 to 350 g)*

Fine sea salt

1½ teaspoons dried oregano

½ teaspoon garlic powder

1. Preheat the oven to 375°F (190°C) and line an extra-large rimmed baking sheet with parchment paper.
2. In a small bowl, stir together the olive oil and grated garlic. Let sit for a few minutes.
3. Meanwhile, cut the baguette crosswise into ½-inch (1 cm) thick slices.
4. Using a silicone pastry brush, brush both sides of the bread slices with a light coating of the garlic-infused oil, placing them on the lined baking sheet as you go. If you run out of oil near the end, simply add a bit more olive oil to the bowl and stir. If you have leftover grated garlic in the bowl at the end, you can rub it onto the bread slices. Garnish each slice with a sprinkling of salt and oregano.

recipe continues

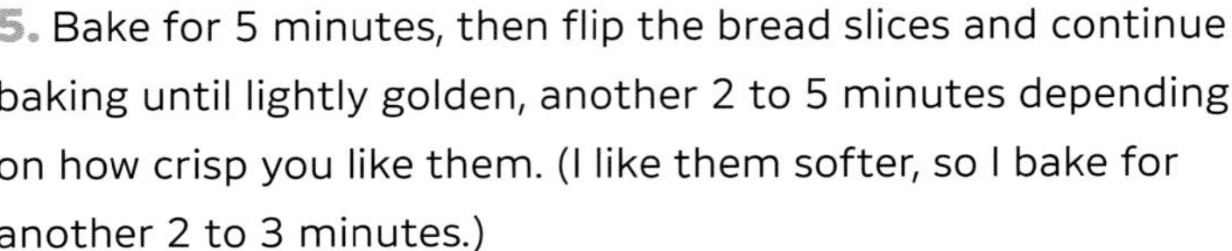

5. Bake for 5 minutes, then flip the bread slices and continue baking until lightly golden, another 2 to 5 minutes depending on how crisp you like them. (I like them softer, so I bake for another 2 to 3 minutes.)

6. After cooking, flip the bread slices so they're oregano side up. For extra garlic goodness, sprinkle garlic powder on each slice. Serve warm (my favorite, but cooled crostini are nice, too).

storage

Store completely cooled crostini in an airtight container at room temperature for up to 3 days or in the freezer for up to 1 month. Reheat from room temperature in a 400°F (200°C) oven for 2 to 4 minutes, and from frozen for 3 to 5 minutes, until warmed through.

tip

* A baguette is shaped like a wand or stick, typically 2 inches (5 cm) across and 20 to 30 inches (50 to 75 cm) long.

vegan • gluten-free option • nut-free • soy-free • kid-friendly • on the glow • one pot

Easy Rustic Double Garlic Croutons

makes 1½ generous cups • prep time: 5 minutes • total time: 12 minutes

3 large garlic cloves (18 g total)

3 tablespoons extra-virgin olive oil*

¼ teaspoon fine sea salt

2 to 3 slices fresh bread (133 g; thick and hearty style preferred)

¼ teaspoon garlic powder

What could be better than lightly salty, delightfully crunchy, entirely just-the-right-amount-of-garlicky croutons on your favorite salad? These croutons work for a number of salads in this cookbook, but I've also found that they are a tasty topper for adding crunch to bowls of soup or stew, or even as a snack all on their own; try dipping them in my Velvety Cashew Garlic Dressing (page 226)—it's better than chips and dip! I prefer these made with a hearty bread, but feel free to use any kind of bread you have on hand. Use them to top my Busy Bee Big Salad (page 69) and Radiant Garden Side Salad (page 89), to name a couple. Even though they only take about 12 minutes from start to finish, I've included a time-saving method in the Tips.

1. Smash the garlic cloves, one at a time, as flat as you can, by laying the flat side of a chef's knife over a clove. Use the heel of your hand to press the blade down on the clove. Remove the peels from the smashed cloves and discard.
2. To a large skillet, add the smashed garlic and olive oil, stirring until combined, then sprinkle with the salt. Cook over medium heat for 2 to 3 minutes, stirring occasionally, until the garlic cloves are softened and very lightly golden in some spots.
3. Meanwhile, slice the bread (or tear it, for a rustic look) into ¾- to 1-inch (2 to 2.5 cm) cubes (you should have 2 cups).

4. Add the cubed bread to the skillet, tossing to coat with the garlic and oil, then spread out into an even layer. Increase the heat to medium-high and cook for 2 to 3½ minutes, until golden on the bottom, watching closely and moving the croutons and garlic around a bit to avoid burning. Using metal tongs or a spatula, flip the croutons over and cook for another 2 to 3 minutes, until the croutons are golden and crispy but still chewy on the inside. When done, toss the croutons with the smashed garlic to infuse a bit more garlic flavor over them.

5. Remove from the heat, sprinkle the garlic powder evenly over the croutons, and serve. Discard (or eat, if you dare!) the smashed garlic.

storage

Store completely cooled croutons in an airtight container in the fridge for up to 4 days. To reheat, add the croutons to a dry skillet over medium-high heat and cook, uncovered, for 4 to 6 minutes, flipping once halfway through, until lightly crispy.

tips

* If you plan on serving the croutons right away, you can use vegan butter instead of oil. However, the butter contains quite a bit of water and the croutons will soften substantially if stored.

Feel free to use garlic-infused extra-virgin olive oil if you have some on hand and skip steps 1 and 2 (except for preheating the pan, for course!).

make it gluten-free

Use your favorite gluten-free bread.

vegan • gluten-free option • nut-free • soy-free • kid-friendly • freezer-friendly • on the glow

Crispy Tortilla Strips

makes 1 heaping cup • prep time: 6 minutes • total time: 14 minutes

1 large (10-inch/25 cm) soft flour tortilla

2 teaspoons extra-virgin olive oil

½ teaspoon garlic powder

¼ teaspoon ground cumin

¼ teaspoon chili powder

⅛ teaspoon fine sea salt

Cayenne pepper (optional)

Crispy, crunchy, spicy, savory, smoky . . . my Crispy Tortilla Strips pack a surprising punch of flavor for their dainty size. It's easy to see why everyone loves these: they are fast, simple, and inexpensive, and use on-hand ingredients. I love serving these sprinkled on top of my Mile-High Warm Portobello Fajita Salad (page 59) and Toppled Taco Salad (page 49). You can even cut them into larger pieces and dip them into my Glow Up Garden Guacamole (page 283). Sometimes I'll tuck them into school lunches with a little container of guacamole or hummus for a fun snack option (omitting the cayenne pepper).

1. Preheat the oven to 375°F (190°C) and line an extra-large baking sheet with parchment paper.
2. Using kitchen shears, cut the tortilla into strips about 1 to 2 inches (2.5 to 5 cm) long by ¼ inch (5 mm) wide. Place them in a large bowl. Toss with the olive oil until coated.
3. To a small bowl, add the garlic powder, cumin, chili powder, and salt. Stir well to combine. Sprinkle the spices over the tortilla strips and toss well with your hands until evenly coated.
4. Spread the tortilla strips in an even layer on the prepared baking sheet, making sure they do not overlap.
5. Bake for 6 to 10 minutes (I bake for 7), flipping the strips and rotating the pan halfway through baking, until lightly golden. Watch closely near the end of baking to avoid burning the strips.
6. After cooking, sprinkle on a tiny bit of cayenne pepper (if using) to taste. (This is a nice way to try a small amount to see if you like it!) Cool on the baking sheet for 5 to 10 minutes. The tortilla strips will firm up after cooling.

Double Batch Variation

For a double batch of tortilla strips, use 2 large (10-inch/25 cm) soft flour tortillas, 4 teaspoons extra-virgin olive oil, 1 teaspoon garlic powder, ½ teaspoon ground cumin, ½ teaspoon chili powder, scant ¼ teaspoon fine sea salt, and cayenne pepper to taste (optional). Follow the recipe as written. Makes 2 heaping cups.

storage

Store completely cooled tortilla strips in an airtight container at room temperature for up to 1 week or in the freezer for up to 7 weeks.

make it gluten-free

Use your favorite gluten-free tortilla. Different brands cook for varying amounts of time, so keep a close eye on them while they cook.

vegan • gluten-free • soy-free • grain-free • raw/no bake • kid-friendly • freezer-friendly • on the glow • one bowl

Ultra-Creamy Flavor Burst Basil Pesto

makes 1⅓ cups • prep time: 12 minutes • total time: 12 minutes

I adore whipping up pesto because it comes together so quickly and adds that main-character flavor energy we all love in a dish. Pine nuts have a rich, lightly sweet, and buttery taste that adds depth and mega creaminess to this herby pesto. Garlic lends a savory kick, and peppery basil creates a bold pesto made vibrant with a healthy dose of fresh lemon juice, all mellowed with cheesy nutritional yeast. I serve savory scoops of this with my Glow Up Pesto Dream Bowl (page 37), Sun-Kissed On the Glow Pasta Salad (page 111), on top of Garlic-Infused Olive Oil Crostini (page 249), and to jazz up rice, quinoa, farro, and more. One of my favorite ways to serve this creamy pesto is to mix a spoonful into a bowl of warm roasted veggies, such as roasted potatoes, carrots, red onion, bell peppers, broccoli, etc.—it's divine!

1 medium garlic clove (5 g)*

2¼ cups packed (68 g) fresh basil leaves

¾ cup (114 g) pine nuts

6 tablespoons extra-virgin olive oil

4½ to 5 tablespoons fresh lemon juice, or to taste** (I like 5 tablespoons)

3½ tablespoons nutritional yeast

½ to ¾ teaspoon fine sea salt, to taste

Freshly ground black pepper***

1 to 3 tablespoons water (optional)

1. In a large heavy-duty food processor, process the garlic and basil until coarsely chopped, about 10 seconds, stopping to scrape down the sides of the bowl if necessary.
2. Add the pine nuts, olive oil, lemon juice, nutritional yeast, salt (starting with ½ teaspoon), and freshly ground black pepper to taste. Process for about 45 seconds, until the pesto is very smooth but still has pretty flecks of basil, stopping to scrape down the sides of the bowl as needed. Taste and adjust the lemon juice and salt, if desired. If you'd like a thinner pesto, add water, a tablespoon at a time, and process again until combined.

storage

Store in an airtight container in the fridge for up to 9 days. The pesto will thicken slightly when chilled, but will soften at room temperature. Freeze for up to 6 weeks. Thaw on the counter for a couple of hours or overnight in the fridge, and add a touch of salt, pepper, and lemon juice to revive the flavors, if desired.

tips

* Add a second medium clove of garlic if you are a garlic lover.

** You may like less or more lemon juice, so add it slowly and keep tasting

*** I find this flavorful pesto can withstand a good amount of freshly ground black pepper; I tend to use about 15 cranks or so, but as always, add slowly, as peppercorns vary in intensity.

vegan • gluten-free • soy-free • grain-free • raw/no bake • kid-friendly • freezer-friendly • one bowl

Sun-Dried Tomato, Walnut, and Basil Pesto

makes 1½ cups • prep time: 14 minutes • total time: 14 minutes

- 2 medium garlic cloves (10 g total)
- 2½ tablespoons (27 g) chopped drained oil-packed sun-dried tomatoes
- ⅓ cup (35 g) raw walnut halves
- ⅓ cup (45 g) raw cashews
- 3 cups packed (90 g) fresh basil leaves
- ½ cup extra-virgin olive oil
- 3 tablespoons fresh lemon juice, or to taste (I often add an extra teaspoon)
- 1 tablespoon water
- 1½ tablespoons nutritional yeast
- ½ teaspoon fine sea salt, or to taste

storage

Store in an airtight container in the fridge for up to 5 days. The pesto will firm up when chilled, but will soften at room temperature. Freeze for up to 6 weeks. Thaw on the counter for a couple of hours or overnight in the fridge.

Peppery basil and tangy, lightly tart sun-dried tomatoes are the heart of this deeply flavored pesto. I love how the sweet cashews balance out the tanginess, while earthy, bitter walnuts add depth and ensure the pesto doesn't end up too sweet. Nutritional yeast adds a cheesy, rich umami to bring it all together. I like to make this pesto with a coarse texture, which allows the individual flavors of the cashews, walnuts, sun-dried tomatoes, garlic, and basil to each shine through, compared with when they are all processed into a very smooth pesto. I encourage you to enjoy this in recipes such as my Zucchini and Carrot Ribbon Pesto Salad (page 65), on my Garlic-Infused Olive Oil Crostini (page 249), or in a simple salad of mixed greens over Easy Garlic-Infused Farro (page 268).

1. In a large heavy-duty food processor, process the garlic and sun-dried tomatoes until coarsely chopped, about 5 seconds.
2. Add the walnuts and cashews. Pulse 30 to 40 times, just until the nuts are coarsely chopped. You still want texture for crunch, so don't process them to fine crumbs. Scrape the mixture into a small bowl and set aside. Return the bowl to the processor; no need to wipe clean.
3. To the processor bowl, add the basil, olive oil, lemon juice, water, nutritional yeast, and salt. Process until the basil mixture is mostly smooth but still has pretty flecks of basil, 20 to 30 seconds, stopping to scrape down the sides of the bowl if necessary.
4. Scrape the sun-dried tomato and nut mixture back into the processor bowl with the basil mixture. Pulse only 10 to 12 times, just enough for the nuts to incorporate into the basil mixture; avoid overprocessing, as you want a textured, coarse pesto. Taste and adjust the lemon juice and salt, if desired.

vegan • gluten-free • nut-free • grain-free • raw/no bake • advance prep required • freezer-friendly • on the glow • one bowl

Vegan Feta Cheese

makes 4 cups • prep time: 10 minutes • total time: 10 minutes, plus pressing and chilling time

My plant-based Vegan Feta Cheese is so close in flavor to feta cheese that you may just win over the skeptics at your table. Once I tried this feta, I started enjoying it on just about everything. It adds such a punch and lively creaminess to salads that I can't resist it. If you can get your hands on store-bought pre-pressed tofu (see "Pantry Staples," page 342), it tends to produce the firmest feta cheese. If not, don't worry, just be sure to buy extra-firm or firm tofu and give it a good press (the longer you press it, the more water will be removed from the end result). Keep this feta in the fridge or store it in the freezer to top your salads and sandwiches for a punch of added herby flavor and a touch of decadence all week long. We always pile it on top of our Busy Bee Big Salad (page 69), Herby Couscous, Sun-Dried Tomato, and Chickpea Salad (page 75), On the Glow Pasta Salad (page 107), and Strawberry Arugula Salad with Feta and Rosemary-Maple Nuts (page 86), as it adds a gorgeous velvety texture and elevated taste. You'll want to try out my scrumptious Dill Version (see page 260), too. If you can't eat soy, I've created a delectable Protein-Powered Cashew-Hemp Cheese (page 197) that can be used in many recipes that call for my Vegan Feta Cheese. While not an exact dupe, it's delicious in its own right. A huge thank you to Rob, Ben, and Alex from A Virtuous Pie, a popular Canadian vegan restaurant, for inspiring this recipe.

1 (12-ounce/350 g) block extra-firm or firm tofu, pressed, at room temperature*

½ cup refined coconut oil, melted**

3 to 5 tablespoons fresh lemon juice, to taste (I use 4½ to 5 tablespoons)

1½ tablespoons apple cider vinegar

1½ to 2 teaspoons fine sea salt, to taste (I use 2 teaspoons)

1 tablespoon dried oregano

1. Press the tofu for at least 30 minutes (see page 357).
2. Line an 8- or 9-inch (2 to 2.5 L) square pan with two pieces of parchment paper placed perpendicular to each other, cut to fit the width of the pan with a few inches of overhang on each side for easy removal.
3. In a small pot, melt the coconut oil over low heat, or simply microwave it in a small dish for 20 to 40 seconds.

recipe continues

storage

Store in an airtight container in the fridge for up to 1 week or in the freezer for up to 2 weeks. I like to cube the feta before freezing and then thaw as many cubes as I need by keeping them in the fridge until thawed.

tips

* It's important to ensure your tofu is pressed very well so most of the water is removed before use; otherwise, the feta won't firm up enough after chilling. It's also important that the tofu is room temperature before you begin the recipe. Using chilled tofu can result in the coconut oil hardening up and not processing properly.

** Be sure to use *refined* (or odorless) coconut oil, as it doesn't have a coconut flavor.

4. To a large heavy-duty food processor, add the pressed tofu, breaking it apart into about 8 chunks. Add the melted coconut oil, lemon juice (starting with 3 tablespoons), apple cider vinegar, and salt (starting with 1½ teaspoons). Process until very smooth, 60 to 90 seconds, stopping to scrape down the sides of the bowl if necessary. The mixture will be thick and smooth.
5. Taste and add more lemon juice and salt, if desired. Process again to combine. It should taste very tangy and salty.
6. Remove the processor blade. Using a spatula, and holding the parchment paper in place with one hand, spread the mixture evenly in the prepared pan until it covers the entire base. Evenly sprinkle with the dried oregano and lightly press down on it so it adheres.
7. Refrigerate, uncovered, for 1½ to 2 hours, until firm to the touch.
8. Using the overhanging parchment, remove the feta from the pan. Cut into small cubes and serve immediately or store in the fridge until ready to use.

Dill Version

For a dill version, swap the oregano topping for an equal amount of dried dill.

vegan • gluten-free option • nut-free • soy-free option • grain-free • oil-free • kid-friendly
on the glow • one pot

Sweet and Tangy No-Chop Barbecue Sauce

makes ¾ cup plus 1 tablespoon • prep time: 7 minutes • total time: 12 minutes

¾ cup ketchup

3 tablespoons packed (40 g) brown sugar

1 to 2 tablespoons apple cider vinegar, to taste

2 teaspoons dry mustard

1½ teaspoons smoked paprika

1 teaspoon garlic powder

½ teaspoon onion powder (or 1 teaspoon dried onion flakes)

½ teaspoon fine sea salt, or to taste

Freshly ground black pepper

2 teaspoons vegan Worcestershire sauce

1 teaspoon pure maple syrup (optional)

Sriracha or other hot sauce, to taste (I use 2 teaspoons sriracha)

I love how my kitchen smells like summer barbecues whenever I make my Tangy No-Chop Barbecue Sauce! It's such a cinch to make, with ingredients I usually have in the pantry, and only takes 12 minutes. Not having anything to chop, mince, or grate and adding the ingredients directly to the pot makes this recipe come together in a flash. Its sweet, tangy flavor means you can enjoy it in any recipe that requires barbecue sauce—and even some that don't! Try it drizzled over sautéed potatoes, as a sauce on your homemade pizza, or stirred into baked beans. It has an enticing sweetness and a super-gentle heat that you can ramp up or omit entirely, depending on your tastes. Toss it with my Crispy and Chewy Barbecue Tofu (page 187), which is out of this world in my Backyard Barbecue Tofu and Jalapeño-Tomato Rice Salad (page 43), The Ultimate Ranch Barbecue Tofu Cobb Salad (page 85), and Dreamy Barbecue Tofu and Roasted Green Bean Salad (page 57), and let's not forget its role in my Barbecue Apple Cider Vinaigrette (page 243).

1. To a small pot, add the ketchup, brown sugar, apple cider vinegar (starting with 1 tablespoon), dry mustard, smoked paprika, garlic powder, onion powder, salt, black pepper to taste, vegan Worcestershire sauce, maple syrup (if using), and sriracha. Whisk until combined.
2. Cover with the lid slightly ajar and cook over low to medium-low heat for 5 to 10 minutes, stirring occasionally, until slightly thickened. Taste and adjust the flavors, such as adding another tablespoon of vinegar for more tanginess or a bit of maple syrup for more sweetness, if desired.

storage

Store in an airtight container in the fridge for up to 9 days.

make it gluten- and soy-free

Use a gluten- and soy-free vegan Worcestershire sauce.

vegan • gluten-free • nut-free • soy-free • grain-free • raw/no bake • kid-friendly • on the glow • one bowl

Luxurious Avocado-Lemon Crema

makes 1 cup • prep time: 11 minutes • total time: 11 minutes

I love creamy, velvety crema dolloped over salads, smashed potatoes, and roasted veggies. It adds a bit of glamor and immense flavor to a dish. My Luxurious Avocado-Lemon Crema is our new favorite; it's tangy from the lemon juice, lightly garlicky, mega creamy from the avocado, and peppery and citrusy from the cilantro. It tastes like spring and summer on your plate and gives any dish staying power due to the healthy fats in its avocado base. Not a cilantro fan? Simply swap it out for fresh parsley. Try this dolloped or piped over my Toppled Taco Salad (page 49), Easy Garlic-Infused Farro (page 268), and Super Green Bean, Rice, and Avocado Salad (page 127) for a fun twist.

2 small garlic cloves (8 g total)

½ cup lightly packed (11 g) fresh cilantro or flat-leaf parsley leaves

1 large ripe avocado (225 g), pitted and peeled (1 cup packed)

2 tablespoons grapeseed oil

2 tablespoons + 2 teaspoons fresh lemon juice, or more to taste

1 teaspoon apple cider vinegar

¼ teaspoon fine sea salt, or to taste

1. In a small food processor, process the garlic until minced, about 5 seconds.

2. Add the cilantro or parsley and process again until minced, 5 to 10 seconds.

3. Add the avocado, grapeseed oil, lemon juice, apple cider vinegar, and salt. Process until very smooth, 25 to 30 seconds, stopping to scrape down the sides of the bowl as needed. Taste and adjust the lemon juice and salt, if desired.

storage

Store in an airtight container in the fridge for up to 4 days.

vegan • gluten-free • nut-free • soy-free option • grain-free • raw/no bake • on the glow • one bowl

Lime and Sriracha Aioli

makes 1 scant cup • prep time: 6 minutes • total time: 6 minutes

2 medium garlic cloves (10 g total), grated on a Microplane

¾ cup Soy-Free Vegan Mayonnaise (page 265) or store-bought

6 to 8 teaspoons fresh lime juice, to taste

3 to 6 teaspoons sriracha, to taste (I use 6 teaspoons)*

Fine sea salt

storage

Store in an airtight container in the fridge for up to 1 week.

tip

* Some brands of sriracha are much spicier than others, so it's always a good idea to add slowly and taste as you go.

make it soy-free

If using store-bought vegan mayo, be sure to select a soy-free variety.

What would my glow-rious Toppled Taco Salad (page 49), Sunny Day Charred Corn and Feta Salad (page 71), and Mile-High Warm Portobello Fajita Salad (page 59) be without this tangy, spicy, lightly sweet, citrusy, and garlicky aioli drizzled over top? Well, they would still be dreamy, but this Lime and Sriracha Aioli really takes them over the top! It whips up in minutes and lasts in the fridge for a week, so you can enjoy it for several days and in as many different dishes as you can think of. Enjoy it on my Backyard Barbecue Tofu and Jalapeño-Tomato Rice Salad (page 43) or as a zesty dip for Crispy and Chewy Barbecue Tofu (page 187). Or, for a delectable side dish, serve it drizzled over my Savory Jalapeño-Tomato Rice (page 270) or Cilantro-Jalapeño Rice (page 273). I like to spoon it on roasted veggies, crispy smashed potatoes, and sandwiches, too.

1. In a medium bowl, stir together the grated garlic, vegan mayonnaise, lime juice to taste, and 3 teaspoons of sriracha until combined. Taste, add more lime juice and sriracha, if desired, and season to taste with salt.

vegan • gluten-free • nut-free • soy-free • grain-free • raw/no bake • kid-friendly • one bowl

Soy-Free Vegan Mayonnaise

makes 1 cup • prep time: 5 minutes • total time: 5 minutes

I love the taste and texture of my favorite store-bought vegan mayonnaise, but I can't always get to the store when I run out. Enter my homemade vegan mayo, which is delightfully similar in both taste and texture. I simply save up the liquid from my canned chickpeas (called aquafaba) and I can whip up this recipe in about 5 minutes. Pro tip: It's important to follow the recipe exactly as written to ensure your mayo thickens properly. There are many delicious uses for your homemade mayonnaise, such as my Sriracha Honey-Mustard Dressing (page 242), Luxurious ACV and Dijon Dressing (page 221), High-Protein No-Egg Egg Salad (page 81), Ranch Buttermilk Dressing (page 232), Creamy Chipotle Dressing (page 237), Glow Girl Kale Slaw (page 39), Lime and Sriracha Aioli (page 264), and Creamy ACV, Shallot, Maple, and Dijon Vinaigrette (page 233).

3 tablespoons aquafaba (chickpea liquid)*

1 tablespoon fresh lemon juice, or more to taste

1 teaspoon apple cider vinegar

1 teaspoon brown rice syrup

¼ teaspoon fine sea salt, or to taste

¼ teaspoon dry mustard

¾ to 1 cup grapeseed oil or pure/refined olive oil**

1. To a tall 2-cup (500 mL) container, add the aquafaba, lemon juice, apple cider vinegar, brown rice syrup, salt, and dry mustard. Using an immersion blender, blend for 10 to 15 seconds, until combined. It will look bubbly. Alternatively, use a blender and blend on low to medium speed until combined.

2. With the blender running, slowly stream in the grapeseed oil or olive oil, 1 or 2 tablespoons at a time, until the mixture thickens into a white, creamy mayo, about 1 minute or so. (I usually use ¾ cup plus 2 tablespoons of oil, but you might need anywhere up to 1 cup.) Taste and adjust the flavors, if desired, such as adding a bit more salt or another teaspoon of lemon juice.

storage

Store in an airtight container or jar in the fridge for up to 9 days.

tips

* For this recipe, use the liquid from a can of chickpeas (and not the liquid from cooking chickpeas from scratch) to ensure the mayonnaise thickens. I love to freeze leftover aquafaba in ice cube trays for handy access (aquafaba cubes can be stored in an airtight container in the freezer for up to 4 months).

What can you make with the leftover chickpeas? Why not make my irresistible Herby Couscous, Sun-Dried Tomato, and Chickpea Salad (page 75), Roasted Chickpea and Parm Romaine Crunch Salad (page 91), or Garlic-Cayenne Roasted Chickpeas (page 202)?

** It's important to use a neutral-tasting oil in this recipe. I don't recommend using extra-virgin olive oil, as it will taste too pungent. Stick with grapeseed oil or pure/refined olive oil (which has a much lighter flavor) for the best outcome.

vegan • nut-free • soy-free • kid-friendly • on the glow • one pot

Lemon and Garlic Pearl Couscous

makes 2¼ cups • prep time: 10 minutes • total time: 23 minutes

- 1 teaspoon lemon zest
- 1 tablespoon fresh lemon juice
- 1 large garlic clove (6 g), grated on a Microplane
- 2 tablespoons extra-virgin olive oil
- 1 cup (154 g) uncooked pearl couscous
- 1¾ cups water
- ½ teaspoon fine sea salt

storage

Store leftovers in an airtight container in the fridge for up to 4 days. Gently reheat in a pot over low to medium heat for a few minutes, stirring occasionally, until heated through.

Pearl couscous, also known as Israeli or giant couscous, is a chewy, soft, and slightly nutty pasta made from semolina flour and water. In this Lemon and Garlic Pearl Couscous, I add a gentle garlicky, citrusy tone with a sweet finish from the lemon zest. It's our go-to pairing with my Herby Couscous, Sun-Dried Tomato, and Chickpea Salad (page 75) and it's tasty as a simple side dish, too. We eat this both warm and chilled, so it works well in any season. To take it up a level, it's fab drizzled with one of my dressings, such as my Immunity-Boosting Tahini Dressing (page 229), Herby Lemon and White Wine Vinaigrette (page 231), or 6-Ingredient Shake-and-Glow Vinaigrette (page 235).

1. Prepare the lemon zest, lemon juice, and garlic. Set aside.
2. In a medium pot, heat the olive oil over medium heat for about 1 minute, until lightly shimmering. Stir in the couscous and toast, stirring frequently, for 2 to 3 minutes, until the couscous is light to medium golden. Be careful not to burn it. Remove from the heat and let the couscous cool, uncovered, for 1 minute.
3. Carefully add the water, lemon juice, grated garlic, and salt to the pot. Stir. Bring to a boil over high heat, uncovered, then immediately reduce the heat to low or medium-low, stir again, and cover with a tight-fitting lid. Simmer for 9 to 12 minutes, stirring occasionally (especially near the end of the cook time), until the couscous is tender yet slightly chewy and a bit firm. Reduce the heat near the end of cooking, if necessary, to prevent sticking.
4. Drain the couscous in a large fine-mesh sieve for 1 to 2 minutes, stirring occasionally.
5. Spoon the couscous into a medium container, then stir in the lemon zest. Cool, uncovered, in the fridge for 10 to 15 minutes before using. The cooked couscous firms up a lot when chilled; simply use a spoon to break it apart and stir it up before using.

vegan • nut-free • soy-free • oil-free • kid-friendly • freezer-friendly • on the glow • one pot

Easy Garlic-Infused Farro

makes 2¼ cups • prep time: 4 minutes • total time: 35 minutes

6 cups vegetable broth or water*

1 cup (184 g) uncooked pearled farro**

3 large garlic cloves (18 g total), grated on a Microplane, divided

Fine sea salt and freshly ground black pepper

I am in love with farro, a hearty and nutty ancient grain that has been enjoyed for thousands of years. Farro is grown in Italian regions such as Tuscany, Lazio, and Umbria, and in many other countries, including here in Canada. It's a great complement to salads due to its distinct chewy texture. I love it not only for its mild flavor that goes with everything and its delectable al dente bite, but also for its protein and fiber content. It's a great source of magnesium, vitamin B, zinc, iron, and more! My Easy Garlic-Infused Farro recipe is a simple and flavorful way to prepare it; you'll be surprised by how the grated garlic adds such a savory punch. Enjoy it in my Glow Up Pesto Dream Bowl (page 37), Fall Crunch Farro Salad (page 121), and as a hearty base for just about any leafy salad you want to add heft to. This farro is also a dream team with my Velvety Cashew Garlic Dressing (page 226) drizzled over top.

1. In a medium pot, add the vegetable broth (or water). (If using water, add ¼ teaspoon fine sea salt.) Bring to a boil over high heat.
2. Rinse and drain the farro. Once the broth (or water) comes to a boil, stir in the farro and two-thirds of the grated garlic, reserving one-third of the garlic for later. Reduce the heat to medium-high and simmer, uncovered, for 30 to 31 minutes, until the farro is tender but still chewy. There will still be liquid after cooking.
3. Drain the farro and return to the pot. Stir in the reserved grated garlic. Season to taste with salt and pepper.

storage

Store in an airtight container in the fridge for up to 5 days or in the freezer for up to 1 month. To reheat from refrigerated, add the farro and a generous splash of water to a medium pot, stirring to combine. Cover and reheat over medium-low heat for 3 to 4 minutes, stirring occasionally, until warmed through. Revive the flavor with a sprinkle of salt and freshly ground black pepper. To reheat from frozen, follow the same directions but increase the heating time to 5 to 6 minutes, or as needed.

tips

* Vegetable broth produces a more savory version with more umami flavor. However, water plus ¼ teaspoon fine sea salt works in a pinch!

** I use Bob's Red Mill organic farro, which is pearled farro. Different varieties of farro have different cook times, so it's important to use pearled farro and not semi-pearled farro or whole farro.

vegan • gluten-free • nut-free • soy-free • freezer-friendly • on the glow • one pot

Savory Jalapeño-Tomato Rice

makes 4 cups • prep time: 7 minutes • total time: 40 minutes

- 1 tablespoon extra-virgin olive oil
- 2 large jalapeño peppers (140 g total), seeded and finely chopped (¾ cup)
- 2 large garlic cloves (12 g total), minced
- 1½ teaspoons chili powder
- ¾ teaspoon smoked paprika
- ½ teaspoon ground cumin
- 1 cup (180 g) uncooked long-grain white rice
- 1¾ cups vegetable broth*
- ¼ cup + 2 tablespoons strained tomatoes**
- ¼ teaspoon fine sea salt, plus more as needed
- Freshly ground black pepper

My Savory Jalapeño-Tomato Rice will wake up your taste buds and lift your mood! That's exactly what happened to me when Eric and I went to Mexico for a winter vacation several years ago, and I have never forgotten how delicious this dish tasted as we sunned, swam, toured, and feasted our way through each sunny, relaxing day. This recipe differs from traditional Mexican rice, called arroz rojo, in a few ways. Traditionally, arroz rojo involves sautéing the uncooked rice and simmering it in flavorful tomato sauce, adding a lot of character and savory richness to simple white rice. The dish is usually flavored only with the tomato (although some cooks choose to spice theirs up). I cook my version in a smoky combo of spices: finely chopped spicy jalapeño is sautéed with garlic and enhanced by aromatic chili powder, smoked paprika, and cumin, and I use vegetable broth to make it vegan. We serve this tasty rice in my Backyard Barbecue Tofu and Jalapeño-Tomato Rice Salad (page 43). Enjoy it as a spicy swap for the seasoned rice in Mile-High Warm Portobello Fajita Salad (page 59), too. The recipe makes a generous amount and is delicious all on its own as a side dish. Try it topped with my irresistible Glow Up Garden Guacamole (page 283).

1. In a medium (3-quart/3 L) pot, stir together the olive oil and chopped jalapeños. Cook for 3 to 4 minutes over medium-low heat, stirring occasionally and reducing the heat, if necessary, until fragrant and softened.
2. Reduce the heat to low. Stir in the minced garlic and cook for another minute, stirring frequently.
3. Stir in the chili powder, smoked paprika, and cumin and cook for 1 minute, until fragrant.

4. Stir in the rice, broth, strained tomatoes, salt, and several cranks of freshly ground black pepper. Increase the heat to high and bring the mixture to a boil. Immediately reduce the heat to low, stir again, scraping the bottom of the pot, and cover with a tight-fitting lid. Cook for 18 to 22 minutes, checking and stirring around the 12-minute mark, until the water has been absorbed and the rice is tender.

5. Remove from the heat and let the rice steam, with the lid on, for another 7 to 12 minutes. Season to taste with more salt and pepper, if needed. Keep covered to keep it warm until ready to use.

storage

Store cooled rice in an airtight container in the fridge for up to 4 days or in the freezer for up to 3 weeks. If frozen, thaw in the refrigerator overnight, or for 8 to 12 hours, in a sealed container. Reheat in a covered pot over low to medium heat, adding a splash of water if necessary to moisten, until warmed through. Season with salt and pepper, if desired.

tips

* If you are out of vegetable broth, an equal amount of water plus ¾ teaspoon of salt works in a pinch!

** Strained tomatoes are also called "tomato purée" or "passata" depending on the brand.

vegan • gluten-free • nut-free • soy-free • freezer-friendly • kid-friendly • on the glow • one pot

Cilantro-Jalapeño Rice

makes 4 cups • prep time: 12 minutes • total time: 31 minutes

Rice is one of my favorite grains to cook with, as it readily absorbs the flavors of the cooking liquid and any mix-ins. This Cilantro-Jalapeño Rice is my plant-based spin on herby and savory arroz verde, a fluffy white rice dish simmered in a cilantro-infused chicken broth. This version differs from traditional Latin American recipes in a few ways: I use vegetable broth, and add earthy cumin and jalapeños for a woody, smoky, lightly spicy side dish that works so deliciously in Toppled Taco Salad (page 49) and Super Green Bean, Rice, and Avocado Salad (page 127). It's a comforting side dish or base for salads, too. We love a squeeze of lemon over top to enhance and brighten the flavors, or if you happen to have my Lime and Sriracha Aioli (page 264) on hand, a dollop on top of this rice is a tangy, spicy delight.

1½ cups packed (51 g) fresh cilantro leaves (1 large bunch)*

3 medium jalapeño peppers (105 g total), quartered lengthwise and seeded**

1 tablespoon extra-virgin olive oil

1½ teaspoons ground cumin

1 cup (196 g) uncooked white basmati rice***

1¾ cups vegetable broth****

¼ teaspoon fine sea salt, plus more as needed

Freshly ground black pepper

1 lemon wedge (optional)

1. Finely chop the cilantro. Set aside.
2. Quarter the jalapeños lengthwise, discard the seeds, and coarsely chop the peppers into pea-size or smaller pieces. You should have ½ heaping cup.
3. In a medium (3-quart/3 L) pot, stir together the jalapeños and olive oil. Cook for 3 to 5 minutes over medium-low heat, stirring occasionally and reducing the heat, if necessary, until fragrant and softened.
4. Sprinkle the cumin over the jalapeños, stir, and cook for a minute, until fragrant.
5. Stir in the cilantro, rice, broth, salt, and several cranks of freshly ground black pepper. Increase the heat to high and bring the mixture to a boil. Immediately reduce the heat to low, stir again, scraping the bottom of the pot, and cover with a tight-fitting lid. Cook for 12 to 20 minutes, checking for doneness and stirring at the 12-minute mark, until the water has been absorbed and the rice is tender.

storage

Store cooled rice in an airtight container in the fridge for up to 4 days or in the freezer for up to 1 month. If frozen, thaw in the refrigerator overnight, or for 8 to 12 hours, in a sealed container. Reheat the rice in a covered pot over medium-low heat, with a little veggie broth added to moisten, until heated through.

recipe continues

tips

* I tend to chop by hand, as it means fewer dishes to clean up, but if you aren't a big fan of chopping, you can use a large food processor to do the work for you. Simply pulse the quartered and seeded jalapeños several times until coarsely chopped, then remove from the processor. Add the cilantro and process for 2 to 4 seconds, until finely chopped.

** Use mild jalapeños for a very mild dish, and use hot jalapeños for a moderate to high spice level.

How to tell if a jalapeño is mild or hot? The milder ones have smoother skin with fewer "stretch marks," while hot jalapeños will be older with more stretch marks. Well, isn't this the most relatable vegetable around?

*** The measurements and cooking times in this recipe are accurate only for white basmati rice. Each rice has a slightly different cooking time and liquid amount, so it's best to use white basmati to ensure success.

**** You can swap the vegetable broth for an equal amount of water plus ½ to ¾ teaspoon of fine sea salt (to taste).

6. Remove from the heat and let the rice steam, with the lid on, for another 3 to 5 minutes. Stir in more salt and pepper to taste (I use another ¼ teaspoon of salt and several cranks of freshly ground black pepper) and a small squeeze of lemon juice for brightness, if desired. Keep covered to keep it warm until ready to serve.

vegan • gluten-free • nut-free • soy-free • grain-free • oil-free • on the glow • one bowl

Community-Fave 10-Spice Mix

makes ¼ cup plus 2 teaspoons • prep time: 3 minutes • total time: 3 minutes

Over a decade ago, I made a big pot of veggie and chickpea soup with cashew cream using this bursting-with-all-the-flavors spice combo. Little did I know that the soup and spice mix would become such beloved recipes in the Oh She Glows community. (If you haven't made my 10-Spice Vegetable Soup with Cashew Cream from *The Oh She Glows Cookbook*, you absolutely must!) Earthy smoked paprika, pungent garlic and onion powders, herby basil and thyme, spicy cayenne, black and white peppers, and a little sea salt make up my spicy, smoky, herby, lightly sweet, and bright Community-Fave 10-Spice Mix. I love using it in my Fiery 10-Spice Roasted Potato Salad (page 165) or sprinkled on top of my Spicy Chipotle Corn Salad (page 53), Sunny Day Charred Corn and Feta Salad (page 71), and Smoky Seasoned Roasted Cauliflower and Potato Salad (page 159).

4 teaspoons smoked paprika
2 teaspoons dried basil
2 teaspoons dried oregano
2 teaspoons garlic powder
2 teaspoons onion powder
1½ teaspoons dried thyme
1 teaspoon freshly ground black pepper
1 teaspoon fine sea salt
½ teaspoon cayenne pepper*
½ teaspoon ground white pepper (optional)*

1. To a small container or jar with a lid, add the smoked paprika, dried basil, dried oregano, garlic powder, onion powder, dried thyme, black pepper, salt, cayenne, and white pepper (if using). Secure the lid and shake to combine. Shake well before each use.

storage

Store in an airtight container in a dark place for up to 3 months.

tip

* The white pepper and cayenne pepper make this spice mix quite spicy and hot, so if you prefer a milder spice mix, simply omit them (or reduce their amounts). It's still fantastic.

vegan • gluten-free • nut-free • soy-free • grain-free • oil-free • raw/no bake • on the glow

Quick-Pickled Sweet Onions (and more!)

makes 1½ scant cups • prep time: 5 minutes • total time: 1 hour and 10 minutes

- 2 cups (155 g) thinly sliced sweet onion (1 large)
- 1 cup water
- ¼ cup distilled white vinegar
- ¼ cup apple cider vinegar
- 1½ tablespoons natural cane sugar
- 1½ teaspoons fine sea salt

I adore pickled onions on top of veggie burgers, avocado toast, roasted veggie salads, and other hearty dishes—you name it! These are wonderful served on my High-Protein No-Egg Egg Salad (page 81), and my Busy Bee Big Salad (page 69). They last up to 3 weeks in the fridge, so feel free to make up a batch just to have on hand. We love them so much around here that I knew I had to create variations that would enhance particular salads and offer up other veggies. My Quick-Pickled Spicy Lime Red Onions variation is the perfect sweet, tangy, and citrusy addition to Easy Breezy Deconstructed Guacamole Salad (page 95) and other recipes that feature avocado, cilantro, and lime flavors. Do you love carrots? Make the sweet Quick-Pickled Carrots (see Variations), too; they're just irresistible in my Summer Roll Salad with Pickled Carrots (page 101).

1. Thinly slice the onion using a mandoline or sharp knife.
2. Place the sliced onion in a 2- to 3-cup (500 to 750 mL) heat-safe glass jar with a lid. Set aside.
3. In a small pot, combine the water, distilled white vinegar, apple cider vinegar, sugar, and salt. Bring to a boil over high heat, then immediately remove from the heat and stir until the sugar and salt have dissolved.
4. Carefully, using a funnel if you have one, pour the hot liquid into the jar over the onion. Use a spoon to gently push the onion down into the liquid until fully submerged.
5. Let the jar sit on the counter, uncovered, for 1 hour. After an hour, you can enjoy the pickled onions or secure the lid and store them in the fridge until chilled and ready to use.

Quick Pickled Variations

Quick-Pickled Carrots: Swap the sliced onions for 2 heaping cups peeled and julienned carrots (you'll need 3 medium carrots, 308 g total). Use a julienne peeler to very thinly peel the carrots into 2- to 3-inch (5 to 8 cm) long strands. The other ingredients remain the same; follow the method as directed.

Quick-Pickled Spicy Lime Red Onions: Swap the sweet onion for red onion. Use 1 cup water, ¼ cup distilled white vinegar, 2 tablespoons apple cider vinegar, 2 tablespoons fresh lime juice, 1½ tablespoons natural cane sugar, and 1½ teaspoons fine sea salt. Follow the method as directed.

Quick-Pickled Red Onions: Simply swap the sweet onion for red onion. The other ingredients remain the same; follow the method as directed.

storage

Store in the jar or an airtight container in the fridge for up to 3 weeks. Be sure to use a clean utensil to remove onions from the jar, to prevent spoilage.

vegan • gluten-free • soy-free • grain-free • raw/no bake • freezer-friendly • on the glow • one bowl

Lime, Cumin, and Red Pepper Parmesan

makes 1½ scant cups • prep time: 8 minutes • total time: 8 minutes

2 medium garlic cloves (10 g total)

2 tablespoons packed fresh cilantro leaves

2 tablespoons fresh oregano leaves (or 1 teaspoon dried oregano)

1 cup (134 g) raw cashews

1 tablespoon nutritional yeast

1 tablespoon extra-virgin olive oil

½ to 1 teaspoon red pepper flakes, to taste*

1 teaspoon ground cumin

1 teaspoon lime zest

½ to 1 teaspoon fresh lime juice, to taste

¼ teaspoon fine sea salt, or to taste

storage

Store in an airtight container in the fridge for up to 4 days or store in a freezer bag with the air pressed out or in an airtight container in the freezer for up to 3 weeks.

tips

* You control the heat level in this parmesan; ½ teaspoon of red pepper flakes is mildly spicy, and 1 teaspoon is mild to moderately spicy.

This recipe can be made using a small (4-cup/1 L) food processor or a large one; I use my small food processor, as it's easier to clean.

This parm could make cardboard taste good! While I don't encourage you to test that theory at home, I assure you that this parmesan elevates the simplest of recipes into something quite special. Earthy from the cumin, with a zesty fresh tone from the lime and cilantro and a hint or kick of heat from the red pepper flakes (chef's choice!), this parm pairs beautifully with my Super Green Bean, Rice, and Avocado Salad (page 127), or you can be like us and eat it out of the bowl with a spoon. Sprinkle it over just about any salad to add a flavorful burst of chewy texture.

1. In a food processor, process the garlic until minced.
2. Add the cilantro and oregano leaves (or dried oregano). Process again until minced, 5 to 10 seconds, scraping down the sides of the bowl if needed.
3. Add the cashews, nutritional yeast, olive oil, red pepper flakes (to taste), cumin, lime zest, lime juice, and salt. Pulse just until a coarse meal forms, 20 to 40 pulses or so. Taste and add more salt and/or lime juice, if needed.

vegan • gluten-free • soy-free • grain-free • oil-free • raw/no bake • kid-friendly • freezer-friendly
on the glow • one bowl

Oregano, Basil, and Lemon Zest Parmesan

makes 1½ cups • prep time: 10 minutes • total time: 10 minutes

2 medium garlic cloves (10 g total)

⅓ cup packed (11 g) fresh basil leaves

1½ tablespoons fresh oregano leaves (or 1 teaspoon dried oregano)

1 cup (134 g) raw cashews

2 tablespoons nutritional yeast

1 teaspoon lemon zest

1 to 2 teaspoons fresh lemon juice, to taste

¼ + ⅛ teaspoon to ½ teaspoon fine sea salt, to taste

storage

Store in an airtight container in the fridge for up to 5 days or in the freezer for up to 3 months.

tip

This recipe works well in either a small (4-cup/1 L) food processor or a large one; I use my small food processor, as it's easier to clean.

This flavorful parmesan adds a bright, herby flavor to salads, cooked potatoes, or even a simple avocado or avocado toast. It is summery and fresh from the lemon juice, lightly sweet from the lemon zest, and green and slightly peppery from the fresh oregano and basil, with a lovely nuttiness from the cashews that form the base of this vegan parmesan. It suits to perfection my Sun-Kissed On the Glow Pasta Salad (page 111) and my Zucchini and Carrot Ribbon Pesto Salad (page 65).

1. In a food processor, process the garlic, basil, and oregano until minced, about 10 seconds, stopping to scrape down the sides of the bowl if necessary.
2. Add the cashews, nutritional yeast, lemon zest, lemon juice, and salt to taste. Pulse about 15 to 40 times, until a coarse meal forms. Be careful not to overprocess—you want lots of texture and some bigger pieces in the mix for a delightful crunch.

vegan • gluten-free • soy-free • grain-free • oil-free • raw/no bake • kid-friendly • freezer-friendly
on the glow • one bowl

Garlic Lovers' Cashew Parmesan

makes 1 generous cup • prep time: 5 minutes • total time: 5 minutes

Quicker than quick, you can have a protein-rich, nourishing, crunchy, and garlicky salad topper ready to go. I love using vegan parmesan on my salads because it's such a simple way to add flavor and texture, and it freezes wonderfully so you can always have some on hand for those busy days. Nutty, buttery cashews, pungent garlic, peppery fresh parsley, and cheesy nutritional yeast, along with a pinch of sea salt, are all it takes to elevate your salad to the next level. Tossed into the salad, scattered on top, served in a cute dish on the side . . . there are so many ways to enjoy it. Try it sprinkled liberally over my Roasted Chickpea and Parm Romaine Crunch Salad (page 91), Busy Bee Big Salad (page 69), Sun-Kissed On the Glow Pasta Salad (page 111), potato salads, and basic green salads (but you know we don't do basic here!).

2 medium garlic cloves (10 g total)*
¼ cup lightly packed (7 g) fresh flat-leaf parsley leaves**
⅔ cup (89 g) raw cashews
2 teaspoons nutritional yeast
1 teaspoon garlic powder
¼ teaspoon Herbamare or fine sea salt, or more to taste

1. In a food processor, process the garlic and parsley until minced, 5 to 10 seconds.
2. Add the cashews, nutritional yeast, garlic powder, and Herbamare (or salt) and process just until a coarse meal forms, 4 to 6 seconds. Be careful not to overprocess—you want a coarse, crumbled texture.

storage

Store in an airtight container in the fridge for up to 1 week or in the freezer for up to 3 weeks. I like to revive the flavors with a sprinkle or two each of garlic powder and fine sea salt.

tips

* If you are sensitive to the flavor of raw garlic, use only 1 medium clove.

** Out of fresh parsley? Not to worry! This recipe tastes great even without it.

This recipe works well in either a small (4-cup/1 L) food processor or a large one; I use my small food processor, as it's easier to clean.

vegan • gluten-free • nut-free • soy-free • grain-free • oil-free • raw/no bake • kid-friendly • on the glow • one bowl

Glow Up Garden Guacamole

makes 2 cups • prep time: 18 minutes • total time: 18 minutes

Creamy, chunky, textured guacamole bursting with summer flavors—that's what this Glow Up Garden Guacamole is all about. We enjoy it all year round, although its ingredients taste even better during their hot growing season. Ripe red tomatoes and velvety avocados add a creamy, sweetish base. Zesty and lightly spicy jalapeño and red onion give it a little crunch and kick up the heat, while the cilantro and lime juice pull it together with a fresh, green finish. Select avocados and tomatoes at their peak ripeness for best flavor. We love serving a big scoop of this on my Backyard Barbecue Tofu and Jalapeño-Tomato Rice Salad (page 43), Mile-High Warm Portobello Fajita Salad (page 59), and Toppled Taco Salad (page 49). You can also serve it with crudités and Crispy Tortilla Strips (page 254), tortilla chips, or Garlic-Infused Olive Oil Crostini (page 249).

2 medium garlic cloves (10 g total), minced

3 medium ripe avocados (525 g total), pitted and peeled

3 small tomatoes (190 g total), diced (¾ cup)*

1 medium jalapeño pepper (40 g), seeded and minced (3 tablespoons)**

3 tablespoons minced red onion**

⅓ cup packed (12 g) fresh cilantro leaves, minced (3 tablespoons)

3 to 4 teaspoons fresh lime juice, to taste

¼ + ⅛ teaspoon to ½ teaspoon fine sea salt, to taste

1. Add the minced garlic to a large bowl.
2. Scoop 1½ packed cups of avocado into the bowl with the garlic and coarsely mash the avocado with a fork to the desired texture (I like to leave it chunky).
3. Prepare the tomatoes, jalapeño, red onion, and cilantro, adding them to the bowl as you go. Stir to combine. Stir in the lime juice and salt to taste.

storage

Store in an airtight container in the fridge for up to 2 days.

tips

* I remove and discard the gelatinous seeds from the tomatoes before dicing them to prevent the guacamole getting watered down in flavor.

** I like to mince the jalapeño and red onion super finely to avoid getting big pieces of them in the guacamole.

desserts

desserts

vegan • soy-free option • kid-friendly • freezer-friendly • on the glow

Autumn Spiced Carr-oat Cake with Vegan Cream Cheese Frosting

makes 1 (8-inch/20 cm) round cake, serves 8 • prep time: 30 minutes • total time: 65 minutes, plus cooling time

I love carrot cake, plain and simple. I don't, however, like my carrot cake to *taste* plain and simple! In my Autumn Spiced Carr-oat Cake recipe, I've added an abundance of comforting carrot cake spices, including spicy cinnamon and allspice, warming nutmeg and ginger, and aromatic cloves. It's like a big hug. Almond flour adds a lightly sweet note, and I also infused the cake with ultra-creamy and wholesome oat milk and oat flour; they complement its rich flavor so beautifully. You can certainly serve this flavor-packed cake on its own (or maybe with Coconut Whipped Cream, page 315), but our favorite way is to frost it with my luxuriously smooth Vegan Cream Cheese Frosting (page 291); the distinctive sweet and tangy flavor is a classic for a reason. A dusting of chopped walnuts around the perimeter of the cake lends a fancy touch and a little crunch for the perfect contrast. Get ready to swoon over every bite!

Dry Ingredients

¾ cup + 2 tablespoons (127 g) all-purpose flour*

½ cup (55 g) oat flour

⅓ cup (33 g) almond flour (not almond meal)

¼ cup (63 g) natural cane sugar

2 teaspoons baking powder

2 teaspoons cinnamon

½ teaspoon ground allspice

½ teaspoon ground ginger

½ teaspoon fine sea salt

¼ teaspoon baking soda

¼ teaspoon ground nutmeg

¼ teaspoon ground cloves

Wet Ingredients

¾ cup unsweetened oat or almond milk

½ cup pure maple syrup

2 tablespoons grapeseed oil

2 tablespoons ground flaxseed

½ tablespoon pure vanilla extract

1 teaspoon apple cider vinegar

Mix-Ins

1 cup packed (130 g) finely grated peeled carrots (about 3 medium/230 g total)**

½ cup (50 g) raw walnut halves, chopped

1. Position a rack in the center of the oven and preheat to 350°F (180°C). Lightly grease the bottom and sides of an 8-inch (1.2 L) round nonstick cake pan. Line the bottom of the pan with a piece of parchment paper cut to fit (see Tips).

2. Mix the Dry Ingredients: In a large bowl, whisk together the all-purpose flour, oat flour, almond flour, sugar, baking powder, cinnamon, allspice, ginger, salt, baking soda, nutmeg, and cloves.

3. Mix the Wet Ingredients: In a medium bowl, whisk together the oat or almond milk, maple syrup, grapeseed oil, ground flaxseed, vanilla, and apple cider vinegar.

4. Pour the wet mixture into the dry mixture and stir just until combined and no dry patches remain.

recipe continues

For assembly

1 batch Vegan Cream Cheese Frosting (page 291)

½ scant cup (43 g) raw or toasted walnut or pecan halves, chopped

storage

Store leftover cake in an airtight container or wrapped in plastic wrap in the fridge for up to 5 days. Freeze, unfrosted, for up to 1 month.

tips

* I suggest weighing the flour for the most accurate result. If you don't have a kitchen scale, use the *scoop-and-shake-until-level* method (see "Measuring Flour," page 29).

** Use the small/fine holes on a box grater to grate the peeled carrots until you have 1 packed cup.

The easiest way to cut your parchment paper so that it fits the bottom of your cake pan is to place the cake pan on the parchment paper and trace around the base with a pencil. Cut out the resulting circle just inside the line and *voilà*, a perfectly fitting round of parchment!

If you don't have an 8-inch (1.2 L) round cake pan, a 9-inch (1.5 L) round cake pan works in a pinch; the cake will just have less height than shown in the photo.

make it soy-free

Use soy-free vegan butter and soy-free vegan cream cheese in the frosting.

5. Add the Mix-Ins: Fold in the carrots and walnuts until just incorporated, being careful not to overmix.

6. Spoon the batter into the prepared cake pan and spread evenly with a spatula.

7. Bake the Cake: Bake, uncovered, for 40 to 50 minutes, until the cake slowly springs back when lightly pressed and a toothpick inserted into the center comes out clean (or with only cooked crumbs on it).

8. Meanwhile, make the Vegan Cream Cheese Frosting: Transfer to an airtight container and chill in the fridge so it can firm up a bit while the cake bakes and cools.

9. Let the cake cool in the pan on a cooling rack for 30 minutes, then carefully run a butter knife around the cake to loosen the edge. Gently and carefully invert the cake onto a plate, then place right side up on the cooling rack. Let sit until completely cool, about 1 hour.

10. Assemble: Once the cake is completely cooled, spoon ¾ to 1 cup of frosting onto the center of the cake. Spread out the frosting with a pastry knife until it's ½ to 1 inch (1 to 2.5 cm) from the edge.

11. Press the chopped walnuts around the edge of the frosting, making a 1-inch (2.5 cm) border of nuts. Slice and serve.

vegan • gluten-free • nut-free option • soy-free option • grain-free • raw/no bake • kid-friendly • on the glow • one bowl

Vegan Cream Cheese Frosting

makes 1½ cups • prep time: 8 minutes • total time: 8 minutes

Is there a better frosting than sweet, tangy, creamy, and velvety Vegan Cream Cheese Frosting? It's a tough call, but this decadent frosting, with its distinct flavor, is the perfect topping for my Autumn Spiced Carr-oat Cake (page 289). The frosting cools and sweetens the warming cinnamon, nutmeg, ginger, allspice, and cloves in the cake and adds that characteristic cream cheese tang. This recipe makes enough frosting to decorate one 8-inch (20 cm) round cake. You can also serve it with my Vanilla Buttermilk Loaf Cake (page 301).

½ cup vegan cream cheese*

2 tablespoons + 2 teaspoons vegan butter**

1¾ to 2 cups (215 g to 246 g) icing sugar***

Non-dairy milk, if needed

Fine sea salt (optional)

1. To a large bowl (or a stand mixer bowl), add the vegan cream cheese and vegan butter. Using a handheld mixer (or the paddle attachment), beat on low speed, gradually increasing to medium, for 30 to 45 seconds, just until smooth and creamy. Be careful not to overmix or the frosting will be runny.

2. Add the icing sugar, ½ cup or so at a time, beating on low speed and gradually increasing to medium, until the frosting is smooth and spreadable, but not too runny or too thick, 45 to 60 seconds. If your frosting becomes too thick while mixing, simply thin it with a bit of non-dairy milk (starting with ½ teaspoon increments) and beat again to combine. If the frosting is too runny, add a touch more icing sugar and beat again until smooth.

3. Add a sprinkle of salt to taste, if desired (I add ⅛ teaspoon), until the flavors pop, beating on low speed to combine.

storage

Store in an airtight container in the fridge for up to 5 days. Place the frosting on the counter for up to 30 minutes to soften slightly before using, if needed.

tips

* I use half a 200 g container of Violife Creamy Original vegan cream cheese, but feel free to use any *plain/unflavored* vegan cream cheese you prefer.

** Vegan buttery spreads or vegan butter sticks will both work fine.

*** Sift the icing sugar before use if necessary.

make it nut-free

Use nut-free vegan cream cheese, non-dairy milk, and vegan butter.

make it soy-free

Use soy-free vegan cream cheese, non-dairy milk, and vegan butter.

vegan • nut-free option • soy-free option • advance prep required • kid-friendly • freezer-friendly • on the glow

Chocolate-Coconut Zucchini Bundt Cake

makes 1 (10-inch/25 cm) bundt, serves 13 • prep time: 45 minutes
total time: 1½ hours, plus chilling and cooling time

How on earth do I make this decadent Chocolate-Coconut Zucchini Bundt Cake, with its rich cocoa and chopped chocolate, so incredibly moist? Believe it or not, I use shredded zucchini and applesauce in the batter. They've always rendered my quick breads so tender without anyone being the wiser, and I love the added nutrition they lend, so why not put them to work in an actual cake? The combo of creamy coconut milk, pure vanilla, cocoa, and melted chocolate (you can spot the little pockets of gooey melted chocolate chunks when you slice the cake!) makes every bite heavenly. If that wasn't enough, each slice is drizzled generously with my luxurious, deeply chocolaty Chocolate-Coconut Glaze (page 295), dolloped with cloud-like vanilla-scented Coconut Whipped Cream (page 315), and scattered with crunchy chopped green pistachios, making it both festive and gorgeous enough for any gathering (or mega chocolate craving).

1. Chill the can of coconut milk in the fridge for at least 12 hours so the cream can solidify.

2. Position a rack in the center of the oven and preheat to 350°F (180°C). Grease a 10-inch (3 L) nonstick bundt pan with oil.

3. Open the chilled can of coconut milk and scoop out *just* 3 tablespoons of the solid white cream from the top into a small bowl, leaving the coconut water behind (you'll need what's left in the can for step 4). Set aside the bowl of coconut cream to use in the chocolate glaze.

4. Prepare the Wet Ingredients: Pour the remaining contents of the can of coconut milk (both the coconut cream and water) into a small pot. Gently heat over medium-low heat until smooth and melted, about 1 minute. Remove from the heat and stir to combine.

Wet Ingredients

1 (14-ounce/398 mL) can full-fat coconut milk, chilled for at least 12 hours*

3 tablespoons ground flaxseed

1 cup (252 g) natural cane sugar

½ cup grapeseed oil**

½ cup unsweetened applesauce

1½ teaspoons pure vanilla extract

1 large zucchini (275 g), trimmed and grated on the large holes of a box grater (2 cups lightly packed/216 g)

Dry Ingredients

2 cups (276 g) all-purpose flour***

½ cup + 2 tablespoons (60 g) unsweetened cocoa powder

2 teaspoons baking powder

1 teaspoon baking soda

½ teaspoon fine sea salt

1 (90 g) bar non-dairy dark or milk chocolate, chopped into pea-size pieces

For assembly

1 batch Coconut Whipped Cream (page 315)

1 batch Chocolate-Coconut Glaze (page 295)

2 teaspoons icing sugar (optional)****

1 cup (140 g) raw pistachios, finely chopped*****

recipe continues

storage

Store unglazed cake in an airtight container in the fridge for up to 4 days or in the freezer for up to 2 months.

tips

* Be sure to use canned coconut milk with guar gum (or other gum) to ensure success; check the ingredient list (see "Pantry Staples," page 342).

**Refined coconut oil can be used instead of grapeseed oil. Gently heat it until melted and ensure all of your ingredients are at room temperature to prevent the oil from solidifying when you mix the batter.

*** I suggest weighing the flour for the most accurate results. If you don't have a kitchen scale, use the *scoop-and-shake-until-level* method (see "Measuring Flour," page 29).

**** Sift the icing sugar before use if necessary.

***** Out of pistachios? Walnuts work well in a pinch!

make it nut-free

Simply omit the pistachios and use nut-free vegan butter in the Chocolate-Coconut Glaze.

make it soy-free

Use soy-free vegan butter such as Melt Organic Buttery Spread or Earth Balance Soy-Free Buttery Sticks in the Chocolate-Coconut Glaze, and use soy-free chocolate in both the cake and the glaze.

5. To a large bowl, add 1 cup of the melted coconut milk (save any leftover milk for another use) and the ground flaxseed. Whisk to combine. Let sit for a few minutes to thicken slightly.

6. To the coconut milk mixture, add the cane sugar, grapeseed oil, applesauce, and vanilla. Whisk to combine.

7. Lay a clean kitchen towel on the counter and cover it with 10 to 15 pieces of paper towel to create a thick absorbent layer. Spread the grated zucchini out onto the paper towel. Fold the towel to cover it. Press down firmly all over the zucchini to absorb as much water as you can. If the towels become too wet, switch to fresh paper towels and repeat the process (or simply use another absorbent kitchen towel). Stir the grated zucchini into the wet mixture.

8. Mix the Dry Ingredients: In a medium bowl, whisk together the flour, cocoa powder, baking powder, baking soda, and salt. Spoon the dry ingredients over the wet ingredients and whisk just until the batter is smooth and no dry patches remain. Fold the chopped chocolate into the batter.

9. Spoon the batter into the prepared bundt pan and spread evenly with a spatula.

10. Bake the Cake: Bake, uncovered, for 45 to 55 minutes (I bake for 50 minutes), until the cake slowly springs back when lightly pressed in the center. Transfer the pan to a cooling rack and let cool for 30 to 45 minutes, until it no longer feels warm to the touch. Carefully invert the pan over the cooling rack and tap the bottom to dislodge the cake. Let sit until completely cooled.

11. Prepare the Coconut Whipped Cream and Chocolate-Coconut Glaze.

12. Assemble: Once the cake is completely cooled, sift the icing sugar (if using) over the cake (or you can leave it plain). Slice and plate the cake (1½-inch/4 cm thick slices will yield about 13 servings). Top each slice with a drizzle of glaze (about 1 generous tablespoon) and a generous dollop of coconut whipped cream (about 1 heaping tablespoon). Top each with 1 to 2 teaspoons of chopped pistachios. (Alternatively, you can drizzle glaze over the entire cake and sprinkle the top with pistachios (as shown in the photo) before slicing and serving. If you have leftover glaze, simply serve it at the table for anyone who wants a little extra chocolate decadence.)

vegan • gluten-free • nut-free option • soy-free option • grain-free • advance prep required • kid-friendly • on the glow • one pot

Chocolate-Coconut Glaze

makes 1¼ scant cups • prep time: 7 minutes • total time: 7 minutes, plus chilling time

Calling all chocolate lovers! This lush Chocolate-Coconut Glaze is made by melting semi-sweet chocolate with thick coconut cream for a smooth, ganache-like texture. A bit of butter creates extra richness and a beautiful glossy finish. Cocoa powder deepens the chocolate flavor, while vanilla adds a soft, rounded note. Sweetened with icing sugar, it strikes a balance that lets the chocolate shine. I love it poured over my Chocolate-Coconut Zucchini Bundt Cake (page 293) or Vanilla Buttermilk Loaf Cake (page 301). Leftovers? Drizzle them over vegan ice cream—or chill it in the fridge until spoonably fudgy.

1 (14-ounce/398 mL) can full-fat coconut milk, chilled for at least 12 hours*

3 tablespoons vegan buttery spread

¾ cup (135 g) semi-sweet chocolate chips

2 tablespoons (12 g) unsweetened cocoa powder

1 tablespoon + 2 teaspoons oat milk**

½ teaspoon pure vanilla extract

Pinch of fine sea salt, or to taste

½ to ¾ cup (62 to 95 g) icing sugar, to taste***

1. Chill the can of coconut milk in the fridge for at least 12 hours so the cream can solidify.
2. Open the chilled can of coconut milk and scoop out *just* 3 tablespoons of the solid white cream from the top into a small pot, leaving the coconut water behind. (Store the remaining contents of the can in an airtight container in the fridge for another use.)
3. To the pot with the coconut cream, add the butter and chocolate chips. Melt over low heat, stirring frequently, until smooth, 3 to 6 minutes. Be careful not to burn the mixture. Remove from the heat.
4. Add the cocoa powder, oat milk, vanilla, salt, and icing sugar. Whisk for 30 to 45 seconds, until very smooth and silky.

make it nut-free

Use nut-free vegan butter.

make it soy-free

Use soy-free vegan butter and soy-free chocolate chips, such as the Enjoy Life brand.

storage

Store in an airtight container in the fridge for up to 2 weeks. The glaze will solidify when chilled. Return the glaze to a liquid state by gently warming it in a pot over low heat for a couple of minutes, stirring until liquid.

tips

* Be sure to use canned coconut milk with guar gum (or other gum) to ensure success; check the ingredient list (see "Pantry Staples," page 342).

** You can use unsweetened or sweetened oat milk, and vanilla-flavored or plain.

*** Sift the icing sugar before use if necessary.

vegan • advance prep required • kid-friendly • freezer-friendly

Triple-Layer Mocha Fudge Torte

makes 1 (8-inch/20 cm) torte, serves 8 • prep time: 45 minutes
total time: 45 minutes, plus soaking and chilling time

This decadent, impressive dessert looks fancy but is actually simple to make. Velvety smooth and rich mocha and chocolate layers are flavored with coffee and cocoa powders and rest on a dark chocolate–coffee cookie crust. The coffee throughout adds a deep dimension to the flavors. I decorate the top with a simple chocolate ganache sprinkled with crunchy chopped pecans or roasted cashews. This deeply luxurious torte literally melts in your mouth . . . I serve this dessert at get-togethers and it's always the star of the show! If you love a chocolaty, caramelly, and dreamy indulgence after a meal or on a special occasion, this torte is for you. This torte can even be fully made and kept in the freezer for up to a month before serving, perfect to make ahead for an occasion. You can serve the torte straight from the fridge for a soft, mousse-like texture, or serve it firm and cold from the freezer (after a gentle counter thaw). Either way, it's a crowd-pleaser!

Crust

2½ cups (215 g) mini chocolate graham crackers*

⅓ cup (72 g) vegan buttery spread, melted

1 teaspoon finely ground fresh coffee beans

3 teaspoons non-dairy milk, or as needed

Two Mocha Layers

1½ cups (201 g) raw cashews, soaked

½ cup virgin coconut oil, melted

½ cup + 2 tablespoons pure maple syrup

½ cup canned coconut cream**

¼ cup non-dairy milk

2 teaspoons instant coffee powder***

2 teaspoons pure vanilla extract

¼ teaspoon fine sea salt

3 tablespoons (18 g) unsweetened cocoa powder

3 tablespoons pure maple syrup

Chocolate Ganache Layer and assembly

¼ cup canned coconut cream**

1 teaspoon virgin coconut oil

½ cup (90 g) semi-sweet chocolate chips

¼ cup (29 g) raw pecan halves or roasted cashews, chopped****

1. Place the cashews in a small bowl and add boiling water to cover. Soak for 1 hour, then drain. (If using a high-speed blender, you can reduce the soaking time to 10 minutes.)

2. Position a rack in the center of the oven and preheat to 350°F (180°C). Lightly grease an 8-inch (2 L) round springform pan. Line the bottom of the pan with a piece of parchment paper cut to fit. (Alternatively, you can use an 8-inch/1.2 L round cake pan, lightly greased and lined with parchment paper, allowing excess paper to hang over each side for easy removal.)

3. Make the Crust: In a large heavy-duty food processor, process the chocolate graham crackers until coarsely chopped, 5 to 20 seconds. Add the melted butter and ground coffee and process again until combined, about 10 seconds. Add the milk, a teaspoon at a time, and process until the mixture is the consistency of wet sand. It should easily hold together when pressed between your fingers. Remove 2 tablespoons of the crust mixture and refrigerate in an airtight container for later.

recipe continues

storage

Store in an airtight container in the fridge for up to 6 days or in the freezer for up to 1 month.

tips

* I use Annie's organic chocolate-flavored Bunny Grahams, but you can use any brand of graham crackers you enjoy. Vanilla- or honey-flavored grahams work well too. Just be sure to use the same weight (215 g) for recipe accuracy.

** From 1 (14-ounce/398 mL) can of coconut cream. Alternatively, you can use 1 (14-ounce/398 mL) can of full-fat coconut milk, chilled in the fridge for at least 12 hours; spoon the solid cream from the top and save the remaining contents of the can for another use. Be sure to use canned coconut milk with guar gum (or other gum) to ensure success; check the ingredient list (see "Pantry Staples," page 342).

*** You can use an equal amount of finely ground fresh coffee beans instead.

**** I slightly prefer pecans over roasted cashews, but both work well.

4. Crumble the remaining crust mixture evenly over the bottom of the prepared pan and press it down firmly into a packed, even layer covering the entire base. It will look oily, but this will absorb while baking. Prick the crust 12 or 13 times with a fork to allow the air to escape while baking.

5. Bake the Crust: Bake uncovered, for 13 to 15 minutes (I bake for 14 minutes), until semi-firm to the touch. Transfer to a cooling rack and let cool for 5 minutes.

6. Meanwhile, make the two Mocha Layers. For the cream-colored layer: To a blender, add the drained cashews, melted coconut oil, ½ cup plus 2 tablespoons of maple syrup, coconut cream (leaving any coconut water behind, and setting aside the remaining coconut cream for the ganache layer), milk, instant coffee powder, vanilla, and salt. Blend on high speed for at least 1 minute, until the mixture is super smooth. Pour 1⅓ cups of the mixture into a small bowl, cover, and set aside.

7. Make the Second Mocha Layer: To the remaining mixture in the blender jar, add the cocoa powder and 3 tablespoons of maple syrup. Blend on high speed for 15 to 30 seconds, until smooth.

8. Fill the Crust and Chill: Pour the chocolate mixture in an even layer over the semi-cooled crust, using a spatula to scoop out every last bit. Freeze, uncovered, on a level surface for 50 to 60 minutes, until it's mostly firm to the touch—the chocolate layer doesn't need to be frozen *solid*, just firm enough for the second layer to sit on top of it.

9. Pour the cream-colored mixture over the frozen chocolate layer. Freeze again, uncovered, on a level surface for 4½ to 5½ hours, until solid.

10. Once frozen, make the Chocolate Ganache Layer: In a small pot, heat the coconut cream (leaving any coconut water behind) and coconut oil over medium heat until fully melted and smooth. Remove from the heat and stir in the chocolate chips until melted, 1 to 2 minutes.

11. Finish and Serve: Slide a butter knife around the inside of the pan to loosen the torte, then remove the sides from the springform pan (or, if using a cake pan, use the parchment paper overhang to lift the torte out of the pan). Carefully lift the torte onto a large plate. (You can leave the torte on the springform base, if preferred.) Spoon the ganache over the top of the torte, leaving about 1 inch (2.5 cm) around the edges without ganache. Immediately scatter the pecans (or cashews) and the reserved 2 tablespoons of crust mixture over the ganache. Return the torte to the freezer, uncovered, for 5 to 10 minutes, until the ganache layer is firm.

12. Let the torte sit on the counter for 10 to 15 minutes so it's easier to slice. Run a sharp knife under hot water for a minute or two, then wipe the blade dry. Slice the torte, slowly letting the hot knife slide through the top chocolate ganache layer, and wiping the knife between each slice. Serve immediately, or transfer the slices to an airtight container and chill in the fridge for 30 to 60 minutes to achieve a softer, mousse-like texture!

vegan • nut-free option • soy-free option • advance prep required • kid-friendly • freezer-friendly • on the glow

Vanilla Buttermilk Loaf Cake with Berries and Cream

makes 1 (9 x 5-inch/2 L) loaf, serves 8 • prep time: 25 minutes
total time: 55 minutes, plus chilling and cooling time

This sweet, moist-beyond-belief loaf cake, with its light tang from homemade buttermilk, is just heavenly, and when you pair it with lightly sweet and fluffy Coconut Whipped Cream (page 315) and sweet and juicy Simple Macerated Strawberries (page 303), it's a delightful little dessert or snack that everyone loves. The first time I made it, my daughter, Adriana, sat up straight in her chair and proclaimed, *"I hereby announce that this yummy, scrumptious loaf will be called Adriana's Favorite Loaf of All Time!"* Could she be any cuter?! If you have a vanilla bean on hand, this loaf is lovely with fresh vanilla; simply scrape the seeds from one vanilla bean and add them to the recipe in place of the vanilla extract. To change it up, we like to dress up this humble loaf with my Vegan Cream Cheese Frosting (page 291) or drizzle it generously with my Chocolate-Coconut Glaze (page 295). So many options, so little time!

1 batch Simple Macerated Strawberries (page 303)

Vanilla Buttermilk Loaf Cake

1 cup unflavored and unsweetened non-dairy milk

1 tablespoon fresh lemon juice

⅓ cup canned coconut cream*

½ cup (104 g) vegan buttery spread

¾ cup (189 g) natural cane sugar

1 tablespoon pure vanilla extract

1¾ cups (265 g) all-purpose flour**

2 teaspoons baking powder

½ scant teaspoon fine sea salt

For assembly

1 batch Coconut Whipped Cream (page 315)

1. Make the Simple Macerated Strawberries up to 6 hours in advance.
2. Position a rack in the center of the oven and preheat to 350°F (180°C). Lightly grease a 9 x 5-inch (2 L) loaf pan.
3. Prepare the Cake Batter: In a small bowl, stir together the milk and lemon juice, and let sit for a few minutes. This makes vegan buttermilk.
4. Scoop out *just* ⅓ cup of coconut cream into a small pot, leaving any coconut water behind. Heat the coconut cream over low heat for 1 to 2 minutes, until melted. Remove from the heat and set aside.

recipe continues

storage

Store the cake, without toppings, in an airtight container in the fridge for up to 5 days or in the freezer for up to 1 month. If your loaf has been in the fridge longer than a couple of days and it starts to dry out, gently heat a slice in the microwave for 10 to 20 seconds to restore the moisture and tenderness. Serve with a fresh batch of Simple Macerated Strawberries, if desired.

tips

* From 1 (14-ounce/398 mL) can of coconut cream. Alternatively, you can use 1 (14-ounce/398 mL) can of full-fat coconut milk, chilled in the fridge for at least 12 hours; spoon the solid cream from the top and save the remaining contents of the can for another use. Be sure to use canned coconut milk with guar gum (or other gum) to ensure success; check the ingredient list (see "Pantry Staples," page 342).

** I suggest weighing the flour for the most accurate results. If you don't have a kitchen scale, use the *scoop-and-shake-until-level* method (see "Measuring Flour," page 29).

Don't have a loaf pan? This works well baked in a 9-inch (1.5 L) round cake pan.

make it nut-free

Use nut-free non-dairy milk and vegan buttery spread.

make it soy-free

Use soy-free non-dairy milk and vegan buttery spread, such as Melt Organic Buttery Spread.

5. To a large bowl, add the butter. Using a handheld mixer, beat on medium speed until smooth and fluffy, about 30 seconds. Add the sugar and beat on low, gradually increasing the speed to medium, for about 15 seconds total, until combined. Add the vanilla, melted coconut cream, and buttermilk and beat again for 10 to 15 seconds, until combined. The mixture will look separated because of the vegan buttermilk, but this is normal.

6. In a medium bowl, whisk together the flour, baking powder, and salt until combined. Gradually add the flour mixture to the wet ingredients while beating on low speed for 15 to 25 seconds, until just combined. Avoid overmixing the batter.

7. Spoon the batter into the prepared loaf pan and spread evenly.

8. Bake the Cake: Bake, uncovered, for 45 to 55 minutes, until golden around the edges, the loaf slowly springs back when lightly pressed in a few places, and a toothpick inserted into the center comes out clean.

9. Transfer the pan to a cooling rack and let cool for 30 minutes. Transfer the pan to the fridge, uncovered, until completely cool, about 45 minutes.

10. Meanwhile, prepare the Coconut Whipped Cream.

11. Assemble: Remove the loaf from the pan and slice. Top each slice with a generous dollop or two of whipped cream and ¼ cup of macerated strawberries.

vegan • gluten-free • nut-free • soy-free • grain-free • oil-free • raw/no bake • kid-friendly • one bowl

Simple Macerated Strawberries

makes 2 cups • prep time: 8 minutes • total time: 2 to 3 hours

This is an incredibly simple way to enhance the lovely flavor of strawberries and takes no longer than slicing a pint of berries. A bit of sugar sprinkled over top draws out their juices, forming a light syrup while the strawberries soften, and everything tastes a touch sweeter, lessening the berries' tartness, which can sometimes be off-putting when they're served alongside a sweet dessert. Serve these juicy macerated strawberries on top of my Vanilla Buttermilk Loaf Cake with Berries and Cream (page 301) for a delightful spring and summer treat. They are also delicious all on their own (my kids go wild for them!). If you have a vanilla bean on hand, stir in the seeds from one for a decadent strawberry-vanilla flavor.

1 pound (454 g) fresh strawberries
2 tablespoons natural cane sugar

storage

Store in an airtight container in the fridge for up to 2 days.

1. Hull the strawberries. Thinly slice the berries, ⅛- to ¼-inch (3 to 5 mm) thick, or chop them into small pieces (you should have about 3½ cups). Place the berries in a large bowl.

2. Sprinkle the sugar over the berries and stir to combine. Cover the bowl with a lid or plastic wrap and let sit on the counter for 2 to 3 hours, until the juices release and the strawberries soften and sweeten. If desired, strain the juices before serving.

vegan • gluten-free • soy-free option • grain-free • raw/no bake • kid-friendly • freezer-friendly

Peanut Butter Cup No-Bake Brownies

makes 16 brownies • prep time: 25 minutes • total time: 35 minutes, plus chilling time

What could be better than the combo of chocolate, peanut butter, maple, and sea salt? Not much, my friends. My delicious no-bake and flour-free brownies are topped with an irresistible "peanut butter cup" topping—you'll wonder how you ever lived without these! With all the healthy fats and protein from the nuts and peanut butter, and the iron and fiber from the dates, you can't go wrong savoring these chocolaty, melt-in-your-mouth delights any time of day. I always sprinkle some chopped walnuts and flaky sea salt over top for the best crunch and salty-sweet flavor. We all love the snappy texture of the top chocolate layer and how it accents the chewy, softer brownie base and creamy "cookie-dough-like" peanut butter middle. If you have a pastry roller, I recommend using it to get the layers even and smooth, but rest assured, simply using your hands works great, too.

Brownie Layer

1½ cups packed (286 g) pitted Medjool dates*

¾ cup (75 g) raw walnut halves

6 tablespoons (59 g) raw whole almonds

3½ tablespoons (21 g) unsweetened cocoa powder

1 tablespoon icing sugar**

¾ teaspoon pure vanilla extract

⅛ teaspoon fine sea salt, or to taste

1 to 2 teaspoons water, if needed

Peanut Butter Cup Layer

½ cup + 3 tablespoons smooth natural peanut butter

2 tablespoons coconut oil, at room temperature

2 tablespoons vegan buttery spread

½ cup + 2½ tablespoons (81 g) icing sugar**

1 tablespoon pure maple syrup***

⅛ teaspoon fine sea salt

Chocolate Topping

1 cup (180 g) semi-sweet chocolate chips

1 teaspoon coconut oil

⅓ to ½ cup (35 to 50 g) raw walnut halves or roasted peanuts, chopped (optional)

Large-flake sea salt, such as Maldon, to taste (optional)****

1. Line an 8-inch (2 L) square cake pan with a piece of parchment paper cut to fit the width of the pan, with a few inches of overhang on each side for easy removal.
2. Make the Brownie Layer: To a large heavy-duty food processor, add the dates, walnuts, almonds, cocoa powder, icing sugar, vanilla, and salt. Process until finely chopped and the mixture starts to come together and can easily stick together when pressed between your fingers, 50 to 70 seconds. Avoid overprocessing or the mixture will release more oils. If it's too dry, add water, a teaspoon at a time, and process again until combined (I typically don't need to add any water, though).
3. Crumble or spread the brownie mixture over the bottom of the prepared pan. With your fingers, press down on the mixture until the base is evenly covered and smooth (if it's too sticky, first cover it with parchment paper), or use a pastry roller to roll it smooth. Transfer the pan, uncovered, to the fridge until ready to use.

recipe continues

storage

Store the brownies (as a slab or sliced into squares) in an airtight container in the fridge for up to 2 weeks or in the freezer for up to 2 months.

tips

* For best results, avoid using overly dried-out and hard Medjool dates and opt for soft, fresh ones.

** Sift the icing sugar before use if necessary.

*** Pure maple syrup is necessary for the peanut butter cup layer, as it makes the mixture "seize up" and thicken to the required texture. I don't recommend omitting it or swapping it for another liquid or dry sweetener.

**** Flaked sea salt, such as Maldon, is wonderful sprinkled on top for a salty-sweet contrast! I skip it for the kids' portions, but I love adding it for the adults.

make it soy-free

Use soy-free vegan chocolate chips, such as the Enjoy Life brand, as well as soy-free vegan buttery spread.

4. Meanwhile, make the Peanut Butter Cup Layer: To a large bowl, add the peanut butter, coconut oil, and butter. Using a handheld mixer, beat on medium speed until smooth, 20 to 30 seconds. Add the icing sugar, maple syrup, and salt and beat on low speed for 10 seconds, until the icing sugar is mostly incorporated, then increase to medium and beat until the mixture thickens into a rollable cookie dough texture, about 20 seconds. Crumble the mixture over the brownie layer and spread it out with your hands until smooth and level. If you have a pastry roller, roll the mixture until super smooth and even. Set aside on the counter.

5. Make the Chocolate Topping: In a medium pot, bring 1 to 2 inches (2.5 to 5 cm) of water to a simmer over medium-high heat. Combine the chocolate chips and coconut oil in a medium heatproof bowl and set it over the simmering water (there should be a gap between the water and the bowl). Heat the chocolate, stirring occasionally with a heatproof rubber spatula or wooden spoon, until most of the chocolate chips have melted, 1½ to 2½ minutes. Using an oven mitt, remove the bowl from the pot and stir until smooth.

6. Assemble and Chill: Pour the melted chocolate over the peanut butter layer and spread it out with the back of a spoon until it evenly coats the entire surface. Give the pan a few gentle shakes to help spread the topping out quickly and evenly. Immediately sprinkle on the walnuts (or roasted peanuts) and/or a sprinkle of large-flake sea salt (if using).

7. Transfer the pan to a level spot in the freezer and freeze, uncovered, for at least 30 minutes to allow the layers to firm up.

8. Serve: Once firm and ready to serve, lift the brownies from the pan and set the slab on a cutting board. If you froze them longer than 30 minutes, let the slab sit at room temperature for 10 to 15 minutes to soften slightly before slicing. Heat a very sharp knife in boiling water for a minute. (This will help the knife slide through the firm chocolate. You can skip this step if you don't mind the chocolate topping cracking.) Slice into 16 squares, slowly letting the blade melt through the top chocolate layer.

vegan • nut-free option • soy-free option • advance prep required • kid-friendly • freezer-friendly • on the glow

Pumpkin Streusel Coffee Cake

makes 1 (8-inch/20 cm) square cake, serves 12 • prep time: 35 minutes
total time: 1 hour 30 minutes, plus cooling time

This cozy cake shakes up traditional coffee cake by using warming pumpkin pie spices, fiber-packed pumpkin purée, and crunchy chopped pecans, and of course it's vegan by doing away with eggs, cow's milk, and dairy-based butter. It's one of my go-to desserts when having friends over in the fall or winter for coffee and tea, because adults and kids alike rave about it. The cake is incredibly soft and tender, and its melt-in-your-mouth texture is contrasted by a buttery, crisp pumpkin pie spice streusel and a scattering of chopped pecans (the nuts are optional if you are not a fan). You can serve this plain or with a dollop of my autumn-scented Pumpkin Delight Coconut Whipped Cream (page 311), or I also love to whip up a simple glaze for drizzling over top made of melted vegan butter, non-dairy milk, and icing sugar. This cake works beautifully when using cake and pastry flour, but not to worry if you don't have any on hand, as all-purpose flour works just as well (be sure to see my Tips).

Pumpkin Pie Spice Streusel

¾ cup unpacked (116 g) brown sugar

1 tablespoon (6 g) pumpkin pie spice

½ cup + 1 tablespoon (72 g) cake and pastry flour*

4½ tablespoons (49 g) chopped vegan butter**

⅛ teaspoon fine sea salt

Coffee Cake

½ cup + 1 tablespoon unsweetened non-dairy milk***

1 tablespoon fresh lemon juice

3 tablespoons water

2 tablespoons ground flaxseed

¾ cup (189 g) natural cane sugar

⅓ cup (72 g) vegan buttery spread****

½ cup unsweetened pumpkin purée

1 tablespoon pure vanilla extract

1 tablespoon pure maple syrup

1½ cups (186 g) cake and pastry flour*

1½ teaspoons baking powder

1 teaspoon pumpkin pie spice

½ scant teaspoon fine sea salt

For assembly

1 batch Pumpkin Delight Coconut Whipped Cream (page 311; optional)

½ cup (58 g) raw pecan halves, chopped (optional)

1. Position a rack in the center of the oven and preheat to 350°F (180°C). Lightly grease the bottom and sides of an 8-inch (2 L) square cake pan. Line with parchment paper, allowing excess paper to hang over each side for easy removal.

2. Prepare the Pumpkin Pie Spice Streusel: In a medium bowl, stir together the brown sugar, pumpkin pie spice, flour, butter, and salt. Using clean, dry hands, pinch the mixture together until the butter mixes with the dry ingredients and small clumps form, 1 to 2 minutes. It should resemble wet sand, and there shouldn't be any flour at the bottom of the bowl. Set aside.

3. Make the Coffee Cake: In a small bowl, stir together the milk and lemon juice, and let sit for a few minutes. This makes vegan buttermilk.

recipe continues

storage

Store in an airtight container in the fridge for up to 3 days or in the freezer for up to 1 month.

tips

* All-purpose white flour can be swapped for the cake and pastry flour: simply use ½ cup plus 1 tablespoon (83 g) for the streusel and 1½ cups (216 g) for the cake batter. I suggest weighing the flour for best results. If you don't have a kitchen scale, use the *scoop-and-shake-until-level* method (see "Measuring Flour," page 29).

** I recommend using 4½ tablespoons of a vegan butter stick or Melt Organic Buttery Spread for the streusel topping. Becel Vegan does not work—it makes the mixture too wet and sticky.

*** This recipe has been tested using unsweetened soy milk and almond milk. Be sure that your non-dairy milk contains a binder, such as xanthan gum or guar gum, as it will help the cake hold together.

**** I use Melt Organic Buttery Spread for the cake batter.

make it nut-free

Omit the optional pecans and use a nut-free non-dairy milk and vegan butter.

make it soy-free

Use soy-free vegan buttery spread and non-dairy plant milk.

4. In a large bowl, stir together the water and ground flaxseed, and let sit for a couple of minutes.

5. To the flax mixture, add the sugar, butter, pumpkin purée, vanilla, and maple syrup. Using a handheld mixer, beat on low speed, gradually increasing to medium, for 45 to 60 seconds total, until smooth and combined.

6. Add the buttermilk and beat on low speed just until combined, about 10 seconds. The mixture will appear curdled because of the buttermilk, but this is normal.

7. In a medium bowl, whisk together the flour, baking powder, pumpkin pie spice, and salt. Sprinkle the flour mixture into the bowl with the wet ingredients, ½ cup or so at a time, while beating on low speed, until all the flour is incorporated and the batter is smooth. Avoid overmixing.

8. Spoon half of the batter (a generous 1½ cups) evenly into the prepared pan. Scatter half of the streusel (about ⅔ cup) evenly over the batter.

9. Spread the remaining cake batter evenly over the streusel until completely covered. This part is a bit tricky, as the streusel can start pulling up, but just go slowly and it'll be fine. Evenly scatter the remaining streusel over the batter.

10. Bake the Cake: Bake, uncovered, for 42 to 52 minutes (I bake for 44 minutes), until the cake slowly springs back when lightly pressed in a few places and a toothpick inserted into the center comes out clean.

11. Cool the cake in the pan on a cooling rack for 45 minutes. Transfer the pan to the fridge and chill, uncovered, for at least 30 to 45 minutes. Lift the cake from the pan and slice into squares.

12. Finish and Assemble: Meanwhile, prepare the Pumpkin Delight Coconut Whipped Cream (if using) and chop the pecans (if using). Plate each slice and top each with a generous dollop of whipped cream and a teaspoon of chopped pecans, if desired.

Cuisinart

vegan • gluten-free • nut-free • soy-free • grain-free • oil-free • raw/no bake • advance prep required
kid-friendly • freezer-friendly • on the glow • one bowl

Pumpkin Delight Coconut Whipped Cream

makes 1½ generous cups • prep time: 10 minutes • total time: 10 minutes, plus chilling time

I just love coconut whipped cream . . . on top of frozen treats, ice cream, baked desserts, and oatmeal, or even on a spoon. During one of my annual pumpkin pie spice kicks, I decided to add pumpkin pie spice to my usual coconut whipped cream, then blended in a bit of pumpkin purée. Wow! These flavors elevate our humble but heavenly Coconut Whipped Cream (page 315) into an autumnal delight. You'll want to dollop this Pumpkin Delight Coconut Whipped Cream on just about everything, but especially on top of my Pumpkin Streusel Coffee Cake (page 307); they go together like sweaters and falling leaves.

1 cup canned coconut cream, chilled for at least 12 hours*

3 tablespoons unsweetened pumpkin purée

3 tablespoons (23 g) icing sugar, or more to taste**

2 tablespoons pure maple syrup

¾ to 1 teaspoon pumpkin pie spice, to taste

Smidgen of fine sea salt

1. Chill the can of coconut cream in the fridge for at least 12 hours. About 1 hour before whipping the cream, chill a large bowl in the freezer (this helps the cream stay cold while you beat it).
2. Make the Whipped Cream: Scoop 1 cup of the solid white coconut cream into the chilled bowl, making sure to leave the coconut water in the can.
3. Using a handheld mixer, beat the cream on medium-high speed until fluffy and smooth, 15 to 30 seconds.
4. Add the pumpkin purée, icing sugar, maple syrup, pumpkin pie spice, and salt. Beat on low, gradually increasing the speed to medium, for 15 to 30 seconds total, until smooth and combined. Taste and adjust the sugar and pumpkin pie spice, if needed.
5. Cover and refrigerate the whipped cream until ready to use.

storage

Store in an airtight container in the fridge for up to 1 week or in the freezer for up to 1 month. After storing in the fridge or freezer, let sit at room temperature until it softens slightly, then rewhip if needed.

tips

* Use 1 (14-ounce /398 mL) can of coconut cream or 1 to 2 (14-ounce/398 mL) cans of full-fat coconut milk and refrigerate the cans for at least 12 hours. Be sure to use canned coconut milk with guar gum (or other gum) to ensure success; check the ingredient list (see "Pantry Staples," page 342).

** Sift the icing sugar before use if necessary.

vegan • nut-free option • soy-free • kid-friendly • freezer-friendly • on the glow

Let It Glow Upside-Down Pear Spice Cake

makes 1 (8-inch/1.2 L) round cake, serves 6 to 8 • prep time: 20 minutes
total time: 65 minutes, plus cooling time

My modern spin on this century-old recipe uses applesauce and pure maple syrup for moisture and sweetness. I've heightened the lovely pear flavor with cinnamon, ground ginger, and cardamom for the perfect seasonal twist, and it's vegan, too, of course! My Let It Glow Upside-Down Pear Spice Cake is also quite fluffy—not white cake fluffy, but unexpectedly light and airy for a wholesome vegan cake. Unlike most sickly-sweet upside-down cakes, mine is lightly sweet, so it won't leave you feeling weighed down, and thanks to the unsweetened applesauce—which acts as an oil replacement and natural sweetener—it needs only a touch of oil. I highly recommend serving it with a big dollop of Coconut Whipped Cream (page 315) on top. It's a wonderful and simple cake to enjoy all fall and winter long, and if it's a warm fall day where you are, serve it à la mode with a scoop of vegan vanilla ice cream for a cooling treat. Dare I say some of us have even enjoyed this cake for breakfast? Oh yes, we sure have!

Dry Ingredients

- 1½ cups (185 g) white/light spelt flour*
- 1 tablespoon arrowroot starch
- 2 teaspoons cinnamon
- 2 teaspoons ground ginger
- 1 teaspoon baking soda
- ½ teaspoon baking powder
- ½ teaspoon ground cardamom
- ½ teaspoon fine sea salt

Wet Ingredients

- 2 large ripe Bartlett pears (400 g total)
- ¾ cup pure maple syrup, divided
- 1¼ cups + 2 tablespoons unsweetened applesauce
- 3 tablespoons grapeseed oil**
- 1 tablespoon fresh lemon juice
- 1 teaspoon pure vanilla extract

For assembly

- Coconut Whipped Cream (page 315; optional, but recommended)
- Cinnamon (optional)
- Toasted chopped pecans (optional)

1. Position a rack in the center of the oven and preheat to 350°F (180°C). Lightly grease the bottom and sides of an 8-inch (1.2 L) round nonstick cake pan. Line the bottom of the pan with parchment paper cut to fit.
2. Mix the Dry Ingredients: In a large bowl, whisk together the spelt flour, arrowroot, cinnamon, ginger, baking soda, baking powder, cardamom, and salt until combined.
3. Prep the Pears: Peel, quarter, and core the pears. Slice lengthwise into ¼-inch (5 mm) thick slices.

recipe continues

storage

Store, wrapped with plastic wrap or foil or in an airtight container, in the fridge for up to 3 days or in the freezer for up to 2 months.

tips

* If you don't have white/light spelt flour on hand, you can swap it for an equal amount of whole-grain spelt flour. I suggest weighing the flour for the most accurate result. If you don't have a kitchen scale, use the *scoop-and-shake-until-level* method (see "Measuring Flour," page 29).

** Virgin coconut oil can be used instead of grapeseed oil. Gently heat it until melted and ensure all of your ingredients are at room temperature to prevent it from solidifying when you mix the batter.

Don't use a springform cake pan, as the maple sauce will leak onto the oven floor. (I speak from experience. Oh, what a disaster that was!) A 9-inch (1.5 L) round cake pan will work in lieu of an 8-inch (1.2 L) round pan, but the cake will have less height than the one shown in the photo.

make it nut-free

Omit the pecans.

4. Arrange the slices of pear in the prepared pan until the base of the pan is covered (I like to make a circular pattern fanning out like a flower). Be sure to cover as much of the base with slices as possible to prevent the batter spreading them out during baking. (Dice any leftover slices of pear and use as a garnish, along with the Coconut Whipped Cream, if using. Or just snack on them!)
5. Pour ¼ cup of the maple syrup evenly over the pears.
6. Mix the remaining Wet Ingredients: In a medium bowl, stir together the applesauce, remaining ½ cup maple syrup, grapeseed oil, lemon juice, and vanilla until combined.
7. Pour the wet mixture over the dry mixture and stir until just combined and no dry patches remain. Be careful not to overmix. Carefully spoon the batter over the pears. The cake pan will be very full, but don't worry!
8. Bake the Cake: Bake, uncovered, for 38 to 48 minutes (I bake for 42 minutes), until the cake slowly springs back when lightly pressed and a toothpick inserted into the center comes out clean. There will likely be a crack or two on the surface.
9. Transfer the pan to a cooling rack to cool for 30 minutes.
10. While the cake cools, make the Coconut Whipped Cream (if using).
11. Finish and Serve: Run a butter knife around the edge of the pan to loosen the cake. Place a large plate upside down over the cake pan. Holding the plate firmly in place, carefully flip the pan over. Lightly tap the bottom of the pan to help release the cake. Once the cake releases onto the plate, lift away the pan and carefully peel off the parchment paper. Behold your beautiful upside-down cake! Serve warm with a dollop of Coconut Whipped Cream (if using), a sprinkle of cinnamon, diced leftover pear (if you have any), and chopped pecans (if using).

vegan • gluten-free • nut-free • soy-free • grain-free • advance prep required • kid-friendly
freezer-friendly • one bowl

Coconut Whipped Cream

makes 1¼ cups • prep time: 5 minutes • total time: 5 minutes, plus chilling time

This luxurious vanilla-scented coconut whipped cream uses canned coconut cream. You can also use the cream from full-fat canned coconut milk, just be sure to use only the solid cream and not any of the coconut water in the can and ensure your can contains guar gum (or other gum) so it whips properly. A little icing sugar sweetens it just right without thinning the whipped cream, and I love adding pure vanilla and a hint of fine sea salt for a lightly sweet and fluffy dessert topper. Dollop it on top of my Vanilla Buttermilk Loaf Cake with Berries and Cream (page 301), Chocolate-Coconut Zucchini Bundt Cake (page 293), Cookies and Fudge Freezer Cake (page 319), or Let It Glow Upside-Down Pear Spice Cake (page 313). You can't go wrong serving it alongside fresh, in-season berries, either!

1 cup canned coconut cream, chilled for at least 12 hours*
3 tablespoons (23 g) icing sugar**
¼ teaspoon pure vanilla extract
Fine sea salt (optional)

1. Chill 1 (14-ounce/398 mL) can of coconut cream in the fridge for at least 12 hours. About 1 hour before whipping the cream, chill a large bowl in the freezer (this helps the cream stay cold while you beat it).
2. Make the Whipped Cream: Scoop 1 cup of the solid white coconut cream into the chilled bowl, making sure to leave the coconut water in the can.
3. Using a handheld mixer, beat the cream on medium-high speed until fluffy and smooth, 15 to 30 seconds.
4. Add the icing sugar, vanilla, and a tiny sprinkle of sea salt to taste (if using) and beat again on medium-high speed until smooth, 10 to 15 seconds.
5. Cover and refrigerate the whipped cream until ready to use.

storage

Store in an airtight container in the fridge for up to 1 week or in the freezer for up to 1 month. Before using, bring to room temperature until it softens slightly, then rewhip if needed.

tips

* Use 1 (14-ounce/398 mL) can of coconut cream or 1 to 2 (14-ounce/398 mL) cans of full-fat coconut milk and refrigerate the cans for at least 12 hours. Be sure to use a canned coconut milk with guar gum (or other gum) to ensure success; check the ingredient list (see "Pantry Staples," page 342).

** Sift the icing sugar before use if necessary.

vegan • gluten-free option • soy-free option • kid-friendly • on the glow

Pecan, Walnut, and Cinnamon Oatmeal Cookies

makes 14 cookies • prep time: 20 minutes • total time: 35 minutes

These nutty cookies are lightly crisp on the outside and chewy on the inside, with little crunchy bits from the pecans and walnuts. White/light spelt flour (or regular all-purpose flour—see my Tips) and quick-cooking oats provide a slightly sweet, wholesome flavor. Light brown sugar lends a toffee tone, and it's all rounded out with cinnamon both in the dough *and* sprinkled on top before baking. I couldn't choose between walnuts and pecans, so I did what all good bakers do and used both! Trust me when I say that if your household is anything like mine, these won't last long, so eat one while you can! A full batch of these delightful cookies adds crunch and bursting-with-cookies flavor to my decadent and creamy Cookies and Fudge Freezer Cake (page 319).

- 1 tablespoon ground flaxseed
- 2 tablespoons water
- ⅓ cup (72 g) vegan buttery spread*
- ½ cup (126 g) natural cane sugar
- 3 tablespoons packed (40 g) light brown sugar
- 1 teaspoon pure vanilla extract
- 1 cup + 2 tablespoons (138 g) white/light spelt flour**
- ½ cup (53 g) quick-cooking oats (not old-fashioned oats)
- 1 teaspoon cinnamon, plus more for dusting
- ½ teaspoon baking powder
- ¼ teaspoon baking soda
- ¼ + ⅛ teaspoon fine sea salt
- ½ cup (58 g) raw pecan halves, coarsely chopped
- ⅓ cup (33 g) raw walnut halves, coarsely chopped

1. Position a rack in the center of the oven and preheat to 350°F (180°C). Line a large baking sheet with parchment paper.
2. Make the Cookie Dough: In a large bowl, whisk together the ground flaxseed and water. Let it thicken for a couple of minutes while you gather the other ingredients.
3. To the flax mixture, add the butter, cane sugar, brown sugar, and vanilla. Using a handheld mixer, beat on medium-low speed until smooth, about 45 seconds.
4. In a medium bowl, whisk together the spelt flour, oats, cinnamon, baking powder, baking soda, and salt.
5. Add the dry ingredients to the wet ingredients and beat on low speed until just combined, with no flour patches remaining, 10 to 15 seconds.
6. Coarsely chop the pecans and walnuts into pea-size pieces. Stir the chopped nuts into the dough just until combined. (I like to knead and press the chopped nuts into the dough with my hands.) Be careful not to overmix the dough.

recipe continues

storage

Store completely cooled cookies in an airtight container at room temperature for up to 2 days. Unless using these cookies in the Cookies and Fudge Freezer Cake (page 319), freezing is not recommended, as it tends to dry them out.

tips

* I use Melt Organic Buttery Spread, but other vegan buttery spreads will work, such as Becel Vegan. Don't use vegan butter *sticks* in this recipe, or the cookies will puff up more and turn out underbaked in the center.

** Be sure to use white/light spelt flour and not whole spelt flour. Whole spelt flour doesn't work in this recipe, as it is too coarse and drying. If you prefer, you can replace the white/light spelt flour with ¾ cup (108 g) of all-purpose flour. I suggest weighing the flour for the most accurate result. If you don't have a kitchen scale, use the *scoop-and-shake-until-level* method (see "Measuring Flour," page 29).

make it gluten-free

Swap the white/light spelt flour for 1¼ cups (137 g) gluten-free oat flour and ½ cup (54 g) gluten-free almond flour (not almond meal). Use gluten-free quick-cooking oats. Bake for 9 to 12 minutes.

make it soy-free

Use soy-free vegan butter.

7. Scoop and Shape the Dough: Using a cookie scoop, spoon about 2 slightly heaping tablespoons of dough and form it into a ball, pressing the ball into any nuts that may have fallen to the bottom of the bowl and rolling the ball in your hands. Place the dough ball on the prepared baking sheet. Repeat, leaving 2 to 3 inches (5 to 8 cm) between each, until you have about 14 balls. If desired, sprinkle a dusting of cinnamon on top of the balls. There's no need to flatten them, as they will spread out while baking.

8. Bake the Cookies: Bake for 10 to 13 minutes (I bake for 12 minutes), until the cookies are spread out and *very* light golden on the bottom and top (they will still be quite pale in color). The cookies will be very delicate when they come out of the oven, but will firm as they cool. Allow the cookies to cool on the pan on a cooling rack for 10 minutes before digging in!

vegan • soy-free option • advance prep required • kid-friendly • freezer-friendly

Cookies and Fudge Freezer Cake

makes 1 (9 x 5-inch/2 L) cake, serves 12 • prep time: 50 minutes (includes cookies)
total time: 1½ hours, plus soaking and chilling time

Close your eyes and picture a fudgy, luxuriously creamy chocolate frozen dessert that has chunks of nutty, chewy baked cookies mixed throughout and cascading fluffy whipped cream over top. *No, you aren't dreaming!* This freezer cake has delightfully crunchy bites from my Pecan, Walnut, and Cinnamon Oatmeal Cookies (page 317), which are chopped and stirred into the rich chocolate mixture before it's frozen. For the chocolate base, I melt coconut cream, chocolate chips, and a little coconut oil, then blend it with soaked lightly sweet cashews and pure maple syrup, chocolaty cocoa powder, aromatic vanilla, and a hint of sea salt. The result? The most irresistible fudgy texture that everyone seems to lose their minds over (me included). After making the chocolate base, just stir in the chopped cookies, chill, and you've got yourself a dessert everyone will be talking about and requesting the recipe for! This is a great recipe to make ahead or simply keep on hand for those fudge-and-cookie cravings, since it stores in the freezer so well.

- 1⅓ cups (180 g) raw cashews
- 1 batch Pecan, Walnut, and Cinnamon Oatmeal Cookies (page 317)
- 1 cup canned coconut cream*
- ⅔ cup (120 g) semi-sweet chocolate chips
- 6 tablespoons coconut oil
- ½ cup + 2 tablespoons pure maple syrup
- ¼ cup (24 g) unsweetened cocoa powder
- 1 tablespoon pure vanilla extract
- ½ teaspoon fine sea salt
- Coconut Whipped Cream, for serving (page 315; optional)
- ¼ cup (34 g) chopped raw pecans or walnuts, for serving (optional)

1. Place the cashews in a small bowl and add boiling water to cover. Soak for 1 hour, then drain. (If you have a high-speed blender, you can get away with a 10-minute soak.)
2. Meanwhile, make the Pecan, Walnut, and Cinnamon Oatmeal Cookies. Pro tip: Bake the cookies at the upper limit of the bake time, as this will ensure they get a bit crispy after cooling, which is the perfect texture for this freezer cake. Cool the cookies for 15 minutes on the baking sheet, then transfer them to a plate and freeze for at least 20 minutes, or until frozen solid.
3. Grease a 9 x 5-inch (2 L) loaf pan and line with a piece of parchment paper cut to fit the width of the pan, with a few inches of overhang on each side for easy removal.

recipe continues

storage

Store leftovers in an airtight container in the freezer for up to 6 weeks.

tip

* From 1 (14-ounce/398 mL) can of coconut cream. Alternatively, you can use 1 or 2 (14-ounce/398 mL) cans of full-fat coconut milk chilled in the fridge for at least 12 hours. Be sure to use canned coconut milk with guar gum (or other gum) to ensure success; check the ingredient list (see "Pantry Staples," page 342).

make it soy-free

Use soy-free chocolate chips, and use soy-free vegan butter in the Pecan, Walnut, and Cinnamon Oatmeal Cookies.

4. Make the Fudge (while the cookies chill in the freezer): Scoop *just* 1 cup of the solid white coconut cream from the can into a small pot, leaving any coconut water behind. Add the chocolate chips and coconut oil and heat over low heat for 2 to 4 minutes, stirring frequently and breaking up the coconut cream with a spoon, until about three-quarters of the chocolate is melted. Remove from the heat and continue stirring until all the chocolate chips are melted and the mixture is completely smooth.

5. To a blender, add the melted chocolate mixture, drained cashews, maple syrup, cocoa powder, vanilla, and salt. Blend on high speed until super smooth and no bits of cashews remain, 45 to 75 seconds. Pour the chocolate mixture into a large bowl, using a silicone spatula to scoop out every last bit into the bowl.

6. Prepare the Freezer Cake: Chop the frozen cookies into 1-inch (2.5 cm) pieces. Set aside a large handful of chopped cookies for the topping. Stir the remaining chopped cookies into the chocolate mixture until the cookies are fully coated. Using the spatula, immediately scrape the mixture into the prepared loaf pan. Smooth it out evenly and scatter the reserved handful of chopped cookies all over the surface. Press down lightly. Place in the freezer on a level surface and freeze, uncovered, for at least 4 to 5 hours or overnight, until completely solid.

7. Meanwhile, make the Coconut Whipped Cream (if using).

8. Finish and Serve: Slide a butter knife around the cake to loosen it. Using the overhanging parchment paper, remove the cake from the pan and set it on a cutting board. Run a sharp knife under very hot water for a minute, then cut the cake into ¾-inch (2 cm) slices (or slice diagonally to create pretty triangles!). Plate each slice and top with a dollop of Coconut Whipped Cream and a teaspoon of chopped pecans or walnuts (if using).

a-to-z guide to recipes you can make ahead and all my tips!

In this section, I share all my tips and helpful hints for making my salads and desserts ahead, either partially or fully. If you ever find yourself craving a spectacular meal-worthy dish but wonder how to best fit it into your busy schedule, then this is just the section for you (and me)! A little secret: when I was super busy cooking and photographing each recipe in this cookbook (yes, I cooked, styled, and shot all the recipe photos myself!), I used this chapter to help me plan and make ahead every single one of my recipes. I can't emphasize enough just how helpful and handy this chapter is if you like to prep things ahead of time!

Bursting with helpful information, I share how recipe components can be made in advance and also how many days they can be made ahead (how's that for easy?), letting you spread out the work if needed. The number of days a sub-recipe can be made in advance takes into account its own storage duration and that of main recipe. For example, if a dressing stores for 7 days and the main dish stores for 3 days, the dressing can be made up to 4 days ahead so it's still fresh when you're enjoying leftovers on day 3. Be sure to read over each recipe's storage tips, as they often contain helpful information about how to revive flavors, such as perking up a stored quinoa salad with a squeeze of lemon or a drizzle of dressing and a sprinkle of salt and pepper. Also, please keep in mind that "prepare/make/cook and refrigerate," assumes the item is refrigerated in an airtight container or wrapped up. Sometimes, you'll see a suggestion to let one or more ingredients come to room temperature (such as for refrigerated uncooked chopped squash or pressed tofu that's been in the fridge), and this is simply to ensure that it cooks within the times given in the recipe (chilled components may require a longer cook time).

B

Backyard Barbecue Tofu and Jalapeño-Tomato Rice Salad (page 43)

Make and refrigerate the Sweet and Tangy No-Chop Barbecue Sauce (page 262; if using) and the Soy-Free Vegan Mayonnaise (page 265; if using) up to 5 days in advance. • Make and refrigerate the Lime and Sriracha Aioli (page 264; if using) up to 3 days in advance. • Press and refrigerate the tofu for the Crispy and Chewy Barbecue Tofu up to 1 day in advance. • Make and refrigerate the Glow Up Garden Guacamole (page 283; if using) up to 6 hours in advance (place in a bowl and cover the surface of the guacamole with plastic wrap to prevent air exposure).

To serve: Set the pressed tofu out on the counter for about 30 minutes, until the tofu is just about room temperature. • Cook the Crispy and Chewy Barbecue Tofu (page 187), bell peppers, and Savory Jalapeño-Tomato Rice (page 270), and prepare the remaining veggies as directed. • Assemble the salads.

Breaded Tofu Tender Salad with Barbecue Apple Cider Vinaigrette (page 79)

Make and refrigerate the Sweet and Tangy No-Chop Barbecue Sauce (page 262, if using) and the Soy-Free Vegan Mayonnaise (page 265; if using) up to 6 days in advance. • Make and refrigerate the Barbecue Apple Cider Vinaigrette (page 243) up to 4 days in advance. • Make and refrigerate the Crispy Breaded Tofu Tenders (page 185) up to 1 day in advance. (Alternatively, if you wish to bake the tofu tenders the same day, you can prepare and store the sauce coating in a small container and the breaded coating in a small container up to 1 day in advance, then simply prepare the tofu as directed the day of.)

To serve: Set the dressing and pressed tofu out on the counter for about 30 minutes, until the dressing is softened and the tofu is room temperature. • Prepare the veggies as directed. • Make the Crispy Breaded Tofu Tenders (page 185), following the storage and reheating instructions in the Storage Tip, if needed. • Assemble the salads.

Busy Bee Big Salad (page 69)

Make and refrigerate the Protein-Powered Cashew-Hemp Cheese (page 197) up to 5 days in advance. • Make and refrigerate the quinoa up to 2 days in advance, and your dressing of choice in advance (storage time is given in individual recipes).

To serve: Set the dressing out on the counter until softened. • Prepare the veggies as directed. • Reheat the quinoa, if desired. • Assemble the salads.

Butternut, Cranberry, and Rosemary-Maple Pecan and Walnut Arugula Salad (page 153)

Make the Rosemary, Maple, and Cayenne Roasted Pecans and Walnuts (page 209) up to 1 week in advance. • Make and refrigerate the Glowing House Vinaigrette (page 230) up to 5 days in advance. • Peel, halve, seed, and chop the squash and refrigerate 1 day in advance.

To serve: Set the dressing and squash out on the counter until room temperature. • Roast the squash as directed. • Assemble the salads.

Cinnamon Sweet Potato Wedge Salad with Sriracha Honey-Mustard Dressing (page 175)

Toast the pepitas up to 1 week in advance, if needed. • Make and refrigerate the Soy-Free Vegan Mayonnaise (page 265; if using) up to 6 days in advance. • Make and refrigerate the Vegan Feta Cheese (page 259; if using) up to 4 days in advance. • Make and refrigerate the Sriracha Honey-Mustard Dressing (page 242) up to 2 days in advance.

To serve: Set the dressing out on the counter until softened. • Cook the sweet potatoes. • Prepare the fresh veggies as directed. • Assemble the salads.

Cozy Potato, Zucchini, and Cannellini Bean Salad with Luxurious ACV and Dijon Dressing (page 147)

Make and refrigerate the Soy-Free Vegan Mayonnaise (page 265; if using) up to 1 week in advance. • Make and refrigerate the Luxurious ACV and Dijon Dressing (page 221) up to 3 days in advance.

To serve: Set the dressing out on the counter until softened. • Prepare and cook the potatoes, zucchini, and cannellini beans as directed. • Prepare the herbs, fresh veggies, and nuts. • Assemble the salads.

Cuddle Up Warm Pesto Dream Bowl (page 133)

Toast the pepitas up to 1 week in advance, if needed. • Make and refrigerate the Ultra-Creamy Flavor Burst Basil Pesto (page 257) up to 5 days in advance.

To serve: Revive the flavors of the pesto, as suggested in the Storage Tip, if needed, and set the pesto out on the counter to soften. • Cook the veggies in the roasted veggies section. • Prepare the salad veggies. • Assemble the salads.

Dreamy Barbecue Tofu and Roasted Green Bean Salad (page 57)

Toast the pepitas up to 1 week in advance, if needed. • Make and refrigerate the Sweet and Tangy No-Chop Barbecue Sauce (page 262; if using) up to 6 days in advance. • Cook and refrigerate the rice and press and refrigerate the tofu up to 1 day in advance.

To serve: Set the pressed tofu out on the counter for about 30 minutes, until room temperature. • Make the Crispy and Chewy Barbecue Tofu (page 187) and green beans and the Creamy Cashew, Garlic, and Lemon Dressing (page 240). • Prepare the remaining veggies as directed. • Reheat the rice. • Assemble the salads.

E

Easy Breezy Deconstructed Guacamole Salad (page 95)

Make and refrigerate the Quick-Pickled Spicy Lime Red Onions (page 276, see Variations) up to 1 week in advance. • Make and refrigerate the 6-Ingredient Shake-and-Glow Vinaigrette, Lime Variation (page 235) up to 5 days in advance.

To serve: Set the dressing out on the counter until softened. • Prepare the veggies. • Assemble the salads.

Edamame and Pistachio Soba Noodle Spinach Salad (page 99)

Toast the sesame seeds, if needed, up to 1 week in advance. • Make and refrigerate the Toasted Sesame, Tamari, and Garlic Dressing (page 219) and chop the pistachios up to 2 days in advance. • Thaw and refrigerate the edamame up to 1 day in advance.

To serve: Set the dressing out on the counter until softened. • Cook the noodles and prepare the veggies. • Assemble the salads.

F

Fall Crunch Farro Kale Salad (page 121)

Make and refrigerate The Crunch Nutty Protein Topper (page 211) and Glowing House Vinaigrette (page 230) up to 5 days in advance. • Make and refrigerate the Easy Garlic-Infused Farro (page 268) up to 3 days in advance. • Chop and refrigerate the kale up to 1 day in advance.

To serve: Set the dressing out on the counter until softened. • Prepare the celery and reheat the farro as suggested in the Storage Tip. • Assemble the salads.

Fiery 10-Spice Roasted Potato Salad (page 165)

Make the Community-Fave 10-Spice Mix (page 275) up to 1 week in advance. • Make and refrigerate the Creamy Cashew, Garlic, and Lemon Dressing (page 240) up to 1 day in advance.

To serve: Set the dressing out on the counter until softened. • Cook the potatoes and prepare the veggies and herbs. • Assemble the salads.

G

Glow Girl Kale Slaw (page 39)

Make and refrigerate the Sticky Roasted Tamari-Maple Almonds (page 203; if using) and the Soy-Free Vegan Mayonnaise (page 265; if using) up to 1 week in advance. • Make and refrigerate the Apple Cider, Shallot, Maple, and Dijon Vinaigrette (page 220) up to 5 days in advance. • Prepare and refrigerate the bulgur and kale up to 1 day in advance.

To serve: Set the dressing out on the counter until softened. • Prepare the veggies. • Stir the bulgur. • Assemble the salads.

Glow Up Pesto Dream Bowl (page 37)

Make and refrigerate the Ultra-Creamy Flavor Burst Basil Pesto (page 257) up to 6 days in advance. • Cook and refrigerate the farro up to 1 day in advance.

To serve: Revive the flavors of the pesto, as suggested in the Storage Tip, if needed, and set the pesto out on the counter to soften. • Prepare the veggies and reheat the farro. • Assemble the salads.

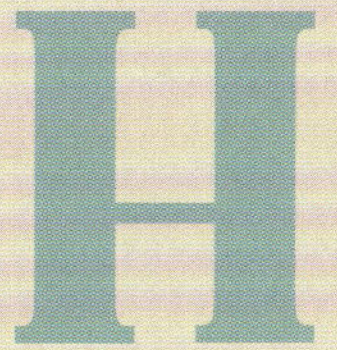

Harvest Roasted Carrot and Herb Salad (page 135)

Toast the pepitas up to 1 week in advance, if needed. • Make and refrigerate the Sweet and Tangy No-Chop Barbecue Sauce (page 262, if using) and the Soy-Free Vegan Mayonnaise (page 265; if using) up to 1 week in advance. • Make and refrigerate the Barbecue Apple Cider Vinaigrette (page 243) up to 5 days in advance. • Cook and refrigerate the quinoa up to 2 days in advance. • Chop and refrigerate the romaine up to 1 day in advance.

To serve: Set the dressing on the counter until softened. • Prepare and roast the carrots, and chop the herbs. • Reheat the quinoa. • Assemble the salads.

Herby Baked Green Bean and Potato Salad (page 169)

Toast the pepitas up to 1 week in advance, if needed. • Make the Garlic Lovers' Cashew Parmesan (page 281; if using) up to 5 days in advance. • Make and refrigerate the Grainy Mustard and Lemon Dressing (page 234) up to 4 days in advance.

To serve: Set the dressing out on the counter until softened. • Cook the potatoes and green beans. • Prepare the onions and herbs. • Assemble the salads.

Herby Couscous, Sun-Dried Tomato, and Chickpea Salad (page 75)

Toast the pine nuts up to 1 week in advance, if needed. • Make and refrigerate the Vegan Feta Cheese (page 259) and Herby Lemon and White Wine Vinaigrette (page 231) up to 4 days in advance. • Make and refrigerate the Lemon and Garlic Pearl Couscous (page 266) up to 1 day in advance.

To serve: Set the dressing out on the counter until softened. • Prepare the veggies and herbs. • Reheat the couscous, if desired, following the instructions in the Storage Tip. • Assemble the salads.

High-Protein No-Egg Egg Salad (page 81)

Make and refrigerate the Soy-Free Vegan Mayonnaise (page 265; if using) up to 5 days in advance. • Press and refrigerate the tofu up to 1 day in advance.

To serve: Prepare the tofu, veggies, and herbs. • Assemble the salads.

Magnificent Miso Salad (page 149)

Toast the pepitas up to 1 week in advance, if needed. • Press and refrigerate the tofu for the Shake-and-Bake Sesame-Crusted Tofu (page 195; if using) up to 1 day in advance. • Make and refrigerate the long-grain white or brown rice (if using) and the Miso, Maple, and Ginger Dressing (page 241) up to 1 day in advance.

To serve: Set the dressing and pressed tofu (if using) out on the counter for about 30 minutes, until the dressing is softened and the tofu is room temperature. • Make the Shake-and-Bake Sesame-Crusted Tofu (page 195; if using) or reheat the rice (if using). • Cook the sweet potatoes. • Prepare the veggies. • Assemble the salads.

Mile-High Warm Portobello Fajita Salad (page 59)

Make the Crispy Tortilla Strips (page 242; if using) and the Lime and Sriracha Aioli (page 264) up to 3 days in advance. • Make and refrigerate the chopped lettuce, sautéed vegetable mixture, and rice up to 1 day in advance. • Make and refrigerate the Glow Up Garden Guacamole (page 283) up to 6 hours in advance (place in a bowl and cover the surface of the guacamole with plastic wrap to prevent air exposure).

To serve: Reheat the sautéed vegetable mixture and rice. • Assemble the salads.

Minty Sesame, Lime, and Ginger Noodle Salad (page 105)

Make and refrigerate the Sesame, Lime, and Ginger Dressing (page 228) up to 4 days in advance. • Chop the pistachios up to 2 days in advance.

To serve: Set the dressing out on the counter until softened. • Cook the soba noodles. • Prepare the veggies. • Assemble the salads.

Mix-and-Glow Roasted Veg Orzo Salad (page 163)

Make and refrigerate the 6-Ingredient Shake-and-Glow Vinaigrette (page 235) up to 3 days in advance. • Press and refrigerate the tofu up to 1 day in advance. • Chop and refrigerate the bell peppers, jalapeño, and zucchini up to 1 day in advance.

To serve: Set the dressing, pressed tofu, and chopped veggies out on the counter for about 30 minutes, until the dressing is softened and the tofu and veggies are room temperature. • Cook the roasted mixture and cook the orzo. • Prepare the salad veggies and herbs. • Assemble the salads.

Nourishing Warm Brunch Salad Bowls (page 113)

Make the Rosemary, Maple, and Cayenne Roasted Pecans and Walnuts (page 209) up to 1 week in advance. • Make and refrigerate the Apple Cider, Shallot, Maple, and Dijon Vinaigrette (page 220) up to 5 days in advance.

To serve: Set the dressing out on the counter until softened. • Cook the potatoes. • Prepare the veggies and fruit. • Assemble the salads.

On the Glow Pasta Salad (page 107)

Make and refrigerate the Soy-Free Vegan Mayonnaise (page 265; if using) up to 6 days in advance.

• Make and refrigerate the Vegan Feta Cheese (page 259) up to 4 days in advance. • Make and refrigerate the Creamy ACV, Shallot, Maple, and Dijon Vinaigrette (page 233) up to 3 days in advance. • Cook and refrigerate the pasta up to 1 day in advance (I don't recommend making the pasta in advance if using a gluten-free or grain-free pasta, as they don't tend to store or reheat well).

To serve: Prepare the remaining veggies and herbs. • Assemble the salad jars or combine the ingredients in one large bowl, as desired.

P

Parsley, Sun-Dried Tomato, and Feta Quinoa Salad (page 63)

Make and refrigerate the Light and Floral Lemony Garlic Vinaigrette (page 238) up to 4 days in advance. • Make and refrigerate the Vegan Feta Cheese (page 259) up to 3 days in advance. • Cook and refrigerate the quinoa up to 1 day in advance.

To serve: Set the dressing out on the counter until softened. Prepare the veggies and herbs. • Assemble the salads.

R

Radiant Garden Side Salad (page 89)

Toast the pepitas up to 1 week in advance, if needed. • Make and refrigerate the Light and Floral Lemony Garlic Vinaigrette (page 238); or dressing of choice up to 5 days in advance (refer to the Storage Tip if making a different dressing). • Make and refrigerate the Protein-Powered Cashew-Hemp Cheese (page 197; if using) up to 4 days in advance. • Make the Easy Rustic Double Garlic Croutons (page 252; if using) up to 1 day in advance.

To serve: Set the dressing out on the counter until softened. • Reheat the croutons and prepare the veggies. • Assemble the salads.

Roasted Chickpea and Parm Romaine Crunch Salad (page 91)

Make and refrigerate the Garlic Lovers' Cashew Parmesan (page 281) up to 5 days in advance. • Make and refrigerate the Velvety Cashew Garlic Dressing (page 226) up to 3 days in advance.

To serve: Set the dressing out on the counter until softened. • Make the Garlic-Cayenne Roasted Chickpeas (page 202; if using). • Prepare the veggies. • Assemble the salads.

Roasted Vegetable Medley with Sun-Dried Tomato, Walnut, and Basil Whipped Feta (page 155)

Make and refrigerate the Perfect Balsamic-Maple Vinaigrette (page 218) up to 6 days in advance. • Make and refrigerate the Sun-Dried Tomato, Walnut, and Basil Whipped Feta Spread (page 247) up to 4 days in advance.

To serve: Set the dressing out on the counter until softened. • Set the whipped feta on the counter for 30 to 60 minutes, until just cooler than room temperature, if desired. • Roast the veggies. • Make the Garlic-Infused Olive Oil Crostini (page 249; if using). • Assemble the salads.

Smoky Seasoned Roasted Cauliflower and Potato Salad (page 159)

Toast the pepitas up to 1 week in advance, if needed. • Make and refrigerate the Velvety Sunflower Garlic Dressing (page 227) up to 2 days in advance.

To serve: Set the dressing out on the counter, until softened. • Make the Addictive Smoky Roasted Cauli, Chickpeas, and Taters (page 200). • Prepare the veggies. • Assemble the salad.

Spicy Chipotle Corn Salad (page 53)

Make and refrigerate the Soy-Free Vegan Mayonnaise (page 265; if using) up to 1 week in advance. • Make and refrigerate the Creamy Chipotle Dressing (page 237) up to 4 days in advance. • Cook and refrigerate the wild rice up to 2 days in advance.

To serve: Set the dressing out on the counter until softened. • Cook the corn and prepare the remaining veggies. • Reheat the rice. • Assemble the salads.

Spring Fever Lentil and Quinoa Salad with Sriracha Honey-Mustard Dressing (page 51)

Toast the pepitas (if using) up to 1 week in advance, if needed. Make and refrigerate the Soy-Free Vegan Mayonnaise (page 265; if using) up to 1 week in advance. • Make and refrigerate the double batch of Sriracha Honey-Mustard Dressing (page 242, see Variation) up to 3 days in advance. • Make and refrigerate the quinoa up to 1 day in advance.

To serve: Set the dressing out on the counter until softened. • Prepare the remaining veggies and reheat the quinoa to room temperature, if desired. • Assemble the salads.

Strawberry Arugula Salad with Feta and Rosemary-Maple Nuts (page 86)

Make the Rosemary, Maple, and Cayenne Roasted Pecans and Walnuts (page 209) up to 1 week in advance. • Make and refrigerate the Perfect Balsamic-Maple Vinaigrette (page 218) up to 1 week in advance. • Make and refrigerate the Vegan Feta Cheese (page 259) up to 5 days in advance.

To serve: Set the dressing out on the counter until softened. • Prepare the veggies and fruit. • Assemble the salads.

Stuffed Butternut Squash Wild Rice Salad (page 129)

Peel, halve, and seed the squash and refrigerate up to 1 day in advance. • Make and refrigerate the double batch of Cold Moon Orange Vinaigrette (page 217, see Variation), cook and refrigerate the rice, and prepare the apricots, cranberries, and pecans up to 1 day in advance.

To serve: Set the dressing and squash out on the counter until room temperature. • Cook the squash and make the wild rice salad. • Assemble the salads.

Summer Roll Salad with Pickled Carrots (page 101)

Toast the sliced almonds up to 1 week in advance, if needed. • Make and refrigerate the 1½ batches of Roasted Almond Butter, Ginger, and Lime Dressing (page 222, see Variation) up to 3 days in advance. Or make and refrigerate the 1½ batches of Nut-Free Sunflower, Ginger, and Lime Dressing (page 224, see Variation) up to 2 days in advance. • Make and refrigerate the Quick-Pickled Carrots (page 276, see Variations) up to 1 day in advance. • Thaw and refrigerate the edamame up to 1 day in advance.

To serve: Set the dressing out on the counter until softened. • Cook the noodles. • Prepare the veggies and herbs. • Assemble the salads.

Sunflower, Ginger, and Lime Crunch Salad (page 45)

Toast the sunflower seeds up to 1 week in advance, if needed. • Cook and refrigerate the brown rice, and make and refrigerate the 1½ batches of Nut-Free Sunflower, Ginger, and Lime Dressing (page 224, see Variation) up to 1 day in advance. • Thaw and refrigerate the edamame up to 1 day in advance.

To serve: Set the dressing out on the counter until softened. • Place the edamame on the counter to come to room temperature. • Prepare the veggies and herbs. • Warm the rice just before serving. • Assemble the salads.

Sun-Kissed On the Glow Pasta Salad (page 111)

Toast the pine nuts up to 1 week in advance, if needed. • Make and refrigerate the Garlic Lovers' Cashew Parmesan (page 281) up to 4 days in advance or the Oregano, Basil, and Lemon Zest Parmesan (page 280), up to 2 days in advance. • Make and refrigerate the Ultra-Creamy Flavor Burst Basil (page 257) up to 2 days in advance. • Cook and refrigerate the pasta up to 1 day in advance (I don't recommend making the pasta in advance if using a gluten-free or grain-free pasta, as they don't tend to store or reheat well).

To serve: Set the pesto out on the counter until softened. • Prepare the veggies and herbs. • Assemble the salad jars or simply serve the salad in one big bowl.

Sunny Day Charred Corn and Feta Salad (page 71)

Make and refrigerate the Soy-Free Vegan Mayonnaise (page 265; if using) up to 1 week in advance. Make and refrigerate the Vegan Feta Cheese (page 259) and the Lime and Sriracha Aioli (page 264) up to 5 days in advance.

To serve: Cook the corn. • Prepare the veggies and herbs. • Assemble the salads.

Super Green Bean, Rice, and Avocado Salad (page 127)

Make and refrigerate the Sesame, Lime, and Ginger Dressing (page 228) up to 1 day in advance. • Make and refrigerate the Lime, Cumin, and Red Pepper Parmesan (page 278) and the Cilantro-Jalapeño Rice (page 273) up to 6 hours before serving.

To serve: Set the dressing out on the counter until softened. • Cook the green beans and prepare the remaining veggies. • Reheat the rice, following the instructions in the Storage Tip. • Assemble the salads.

Sweater Weather Toasted Sesame, Tamari, and Garlic Kale Salad (page 123)

Toast the pepitas up to 1 week in advance, if needed. • Prepare and refrigerate the Toasted Sesame, Tamari, and Garlic Dressing (page 219), quinoa, and kale up to 1 day in advance.

To serve: Set the dressing out on the counter until room temperature. • Cook the sweet potatoes. • Make the Garlic-Cayenne Roasted Chickpeas (page 202). • Prepare the remaining veggies and reheat the quinoa until warm, if desired. • Assemble the salads.

Sweet Potato and Edamame Salad with Roasted Almond Butter, Ginger, and Lime Dressing (page 143)

Make and refrigerate the Sticky Roasted Tamari-Maple Almonds, Sliced Version (page 203) up to 1 week in advance. • Make and refrigerate the Roasted Almond Butter, Ginger, and Lime Dressing (page 222) up to 3 days in advance. Thaw and refrigerate the edamame up to 1 day in advance.

To serve: Set the dressing out on the counter until softened. • Place the edamame on the counter to come to room temperature. • Cook the sweet potatoes and prepare the remaining veggies. • Assemble the salads.

T

The Ultimate Ranch Barbecue Tofu Cobb Salad (page 85)

Make and refrigerate the Sweet and Tangy No-Chop Barbecue Sauce (page 262; if using) and the Soy-Free Vegan Mayonnaise (page 265; if using) up to 5 days in advance. • Make and refrigerate the Vegan Feta Cheese (page 259; if using) up to 3 days in advance. • Make and refrigerate the Ranch Buttermilk Dressing (page 232) up to 2 days in advance. • Press and refrigerate the tofu up to 1 day in advance.

To serve: Set the dressing and tofu out on the counter for about 30 minutes, until the dressing is softened and the tofu is room temperature. • Make the Double Batch Crispy and Chewy Barbecue Tofu (page 190) and prepare the veggies. • Assemble the salads.

Toppled Taco Salad (page 49)

Make and refrigerate the Soy-Free Vegan Mayonnaise (page 265; if using) up to 5 days in advance. • Make and refrigerate the Lime and Sriracha Aioli (page 264) up to 3 days in advance. • Press and refrigerate the tofu up to 1 day in advance.

To serve: Set the pressed tofu out on the counter for about 30 minutes, until the tofu is room temperature. • Make the Taco Tofu Crumble (page 193) and the Cilantro-Jalapeño Rice (page 273). • Prepare the veggies and herbs. • Assemble the salads.

Warm and Cozy Roasted Mediterranean Lentil Salad (page 141)

Make the Zesty Lemon, Dill, and Oregano Dressing (page 239) up to 2 days in advance. • Chop and refrigerate the zucchini, grape tomatoes, and bell peppers up to 1 day in advance.

To serve: Set the zucchini, grape tomatoes, and bell peppers out on the counter to come to room temperature. • Set the dressing out on the counter until softened. • Chop the potatoes, then cook the veggies and prepare the sun-dried tomatoes and herbs. • Assemble the salads.

Warm Mushroom and Spinach Pasta Salad (page 177)

Slice and refrigerate the mushrooms up to 1 day in advance. Make and refrigerate the Creamy Cashew, Garlic, and Lemon Dressing (page 240) up to 6 hours in advance.

To serve: Set the dressing out on the counter until softened. • Cook the pasta and the veggie mixture. • Assemble the salads.

Wintry Day Two-Potato, Apple, and Cranberry Kale Salad (page 171)

Make and refrigerate the Cold Moon Orange Vinaigrette (page 217) up to 4 days in advance. • Prepare and refrigerate the kale and chop the nuts up to 1 day in advance.

To serve: Set the dressing out on the counter until softened. • Cook the potatoes. • Prepare the remaining veggies and fruit. • Assemble the salads.

Z

Zucchini and Carrot Ribbon Pesto Salad (page 65)

Make and refrigerate the Sun-Dried Tomato, Walnut, and Basil Pesto (page 258) and the Oregano, Basil, and Lemon Zest Parmesan (page 280) up to 4 days in advance. • Cook and refrigerate the quinoa (if using) up to 1 day in advance.

To serve: Set the pesto out on the counter until softened. • Prepare the veggies. • Assemble the salads.

DESSERTS

Autumn Spiced Carr-oat Cake with Vegan Cream Cheese Frosting (page 289)

Chop the nuts up to 2 days in advance. • Make and refrigerate the Vegan Cream Cheese Frosting (page 291) up to 6 hours in advance.

To serve: Prep and bake the cake. • Cool the cake fully. • Set the frosting on the counter for up to 30 minutes to soften slightly, if needed, then frost and decorate as directed.

Chocolate-Coconut Zucchini Bundt Cake (page 293)

Make and refrigerate the Chocolate-Coconut Glaze (page 295) up to 1 week in advance. • Make and refrigerate the Coconut Whipped Cream (page 315) and chop the pistachios up to 3 days in advance.

To serve: Prep and bake the cake. • Return the glaze to a liquid state by gently warming it in a pot over low heat for a couple of minutes, stirring until liquid. • Cool the cake fully, then slice it and garnish with the Chocolate-Coconut Glaze, Coconut Whipped Cream, and chopped pistachios as directed.

Cookies and Fudge Freezer Cake (page 319)

Refrigerate the can of coconut cream or milk at least 12 hours in advance. • Prepare and freeze the cake up to 2 weeks in advance. • Prepare and refrigerate the whipped cream up to 2 days in advance. • Note: If making the freezer cake 2 weeks in advance, the freezer storage time for the cake reduces from 6 weeks to 1 month.

To serve: Rewhip the cream for 5 to 10 seconds just before serving. • Slice and serve as directed in the recipe.

Let It Glow Upside-Down Pear Spice Cake (page 313)

Toast the pecans up to 1 week in advance (if using). • Make and refrigerate the Coconut Whipped Cream (page 315; if using) up to 4 days in advance.

To serve: Prep and bake the cake. • Rewhip the cream for 5 to 10 seconds just before serving. • Cool the cake fully and serve as directed.

Peanut Butter Cup No-Bake Brownies (page 305)

Prepare and freeze the recipe up to 1 week in advance.

To serve: Place the pan on the counter for about 15 minutes to thaw and soften slightly before slicing.

Pecan, Walnut, and Cinnamon Oatmeal Cookies (page 317)

Chop and store the nuts up to 1 week in advance. • Add the flour, quick-cooking oats, cinnamon, baking powder, baking soda, and salt to an airtight container, whisk until combined, and store at room temperature up to 1 week in advance.

To serve: Whisk the dry ingredients in the container to recombine and proceed with the recipe as directed.

Pumpkin Streusel Coffee Cake (page 307)

Make and refrigerate the Pumpkin Delight Coconut Whipped Cream (page 311) up to 4 days in advance. • Prep, bake, and cool the cake the day before you plan to serve it.

To serve: Rewhip or stir the whipped cream just before using. Serve as directed.

Planning to take this cake to a gathering? Simply make the recipe in full, top each cooled square with a generous dollop of Pumpkin Delight Coconut Whipped Cream and chopped pecans (if using), then freeze the ready-to-serve squares in a large container with a lid for up to 1 month (be careful not to squish the whipped cream topping). On the day of your gathering, set the container of frozen squares on the counter to thaw and come to room temperature or just cooler, 1 to 3 hours.

Simple Macerated Strawberries (page 303)

Prepare and refrigerate the macerated strawberries up to 6 hours before you plan to use them.

To serve: Follow the recipe as directed.

Triple-Layer Mocha Fudge Torte (page 297)

Prepare and freeze the torte up to 2 weeks ahead. • Note: If making the torte 2 weeks in advance, the freezer storage time for the torte reduces from 1 month to 2 weeks.

To serve: Let the torte sit on the counter for 10 to 15 minutes so it's easier to slice.

Vanilla Buttermilk Loaf Cake with Berries and Cream (page 301)

Make and refrigerate the Coconut Whipped Cream (page 315) up to 2 days in advance. • Make and refrigerate the Simple Macerated Strawberries (page 303) up to 6 hours before serving.

To serve: Prep, bake, and cool the cake as directed. Rewhip or stir the whipped cream just before serving. Slice the cake, then top with the whipped cream and Simple Macerated Strawberries as directed.

helpful recipe lists

I came up with this handy cheat sheet to help you narrow down and select recipes lightning fast. Having the recipes grouped all in one place means skimming only one or two pages (instead of an entire book), which is so quick and convenient. Use this guide when you're searching for recipes that are *speedy* (prepped in 20 minutes or fully ready in 35 minutes or less), *big batch* (over 8 cups of tasty salad that you can enjoy all week long!), *protein-packed* (lentils and beans, or tofu, feta, and edamame), *served warm* or *on the side*, for a *special occasion* meal, or when you want to *get glowing and feed good*! For brevity's sake, this collection doesn't include the recipes from the "Dressings and Vinaigrettes" or "Flavor Boosters" sections, but rest assured that many of those fall under these categories as well.

Speedy

20 minutes or less prep time or 35 minutes or less total time

Big Batch

Makes 8 cups or more, or 10+ servings

Protein-Packed: Lentils and Beans

Protein-Packed: Tofu, Feta, and Edamame

Served Warm

Pro tip: Many of these are great served chilled, too!

On the Side

Special Occasion

get glowing and feel good

While virtually every salad recipe in this book will get you glowing (go, plants!!), here is my list of some of the best glow-promoting recipes. These are the ones you'll rely on when you need a major glow up. They're especially great for those weeks when you have a to-do list longer than your sanity, sleep is hard to come by, and you feel pulled in all directions (or is that every week?!). Eating these top feel-good salads can help you get your glow back, give the skin a glow, and put a pep to your step! Sign me up.

Nutrients and ingredients

that promote healthy, glowing skin: *vitamin C* (e.g., citrus fruits and bell peppers) supports collagen formation for firmer skin; *vitamin E* (e.g., nuts, seeds, and avocados) helps protect against oxidative damage that ages skin, *omega-3 fatty acids* (e.g., hemp seeds, walnuts, and olive oil) help balance hydration and moisturize from the inside out; *beta carotene* (e.g., sweet potatoes and carrots) converts to vitamin A for skin elasticity and cell turnover; *folate* (e.g., broccoli and leafy greens like spinach, romaine, and kale) helps repair and renew the skin; *zinc* (e.g., beans, seeds, and nuts) helps prevent acne and promotes collagen production; *lutein* (e.g., tomatoes and cruciferous veggies like cauliflower, kale, and broccoli) can help protect cells against UV damage and improve skin tone; and, lucky us, dark chocolate is rich in *antioxidants* that help protect the skin from damage, and you know what that means . . . Chocolate-Coconut Zucchini Bundt Cake (page 293)!

Get Glowing and Feel Good: Spring and Summer Recipes

Get Glowing and Feel Good: Fall and Winter Recipes

pantry staples

Here is a handy quick-reference guide to the pantry ingredients most commonly used in this book. I share details about the ingredients, tips for selecting the best options, and the brands I reach for.

Acids

Acidic ingredients, such as lemon juice or various types of vinegar, add vibrant, fresh notes to a dish and enhance the flavor of other ingredients. They awaken salads and dressings while balancing the bitterness, sweetness, and oleogustus (the taste of fat). An important job!

Apple Cider Vinegar: Made from fermented apple juice, this vinegar has a sweet and crisp flavor that is wonderful in dressings like my Apple Cider, Shallot, Maple, and Dijon Vinaigrette (page 220) and in baked goods. My preferred brands are President's Choice Organics Apple Cider Vinegar and Fairchild's Organic Apple Cider Vinegar, which are raw and unfiltered.

Balsamic Vinegar: This dark, intensely flavored vinegar originated in Modena, Italy. It grew to fame for good reason: its rich flavor is sweet, tangy, and distinctive. Try it in my Perfect Balsamic-Maple Vinaigrette (page 218). Because it's often used as a finishing acid in dressings and sauces, it's worthwhile to invest in the highest-quality balsamic that falls within your budget.

Lemon Juice: Lemon juice adds brightness to dishes and can even lighten them by cutting down on the oily feel of a dish. Lemon adds vibrance to my Zesty Lemon, Dill, and Oregano Dressing (page 239). The zest—the peeled skin without the pith—is often used to add a tangy sweetness, such as in my Lemon and Garlic Pearl Couscous (page 266).

Lime Juice: Similar to lemon juice but with floral citrus, orange, and sweet notes. Some say lime juice is sweeter than lemon juice, while others claim it is more bitter. Either way, it adds a distinctive brightness to dressings like my Cilantro, Lime, Cumin, and Jalapeño Dressing (page 236). The zest—the peeled skin without the pith—is sweeter and adds a punch of flavor, such as in my Lime, Cumin, and Red Pepper Parmesan (page 278).

Orange Juice: Orange is the sweetest of the citruses, and its sweet yet gently tart, bright flavor awakens the taste buds. I love using orange juice in my Cold Moon Orange Vinaigrette (page 217) for a lightly sweet flavor that works so well in fall and winter salads like my Stuffed Butternut Squash Wild Rice Salad (page 129) and Wintry Day Two-Potato, Apple, and Cranberry Kale Salad (page 171).

Red Wine Vinegar: Made from fermented red wine, this vinegar lends its robust, tangy, fruity, and acidic flavor to dressings when you want the flavor of the acid to shine through. (A little bit goes a long way!) Try it in my Zesty Lemon, Dill, and Oregano Dressing (page 239).

Seasoned Rice Vinegar: The addition of sugar makes this sweeter and more flavorful than unseasoned rice vinegar, but it is still milder and less acidic than most vinegars. I love using it to add a subtle sweet tang to my Roasted Almond Butter, Ginger, and Lime Dressing (page 222).

White Wine Vinegar: Similar to red wine vinegar but more delicate in flavor, being made from fermented white wine. I love pairing it with zesty, bright fresh herbs, like in my Herby Lemon and White Wine Vinaigrette (page 231) and my Light and Floral Lemony Garlic Vinaigrette (page 238).

Produce

Chives, freeze-dried: Fresh, sharp-tasting chives are freeze-dried to preserve their bright green color and mild onion flavor. The onion taste is quite concentrated, so a little goes a long way, making them an easy-to-use flavor booster when sprinkled over dishes like my Protein-Powered Cashew-Hemp Cheese (page 197).

Cucumbers, Persian (mini): These 5- to 6-inch (12 to 15 cm) long cucumbers are thin-skinned and quite narrow. Wonderfully crisp rather than watery, with a mild, sweet flavor, they are ideal in salads. You'll usually find them in packages of six. I love them in my Spring Fever Lentil and Quinoa Salad with Sriracha Honey-Mustard Dressing (page 51).

Dates, Medjool: Antioxidant-rich Medjool dates are native to Morocco and have been eaten for millennia. Naturally sweet and gooey, with a rich caramel-like flavor, they add fiber and sweetness to baked goods and act as a binder in no-bake crusts, such as in my Peanut Butter Cup No-Bake Brownies (page 305).

Garlic, raw: When the ingredient list instructs you to "mince" garlic, this means to finely chop the garlic clove with a sharp knife, whereas "grated" means to grate it on a Microplane grater or on the small holes of a box grater. The difference is important, as grated garlic is much more potent and intense than minced, and some salad dressings can't handle that intensity. In my recipes, I tell you how much a small, medium, and large garlic clove weigh (4 g, 5 g, and 6 g, respectively); if you are unsure of the size of your garlic clove, I recommend weighing it.

Ginger Root, fresh: Fresh ginger is spicy, warming, digestive-soothing, and packed with a punch of flavor. It lightens rich ingredients such as the seed butter in my Nut-Free Sunflower, Ginger, and Lime Dressing (page 224) and adds its distinctive taste to my Sesame, Lime, and Ginger Dressing (page 228). I love to grate it to bring out the most intense flavor.

Jalapeño Peppers, green: I love to use these spicy peppers in grain dishes like Savory Jalapeño-Tomato Rice (page 270), dips like my Glow Up Garden Guacamole (page 283), and dressings such as Cilantro, Lime, Cumin, and Jalapeño Dressing (page 236). These gorgeously green peppers vary a lot in heat level. For a milder-tasting pepper, select smooth and firm jalapeños without "wrinkles" and be sure to remove the seeds and veins when preparing. If you'd like extra-spicy, go for the wrinkled jalapeños (they are older and have a more intense heat).

Onions, green, red, yellow, and sweet: Onions are known for their assertive taste and pungent aroma. Of the onions used in this cookbook, green onions have the mildest taste and a light crunch when scattered over salads like my Fiery 10-Spice Roasted Potato Salad (page 165). Red onions can be quite sharp-tasting depending on what they are served with, so in some salads, I like to soak them first in cold water, resulting in a gentler taste, like I do in Spicy Chipotle Corn Salad (page 53). Yellow, or cooking, onions have the most flavor, and I prefer them cooked, like in my Stuffed Butternut Squash Wild Rice Salad (page 129). Sweet onions are sweeter and milder than yellow, and we love them in my Quick-Pickled Sweet Onions (and more!) (page 276).

Shallots: Sweet and garlicky shallots taste like a cross between a red and a yellow onion but are a bit less punchy in flavor. They are my go-to when I want to add just a tiny bite of onion flavor to my salad dressings, like my Cold Moon Orange Vinaigrette (page 217), where they provide just the right contrast to the sweet ingredients. The acids in dressings gently pickle them, resulting in an even milder taste. Bonus: minced shallots add a pretty purple color element to the dressing, too!

Sun-Dried Tomatoes, oil-packed: These are tomatoes that have been dehydrated over the course of days, whether in the sun or in a dehydrator, resulting in an intensified, condensed, umami flavor that's further enhanced by the herbs in their packing oil. I use them to add tons of explosive flavor to my Parsley, Sun-Dried Tomato, and Feta Quinoa Salad (page 63) and Sun-Dried Tomato, Walnut, and Basil Whipped Feta Spread (page 247).

Sweet Bell Peppers: Bell peppers add vibrance to salads, both in taste and color. When used raw, they add a sweet, zesty, and delightful crunch to any salad. Try them in my Glow Girl Kale Slaw (page 39). When roasted, they mellow in flavor, becoming sweeter, caramelized, and wonderfully soft yet chewy, like in my Mix-and-Glow Roasted Veg Orzo Salad (page 163). If a recipe doesn't specify a color, you can use red, orange, or yellow bell peppers interchangeably. I don't suggest using green bell pepper, as it has a more bitter and less sweet flavor profile.

Miscellaneous

Aquafaba: Aquafaba is the liquid found in a can of pulses, such as chickpeas, or the liquid left over after cooking your beans from scratch, cooked down until it's a similar thickness to canned aquafaba. It'll keep in an airtight container in the fridge for at least two weeks. I use it as an egg replacer in my Soy-Free Vegan Mayonnaise (page 265). Note that for the recipes in this cookbook, we used aquafaba from a can and did not test the recipe using homemade aquafaba.

Beans and Lentils: Black beans, brown lentils, edamame, chickpeas, peas, peanuts, and cannellini beans are the legumes you'll find in this salad collection. If the ingredient list calls for cooked beans and legumes, you may use an equal amount of canned rather than home-cooked. For reference, a 14-ounce (398 mL) can of lentils or beans is equal to about 1½ cups cooked. About ½ cup plus 2 tablespoons dried green or brown lentils yields about 1½ cups cooked.

Black Pepper: This versatile seasoning adds piney, citrusy notes to all kinds of dishes. In larger amounts, it adds a bit of heat, like in my Community-Fave 10-Spice Mix (page 275). I like to use my pepper grinder to freshly grind peppercorns rather than using pre-ground pepper, as I prefer the flavor and texture of the freshly ground.

Black Salt (Kala Namak): This kiln-fired rock salt has a sulfurous, pungent scent that adds a lovely eggy taste to vegan dishes like my High-Protein No-Egg Egg Salad (page 81).

Brown Rice Syrup: Also called rice syrup or malt syrup, this plant-based sweetener is made by exposing cooked brown rice to natural enzymes that break down and convert the rice's starch into a sweet liquid, which is then reduced to a syrup. It imparts a very subtle sweet flavor, making it perfect for using in my Soy-Free Vegan Mayonnaise (page 265).

Chocolate, semi-sweet, bar, and unsweetened cocoa powder: Who doesn't love the decadent flavor of chocolate? The chocolate desserts in this book feature vegan dark or milk chocolate bars, semi-sweet chocolate chips, and unsweetened cocoa powder. I like that I can break vegan chocolate bars (either dark or slightly sweeter and mild-flavored milk) into custom-sized pieces to add addicting spots of gooeyness to my Chocolate-Coconut Zucchini Bundt Cake (page 293). Semi-sweet chocolate chips are so handy for melting into a shiny glaze, such as my Chocolate-Coconut Glaze (page 295), or into velvety fudge, like in my Cookies and Fudge Freezer Cake (page 319). To add a deep flavor to crusts, cakes, and glazes, I use unsweetened cocoa powder. A little goes a long way in my Peanut Butter Cup No-Bake Brownies (page 305)!

Cinnamon (Ceylon): This is one of my favorite spices for autumn baking. I love using it in my Let It Glow Upside-Down Pear Spice Cake (page 313) and Pecan, Walnut, and Cinnamon Oatmeal Cookies (page 317). You might be surprised to hear that cinnamon is delicious in savory recipes, too, like my Cinnamon Sweet Potato Wedge Salad with Sriracha Honey-Mustard Dressing (page 175). Give it a try!

Coconut Aminos: Also known as soy-sauce substitute and soy-free seasoning, this soy-free seasoning sauce is made from nutrient-rich coconut tree sap. I sometimes use it as a soy-free swap for light tamari, such as in my Sticky Roasted Tamari-Maple Almonds (page 203).

Cream Cheese, vegan: This creamy, tangy spreadable cheese is usually made with soy or nuts, oil, and an acid. I love to use it in my velvety Vegan Cream Cheese Frosting (page 291), and it tastes divine over Autumn Spiced Carr-oat Cake (page 289)!

Fine Sea Salt: This finely ground salt is produced by evaporating water from oceans or saltwater lakes. It's less processed and tastes a little less salty than table salt, and it retains trace minerals. It's used in all of this book's recipes as a flavor enhancer, as I find it brings out the flavor of the other ingredients rather than adding a salty taste.

Honey, vegan: Vegan honey adds sweet flavor to salad dressings and baked goods. I find it irresistible in my Sriracha Honey-Mustard Dressing (page 242). I like using an apple-based honey alternative, such as BlenditUp organic vegan honey. Use whatever liquid honey you prefer, though!

Maple Syrup, pure: My beloved sweetener of choice. I love using Grade A amber pure maple syrup, which is robust and rich-tasting. It balances the flavors in dressings, desserts, and more.

Mustard, old-fashioned Dijon: In addition to adding its distinctive tang, mustard works as an emulsifier in dressings, helping prevent the blended ingredients from separating. Old-fashioned Dijon—also known as whole-grain, stone-ground, old-style, and old-fashioned mustard—is a pungent, spicy mustard made from whole mustard seeds, vinegar, water, and sea salt. It imparts a tangy, distinctive flavor to salad dressings. On the other hand, smooth Dijon (see below), tastes intense and sharp; don't swap the two in my salad recipes, as the smooth version is much more potent and will change the flavor profile of your dressing. I use old-fashioned Dijon in several dressings, including Creamy ACV, Shallot, Maple, and Dijon Vinaigrette (page 233) and Luxurious ACV and Dijon Dressing (page 221). My brand of choice is President's Choice Old-Fashioned Dijon.

Mustard, smooth Dijon: This totally smooth Dijon mustard tastes very pungent compared with old-fashioned Dijon. Be sure not to substitute smooth Dijon for old-fashioned Dijon in my recipes, as smooth Dijon has a much stronger flavor. I add just a touch of smooth Dijon to my Light and Floral Lemony Garlic Vinaigrette (page 238) and a more generous amount, combined with old-fashioned Dijon, to add a big kick to my Grainy Mustard and Lemon Dressing (page 234). My go-to brand is President's Choice Dijon.

Nutritional Yeast: This deactivated bread yeast is my go-to when I want to add a cheesy flavor to dressings, sauces, or a vegan parmesan like Garlic Lovers' Cashew Parmesan (page 281). It replaces the parmesan in pestos, like in my Sun-Dried Tomato, Walnut, and Basil Pesto (page 258). Pair it with acids and an oil for texture (along with a few other magical ingredients) to create a deliciously flavored salad dressing. Try it in Velvety Cashew Garlic Dressing (page 226).

Panko Breadcrumbs: Made from crustless white bread, these crumbs are processed into flakes that are then dried. They are drier and flakier than regular breadcrumbs, absorbing less oil when they cook so they impart a crunchier, lighter-than-air texture. Try them on my Crispy Breaded Tofu Tenders (page 185) and don't look back!

Rice: In this book, I use wild rice blend, basmati rice, and long-grain brown and white rice. Brown rice hasn't had its husk, germ, and bran removed, so it provides more fiber, aroma, and flavor and a chewier texture than white rice. I use it in my Savory Brown Rice and Lentils (page 207), which makes a hearty and nourishing base for salads. Wild rice blend generally features brown rice, various other rices such as red, and wild rice. Compared with brown rice alone, it has more fiber, flavor, and aroma, and a chewier texture, and I love using it in Stuffed Butternut Squash Wild Rice Salad (page 129) for a fantastic texture. Basmati rice and long-grain white rice have had their husk, germ, and bran removed, resulting in a fluffy, light, and soft rice that lets the flavors of the other ingredients shine. Basmati is slightly more aromatic and nutty in flavor, and I use it in Cilantro-Jalapeño Rice (page 273). Long-grain white's fluffy texture is just lovely in my Mile-High Warm Portobello Fajita Salad (page 59).

Soba Noodles: Made from buckwheat, a gluten-free grain, these noodles taste nutty and have a satisfying substantial texture. I love using these delicate noodles, which cook up in minutes, in salads that feature raw crunchy veggies, such as Minty Sesame, Lime, and Ginger Noodle Salad (page 105). Note that they often contain some wheat, so if gluten is a concern for you, be sure to read the ingredients label on your package.

Sriracha: This hot sauce, which originated in Thailand, is made from a paste of chili peppers, garlic, sugar, water, and sometimes vinegar, and it's the hot sauce used throughout this book. Sriracha can vary in heat from brand to brand, so if you prefer a milder dish, I recommend adding it a little at a time, tasting as you go. I love Natural Value Organic Sriracha Sauce.

Vegetable Broth: When used in place of water, vegetable broth adds flavor and savoriness to grains like pasta, rice, quinoa, and farro. I use full-sodium broth in my recipes, as I find that it improves the dish in subtle yet flavorful ways. Try it in my Savory Brown Rice and Lentils (page 207), Sweater Weather Toasted Sesame, Tamari, and Garlic Kale Salad (page 123), and Easy Garlic-Infused Farro (page 268). If you use a low-sodium broth, you'll likely need to add more salt than called for in the recipe; add it slowly, to taste.

Vermicelli Noodles: These are a slender yet strong noodle made from white rice. I love that their neutral taste takes on flavor from dressings and, when chopped, they don't add a lot of chewiness to otherwise highly textured salads like my vibrantly flavored Summer Roll Salad with Pickled Carrots (page 101). Note that some vermicelli noodles are made using wheat so if gluten is a concern for you, be sure to read the ingredients label on the package.

Worcestershire Sauce, vegan: Savory with a deep umami flavor, this vegan version of a classic lends depth, complexity, and a distinctive tangy, sweet, and salty hint to sauces. I love to use this sauce in my Sweet and Tangy No-Chop Barbecue Sauce (page 262) and Taco Tofu Crumble (page 193). I love The Wizard's Organic Gluten Free Vegan Worcestershire Sauce. Some vegan Worcestershire sauces contain gluten and/or soy, so be sure to check the labels if this is a concern for you.

Non-Dairy Milks

Non-dairy milks add moisture and creaminess to dressings and desserts in this book. Used in place of water or dairy milk, they impart a sweetness, richness, or neutral flavor, depending which kind is used. You can make vegan buttermilk by combining plant milk with an acid such as lemon juice or apple cider vinegar; in my baking recipes vegan buttermilk activates baking soda to make the batter rise during cooking and adds a subtle tang that plays against the sweetness.

Almond Milk, unsweetened and unflavored: Almonds are blended with water and strained to create this lightly creamy "milk" that imparts a slightly sweet taste to dishes. I use it in my Pumpkin Streusel Coffee Cake (page 307). I love Earth's Own Unsweetened Original.

Coconut Cream, canned: After coconut flesh is simmered in water and strained, the resulting liquid is left to separate into thick, white coconut cream and translucent coconut water. Cans of coconut cream contain little or no water and are sometimes ready to use without needing to chill the can (although I still recommend chilling when making a coconut whipped cream, as it's more pleasant served cold). Alternatively, you can refrigerate a can of full-fat coconut milk overnight (choose one that contains guar or other gums so the cream separates from the water and it whips properly) and scoop the semisolid cream portion from the can until you have the amount needed for the recipe. Use coconut cream to make whipped creams like my Pumpkin Delight Coconut Whipped Cream (page 311), and cakes and glazes like my Chocolate-Coconut Zucchini Bundt Cake (page 293) and its Chocolate-Coconut Glaze (page 295). Coconut whipped cream also adds a rich flavor and velvety texture to desserts like my Cookies and Fudge Freezer Cake (page 319). When using full-fat coconut milk, I love Native Forest brand.

Oat Milk, unsweetened: Oats and water are blended together, then strained, to create this rich-tasting "milk." Its oat taste works beautifully in baked goods and enhances the oaty flavor of my Autumn Spiced Carr-oat Cake (page 289). My go-to brand is Earth's Own Original.

Oils

In salad dressings, oils are the magic ingredient that gives dressings and sauces their silkiness and allows their flavors to coat the leaves rather than just creating a liquid "soup" at the bottom of your bowl. Thank you, oils!

Avocado Oil, pure (100%): The oil pressed from avocado flesh has a light, neutral taste that is perfect in dressings where you want the other flavors to shine through, like my 6-Ingredient Shake-and-Glow Vinaigrette (page 235). I love Chosen Foods 100% Pure Avocado Oil.

Butter Sticks, vegan: These provide the same qualities as vegan buttery spread (see below) but with a more solid texture when chilled, giving thickness and body to desserts like fluffy whipped frostings. I use vegan butter sticks in my Vegan Cream Cheese Frosting (page 291).

Buttery Spread, vegan: Plant-based buttery spreads are spreadable even when chilled and can be used in many foods and baked goods that call for dairy butter. They add creaminess and that unmistakable rich, buttery flavor. I love using vegan buttery spreads, such as Melt Organic Buttery Spread (labeled Melt Organic Plant Butter in the United States), in cookies like my Pecan, Walnut, and Cinnamon Oatmeal Cookies (page 317).

Coconut Oil, refined: Refined coconut oil doesn't have any coconut flavor or aroma, and it has a higher smoke point (400°F/200°C) than unrefined virgin coconut oil. I use it in recipes when I don't want any hint of coconut flavor, like in my Vegan Feta Cheese (page 259). Both refined and virgin coconut oil harden in the freezer, making them an excellent addition to frozen no-bake desserts.

Coconut Oil, virgin: Virgin coconut oil is extracted from coconut meat and doesn't undergo refining. It has a light coconut taste and aroma, which make it lovely in dessert or snack recipes like my Triple-Layer Mocha Fudge Torte (page 297). Both refined and virgin coconut oil harden in the freezer, making them an excellent addition to frozen no-bake desserts.

Extra-Virgin Olive Oil: A staple in the Mediterranean diet, extra-virgin olive oil is a go-to for its health benefits and for the robust flavor it adds to salad dressings. Higher-quality extra-virgin olive oils have a fruity, herbal taste (just like wine!), so it's worth the investment if you're using it in dressings, as its flavor is a key component. I use it in several dressings, including Creamy ACV, Shallot, Maple, and Dijon Vinaigrette (page 233).

Grapeseed Oil: I love using neutral-tasting grapeseed oil in dressings where I want the acids and herbs to shine as the prominent flavors. This quality makes it ideal for baking as well. Try it in desserts like Autumn Spiced Carr-oat Cake (page 289) and Chocolate-Coconut Zucchini Bundt Cake (page 293), and in dressings like my Sesame, Lime, and Ginger Dressing (page 228). It's a key ingredient in my Soy-Free Vegan Mayonnaise (page 265), too!

Mayonnaise, vegan: Velvety, delicious mayo without the eggs adds creaminess and thick texture to dressings and holds together ingredients in a chunky salad (think potato salad!). It's a breeze to make at home, too. Try my Soy-Free Vegan Mayonnaise (page 265) in High-Protein No-Egg Egg Salad (page 81).

Toasted Sesame Oil: Sesame oil is one of the oldest documented vegetable oils, used in Chinese, Japanese, and Middle Eastern cuisines. Toasting the sesame seeds before pressing out the oil gives added nuttiness to the flavor, making this a robust flavoring agent for dressings and other recipes. Because it has already been heated, it isn't used as a cooking oil, since double-cooking could burn it, resulting in an acrid-tasting dish. Instead, use it as a finishing oil in dressings like my Toasted Sesame, Tamari, and Garlic Dressing (page 219) and Nut-Free Sunflower, Ginger, and Lime Dressing (page 224).

Untoasted (unrefined) Sesame Oil: Pressed from tiny raw sesame seeds, untoasted sesame oil is good for medium heat (350°F/180°C), making it ideal for stir-fries as well as salad dressings. I love to use it in my Miso, Maple, and Ginger Dressing (page 241) and Addictive Smoky Roasted Cauli, Chickpeas, and Taters (page 200).

Flours

All-Purpose White Flour: Made with a blend of hard and soft red wheats, all-purpose flour contains about 75 percent of the wheat grain, with most of the bran and germ removed. It adds structure and a light texture, without adding flavor. It is most often used in cakes, pastries, and cookies, and as a thickening agent. I use it in my Chocolate-Coconut Zucchini Bundt Cake (page 293).

Almond Flour: This gluten-free flour is made by finely grinding blanched almonds. It is high in protein and adds a tenderness and subtle nutty sweetness to baked goods. When used in combination with wheat flour, it lightens the texture of baked goods. Don't use almond meal as a swap for almond flour in my recipes; it has a coarser texture and often contains the skins, resulting in a much different finished product. I use almond flour along with oat flour and all-purpose flour in my Autumn Spiced Carr-oat Cake (page 289).

Cake and Pastry Flour: This fine-textured flour is made from soft wheat. With its low protein (and therefore low gluten) content, it is perfect for baking lightly textured and high-rising cakes and flaky pastries that are both tender and crumbly. I love it in my Pumpkin Streusel Coffee Cake (page 307).

Oat Flour: Made from only oats, this flour adds a lightly toasty, rounded flavor to baked goods. You can easily make your own by simply processing rolled oats in a large food processor to a fine powder. Or you can purchase it pre-ground from most grocery stores. I use it in my Autumn Spiced Carr-oat Cake (page 289) for the most tender vegan carrot cake you ever did taste! Oat flour is gluten-free when made with certified gluten-free oats.

White/Light Spelt Flour: Made from the ancient grain spelt, white/light spelt flour is more refined than whole spelt flour, so it is much softer, lighter, and less dense. I love it in my Pecan, Walnut, and Cinnamon Oatmeal Cookies (page 317). My brand of choice is Hockley Valley Whole Foods Premium Light Spelt Flour.

Nuts and Seeds, Butters, and Pastes

Almonds, sliced: Sliced almonds are an excellent way to enjoy the delicate crunch of sweet, nutty almonds on your salad when whole nuts would overwhelm the texture of the dish. I use them in the sliced version of my Sticky Roasted Tamari-Maple Almonds (page 203), and I toast them to scatter over Summer Roll Salad with Pickled Carrots (page 101). To toast sliced almonds: Preheat a small dry skillet over medium heat. Add the sliced almonds and cook, tossing or stirring occasionally, for 3 to 5 minutes, until lightly golden and fragrant. Watch closely to avoid burning, and reduce the heat if necessary.

Pine Nuts: I love using raw pine nuts in my pestos. Their soft texture and sweet, nutty, buttery taste work so well with grassy herbs and greens. When toasted, they take on a lightly crunchy texture and their flavor is even richer. I love using them this way as a salad topper. To toast pine nuts: Preheat a small dry skillet over medium-low to medium heat. Add the pine nuts and cook, tossing or stirring frequently, for 3 to 5 minutes, until lightly golden and fragrant. Watch closely to avoid burning, and reduce the heat if necessary.

Pepitas: I like to keep raw pepitas on hand. To toast raw pepitas at home, preheat a small dry skillet over medium heat. Add the pepitas and cook, tossing or stirring occasionally, for 3 to 5 minutes, until fragrant and slightly puffy. Watch closely to avoid burning, and reduce the heat if necessary. For convenience, I love having a bag of salted roasted pepitas on hand in my pantry as they are so speedy for scattering on top of salads.

Roasted Almond Butter: This nut butter is made by processing roasted almonds into a paste. I love to use it in salad dressings; it adds a deep, rich, nutty flavor to my Roasted Almond Butter, Ginger, and Lime Dressing (page 222).

Sesame Seeds: Tiny sesame seeds are often underestimated, but don't let their diminutive size fool you! They add mega flavor, pops of crunch, and nutty sweetness to a range of dishes, such as my Crispy and Chewy Barbecue Tofu (page 187). I like to toast them to bring out their flavor even more and scatter them over salads like my Edamame and Pistachio Soba Noodle Spinach Salad (page 99). To toast raw sesame seeds: Preheat a small dry skillet over medium heat. Add the sesame seeds and cook, stirring frequently, for 3 to 4 minutes, until fragrant and most of the seeds are lightly golden. Watch closely to avoid burning, and reduce the heat if necessary.

Sunflower Seed Butter, natural smooth roasted: This creamy seed butter is made by processing roasted sunflower seeds into a paste. Its creaminess and mild flavor make it the perfect nut-free substitute for almond or peanut butters in many recipes. I love using it to make my silky-smooth Nut-Free Sunflower, Ginger, and Lime Dressing (page 224). Be sure to use one that doesn't contain added sweetener or emulsifiers.

Sunflower Seeds: These little seeds pack a nutritional punch and are a great option for nut-free diets. Raw sunflower seeds can be soaked and blended into luxurious dressings, like my Velvety Sunflower Garlic Dressing (page 227). I like to toast them lightly to bring out their naturally mild nutty flavor and then scatter them over salads for crunch, like in my Sunflower, Ginger, and Lime Crunch Salad (page 45). To toast raw sunflower seeds: Preheat a small dry skillet over medium to medium-high heat. Add the sunflower seeds and cook, stirring frequently, for 5 to 7 minutes, until lightly golden brown. Season with a sprinkle of salt to enhance their flavor.

Tahini: Grinding sesame seeds turns them into a mineral-rich paste full of healthy fats. I love how tahini adds richness, creaminess, a toasty flavor, and a ton of personality to salad dressings like my Miso, Maple, and Ginger Dressing (page 241) and a creaminess when drizzled over salads, like with my Mix-and-Glow Roasted Veg Orzo Salad (page 163).

LE CREUSET

Soy Products

Soy products are derived from soybeans, a flowering plant in the pea family that is high in protein and processed and served in a variety of ways.

Light Tamari: My favorite liquid soy seasoning, light tamari adds a ton of rich, lightly salty, and umami flavor to dressings and sauces. Try it in my Toasted Sesame, Tamari, and Garlic Dressing (page 219). I use San-J brand light tamari, which has 710 mg of sodium per tablespoon (that's 28 percent less sodium than their regular tamari). It adds deep flavor to my Super Green Bean, Rice, and Avocado Salad (page 127). I *always* use light tamari in my recipes. I don't recommend swapping light tamari for regular tamari—in most cases, it will make the dish much too salty.

Tofu, extra-firm: The amazing thing about tofu is that it is essentially flavorless but takes on the flavor of whatever spices, marinades, or sauces you cook it with. I love to create tofu recipes that burst with flavor, like my Crispy and Chewy Barbecue Tofu (page 187). The recipes in this book require the tofu to be pressed to remove the excess water. To save time, you can purchase pre-pressed tofu, such as Soyganic organic pressed tofu or Nasoya super-firm organic tofu. Using store-bought pre-pressed tofu tends to result in an even firmer Vegan Feta Cheese (page 259) and Crispy Breaded Tofu Tenders (page 185), so it's my preference when making these recipes. If you'd like to press tofu at home, you can use a tofu press (which is what I use) or the book-stacking method: Rinse the tofu, pat it dry, and slice it lengthwise into two thin slabs. Lay two dishcloths on the counter and top them with a few sheets of paper towel. Top these with the tofu slabs, then cover the slabs with a few more sheets of paper towel and two more dishcloths. Carefully stack several very heavy books on top of the covered tofu, and allow it to sit for at least 30 minutes.

White Miso (shiro): White miso, also known as shiro miso, is less salty and potent-tasting and sweeter than red miso due to differences in processing. White miso is fermented for the shortest amount of time, resulting in the mildest flavors. Use it in my Miso, Maple, and Ginger Dressing (page 241). I use Amano brand organic shiro miso, which has 440 mg of sodium per tablespoon.

heartfelt

To my dear readers, each and every one of you has changed my life for the better in so many ways. Your support and kindness have brought me so much joy, love, new interests and hobbies, friendships, and more since I started my blog in 2008. I will never be able to say thank you enough for those of you who support what I do, everything *Oh She Glows*, and this wonderful journey that we're on together! Thank you for your understanding when I seemingly fall off the face of the earth and struggle to keep all the balls in the air at once, caught up in the whirlwind of raising three kids. I am my own toughest critic, and your kind words and comments over the years have lifted me up in ways you may never know.

Eric, thank you for always believing in me and for encouraging me to silence the self-doubt and just go for it. You have this unbelievable knack for lifting me up whenever I'm on the verge of throwing in the tea towel. Your encouragement, sacrifices, support, and enthusiastic taste-testing have made all of this possible! To Adriana, Arlo, and Levi for giving me my proudest, most joyful, and oh-so-humbling role as your mama. I love seeing you follow your own passions in life and hope more than anything that you feel the freedom to shine your unique light in the world! To my mom, I'm so grateful for the sacrifices you've made for me and your immense support over the years. Your Instagram handle, @OSGMOM, just says it all. To all of my family and friends, of whom there are too many to individually name—I love you and truly appreciate your love and encouragement!

thanks

A huge thank you to my incredibly talented group of recipe testers. Nicole White, my Head Recipe Tester and Right-Hand Gal and one of my BFFs in this life, I hate to think what life would be like if *Oh She Glows* hadn't brought us together. You are a kindred spirit. There's no doubt in my mind that I wouldn't have been able to create this cookbook without your dedication, hard work, feedback, hilarious sense of humor, countless hours of recipe tests, cheerleading, and the list goes on. I'm also super grateful for Anne Boyd, Lynn Isted, Tana Gilberstad, Caroline Dufresne, Carin Weisman, Danielle Pixley Wilkerson, Laura Beizer, Heather Bock, Erin Hansuld, Stephanie Regis, Adrienne Brown, Anna Gunn, Vanessa Gilic, Kirsten Tomlin, Kathy Hawkins, Suzanne Poldon, Beth Miller Erman, Audrey Singaraju, Tammy Root, Stephanie Steenhuis, and Stephanie Scilingo. If it wasn't for all of your helpful recipe testing and feedback, I would be working on this cookbook until I was eighty years old, no doubt!

To my editor, Andrea Magyar, thank you for believing in me all these years and for planting the seed for a salad cookbook, which has been my favorite to create thus far! I'm so grateful for all your hard work on this book. A huge thanks to our incredible Penguin Random House Canada team for all of your dedication and dedicated effort on this cookbook, including Terri Nimmo for the gorgeous design and Shaun Oakey for your meticulous copyediting!

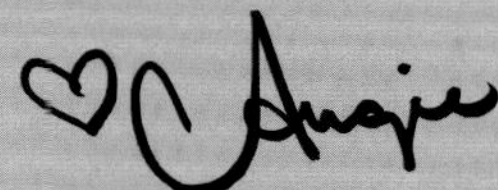

glow index

I created this handy index when you are looking for recipes in the book that are gluten-free, nut-free, freezer-friendly, and on the glow (great for travel and transporting). Please note that to keep this section as concise as possible, dressings and vinaigrettes are not included (please see the recipe itself for this information).

Gluten-Free and Gluten-Free Option

These recipes are gluten-free as written, or if they contain gluten, I have provided a suggestion for how to make the recipe gluten-free. Be sure to check the labels of your ingredients, too.

Spring and Summer

Grain Salads

Beans, Lentils, and Tofu Salads

Pasta and Potato Salads

Fall and Winter

Grain Salads

Beans, Lentil, and Tofu Salads

Pasta and Potato Salads

Protein Toppers

Flavor Boosters

Desserts

Nut-Free and Nut-Free Option

These recipes do not contain nuts, or if they do, I have provided an easy tip for how to make the recipes nut-free. As explained on page 27, I do not classify coconut as a nut product. Always check the ingredients and product labels if you have a nut allergy, and follow your physician's recommendations.

Spring and Summer

Grain Salads

Beans, Lentil, and Tofu Salads

Pasta and Potato Salads

Fall and Winter

Grain Salads

Beans, Lentil, and Tofu Salads

Pasta and Potato Salads

Protein Toppers

Flavor Boosters

Desserts

Freezer-Friendly

These recipes store well in the freezer. Be sure to see the recipe's Storage information for instructions on freezing the recipe.

Fall and Winter

Grain Salads

Protein Toppers

Flavor Boosters

Desserts

On the Glow

These recipes transport well for work or school lunches, and they are great for travel, too!

Spring and Summer

Grain Salads

Bean, Lentil, and Tofu Salads

Pasta and Potato Salads

Fall and Winter

Grain Salads

Bean, Lentil, and Tofu Salads

Pasta and Potato Salads

Protein Toppers

Flavor Boosters

Desserts

index

c

D

E

F

M

N

O

Q

R

S

T

U